THE
LITVINENKO FILE

Also by Martin Sixsmith

MOSCOW COUP
The Death of the Soviet System

SPIN

I HEARD LENIN LAUGH

THE
LITVINENKO FILE

The True Story of a Death Foretold

Martin Sixsmith

MACMILLAN

First published 2007 by Macmillan
an imprint of Pan Macmillan Ltd
Pan Macmillan, 20 New Wharf Road, London N1 9RR
Basingstoke and Oxford
Associated companies throughout the world
www.panmacmillan.com

ISBN 978-0-230-53154-3

1 3 5 7 9 8 6 4 2

A CIP catalogue record for this book is available from
the British Library.

Typeset by SetSystems Ltd, Saffron Walden, Essex
Printed and bound in Great Britain by
Mackays of Chatham plc, Chatham, Kent

Contents

Contents

PART THREE

PART FOUR

Contents

Contents

PART ONE

1

A FUNERAL IN LONDON

The afternoon was tinged with the unreal. Riding the Underground to London's Highgate Cemetery, I caught myself reliving Russian funerals from my past. Andrei Sakharov's emotional leave-taking in 1989, when weeping thousands lined the streets of Moscow; the murdered Russian *mafiosnik* whose burial party I saw decimated by a graveside bomb ... severed limbs on the cemetery path, a shin and foot in the branches of a tree, the foot still sheathed in one expensive loafer.

I shook myself. This was December 2006; north London on a drizzly Thursday. What could the funeral of an exiled former KGB man offer that I hadn't seen before? Highgate Cemetery was drenched in dark December rain. The funeral procession straggled through the puddles of a tree-lined avenue, an outsized coffin perched precariously on the shoulders of eleven ill-matched pall-bearers. So here he was. Encased in lead, wrapped in oak, adorned with gleaming brass. More resplendent in death than ever he was in life, here was Sasha Litvinenko, the boy from the deep Russian provinces who rose through the ranks of the world's most feared security service; the man who alleged murder and corruption in the Russian government, fled from the wrath of the Kremlin, came to London and took the shilling of Moscow's avowed enemy. Now he was a martyr, condemned by foes unknown to an agonizing death in a hospital bed many miles from home; now he would lie in foreign soil, in an airtight casket to preserve his body for a thousand years. A hundred yards away, the grey granite statue of Karl Marx rose above the grave of the father of world revolution.

★

Sasha's coffin was heavy; Boris Berezovsky couldn't hide his relief as the weight was lifted from his back. In the greenery and the fresh air Berezovsky seemed somehow diminished, subdued, not his usual combative self. It came to me that all the times I had met Berezovsky it was always inside, away from the light – under the fluorescent strips of his claustrophobic Down Street office or at the shielded corner table of the Al Hamra restaurant with his bodyguards surrounding us, watching all the doors at once.

Now there was something odd. Why was Berezovsky not exploiting the moment? Ever since I had known him, he had seized every opportunity to blacken the hated name of Vladimir Putin. In the late 1990s Berezovsky had been Russia's richest and most powerful man. He had established such a financial and political stranglehold over the weak Boris Yeltsin that he had virtually run the country. But Putin had dethroned him, stripped him of his power and much of his wealth. In a boiling fury Berezovsky had fled to London and appeared to have devoted his life to an obsessive quest for revenge. Sasha Litvinenko was Berezovsky's lieutenant in a bitter propaganda campaign against Putin and his regime. But now, as the world reviled Putin as the hidden hand behind Sasha's murder, Berezovsky was retreating into his shell. I wondered what he had on his mind as he watched the coffin poised over the open grave. Why did the leader and financier of the anti-Kremlin opposition seem so preoccupied?

Sasha's father, Walter Litvinenko, was talking, his face etched with the uncomprehending pain of an old man contemplating the brutal death of a son. As he spoke, his pain turned to anger. 'My son was killed,' he said. 'Killed by those who had every reason to fear what he knew. To fear the truth he told. They wanted to silence him in the cruellest fashion.'

There was nothing suspect about Walter Litvinenko's grief. His was a human personal tragedy. But what of the men he blamed for it? What about Putin, the president who gave his security services the legal right to assassinate political enemies on Russian soil or abroad? What about Sasha's former colleagues in the KGB – now renamed the Federal Security Service or FSB? As the mourners filed past, I picked out some unknown faces among the familiar crowd of exiled oligarchs and their acolytes – one unknown man in a leather jacket, another smoking a cigarette despite the solemnity of the occasion. Who were they? Sasha's friends from far away? Kremlin envoys sent to gather intelligence on its enemies abroad?

Akhmed Zakayev, a powerful member of the Berezovsky camp with sad southern eyes in a face etched by the grief of his nation, nodded to a man with a beard and Islamic skullcap. The imam intoned a Muslim prayer and Zakayev made the ritual motion of washing his face with both hands. Another odd moment this, in an increasingly puzzling day. I had first met Akhmed Zakayev in 2003, when he was campaigning to avoid extradition from Britain to Russia. As Chechen foreign minister, he had angered the Kremlin by wooing the foreign media with tales of Russian atrocities in his homeland; Putin in return accused him of terrorist crimes. A PR campaign led by Tim Bell and Vanessa Redgrave swayed the British press and – just as it had done with Zakayev's protector Berezovsky – the High Court rejected the extradition request. Zakayev got the right to stay in Britain, in a London that disaffected Russians have made the headquarters of anti-Putin opposition.

He and Berezovsky persuaded Sasha Litvinenko to settle in London with them. They found him a house next door to Zakayev, gave publicity to his accusations of FSB villainy and offered him protection – how ironic that now seemed – against the avenging agents of his enemies. In return, Litvinenko told the world that President Putin had plotted to murder Berezovsky; that Putin had conspired with the FSB to blow up Moscow apartment blocks and blame the attacks on Chechen separatists to justify the second invasion of Chechnya. Over time, Sasha's allegations had grown increasingly outrageous, including claims that Putin had regular sexual relations with young boys – all, in retrospect, potential motives for a murder.

Litvinenko's former wife, his widow and three orphans stood in silence as the Muslim prayers droned on. His widow, Marina, still living in the suburban London house Berezovsky had bought for them, was unhappy with the Islamic element. She disputed the account of Sasha's alleged deathbed conversion and had wanted a non-denominational service. But families must come second to the demands of the political struggle, and Marina kept quiet. What were her feelings as she walked over to embrace Zakayev after the service? Was she acknowledging that her husband's life and tortured death had been a necessary sacrifice, a martyrdom in the covert war between the Kremlin and its political opponents?

It is a war that has blown hot and cold since hostilities were declared in 2000 and has pitted some of Russia's strongest, richest men against the most powerful president since Josef Stalin. But a war it most certainly is; a war in which each side accuses the other of the darkest acts, where claims and counter claims are made, sometimes without the slightest basis in fact, and the hand of Putin or Berezovsky is seen behind every evil.

2

EMISSARIES FROM RUSSIA

It was hard to imagine that five weeks earlier, at the beginning of November, the world had never heard of Alexander Litvinenko, or Sasha as he was known to his friends. As an old Russia hand and an habitué of Russian exile circles in London, I knew who he was and that he was closely associated with the kingpin of the exiles, Boris Berezovsky. I had had dealings with Berezovsky over the years.

Sasha Litvinenko was both a complex and a very simple man. Those who knew him well speak unfailingly of his naivety and an unrelenting stubbornness which made many regard him as an obsessive. His widow Marina describes him as boyish and emotional, but she says he had ruthlessness in him too. He was no angel. Even his closest friends say he probably had the blood of more than one victim on his hands. But they were victims he dispatched while carrying out his duty. And duty was important to Litvinenko; his constant refrain to those who would listen was that he had always behaved loyally and honestly. He spent his youth and most of his adult career being loyal to the authorities in his country, whoever they were: first to the communists, then to Boris Yeltsin's reformers, and then to the hardline autocracy imposed by Vladimir Putin, Sasha's former boss at the FSB. But in the course of a few turbulent weeks in 1998 he was transformed from a Putin ultra-loyalist to an acrimonious, diehard foe. As we will discover, Litvinenko challenged Vladimir Putin in the most bizarre circumstances; Putin rebuffed him, and Sasha felt slighted. His hurt – and his obsessive nature – meant he would not sue for peace, even when his comrades in arms were doing so. He threw in his lot with the Kremlin's public enemy number one, Boris Berezovsky. When Berezovsky fled to England in 2000, he fled with him. Since then Litvinenko had been venting his bile on Putin, hurling ever more outrageous accusations and insults at the man he used to speak of as his own role model, the man he once idolized with an intensity bordering on love. From London he had directed increasingly bitter polemics at his former colleagues in the FSB. He had become involved in murky business dealings, with dark suggestions of blackmail plots. And he had exasperated and finally fallen out with Berezovsky himself. Many had a motive for murder. In the end, someone's patience snapped.

The aim of this book is to discover who that someone was. Who had the motive, and the means, to carry out a murder that was for all intents and purposes the world's first act of international nuclear terrorism? This account will examine the movements and actions of a key group of players, both friends and suspects. It will weigh, and ultimately pronounce on, their guilt or their innocence. And it will look beyond the hired hands and killers to those who gave the orders. The truth behind the Litvinenko story lies in the dubious and colourful past of the man himself, the battles he fought and the enemies he made; it lies in the years of social and political upheaval which have shaped today's Russia and brought the current regime to power; it lies in the murky economic and business conflicts, the vested interests and the corruption of the body politic, which have divided a great nation into warring camps. All this has forced men like Sasha Litvinenko to take sides in a confrontation where they are the expendable pawns of ruthless masters. When pawns threaten – or when they lose their usefulness – they can easily be sacrificed . . .

*

Back on 1 November 2006 neither I nor anyone except a small, secretive group of conspirators had any idea that the fate of this fugitive from the Russian secret services was about to change the face of international politics and strain relations between Russia and the West.

That evening, I was invited to the Emirates soccer stadium in north London to see the London team Arsenal play the Russian champions CSKA Moscow. It was an important game, with both sides seeking a victory that would guarantee their safe passage to the knockout stages of the prestigious and lucrative European Champions League. Two weeks earlier, Arsenal had lost 1–0 in Moscow and they were out for revenge. Other people in the crowd that evening may have had revenge on their minds too. Within weeks, some of them were to become the focus of attention in one of the most spectacular murder inquiries the world of international espionage has ever witnessed.

The new 60,000-seat stadium was filling up with expectant Arsenal fans in red and white shirts and scarves, their chants rolling noisily round the banks of spectators. In one corner of the ground, less garishly clad and very much quieter, a small throng of visiting Russian supporters struggled to make their voices heard. In the Soviet era there had been no tradition of fans chanting or singing at Russian soccer matches; the stadiums were largely quiet and respectful.

The CSKA fans there that night belonged to the small minority of Russians who had the financial means to pay for a trip to London. Some came for the soccer; some for the bright lights and shopping; some perhaps for less innocent purposes.

Dmitry Kovtun, a burly, rather handsome man in his early forties, had flown into London that morning from Hamburg on the 6.40 a.m. Germanwings flight, a low-cost subsidiary of the German airline Lufthansa, but there was nothing low-cost about his accommodation plans. Kovtun travelled from London's Gatwick Airport directly to the swanky Mayfair district in the city centre and checked in at the Millennium Hotel, where rooms start at £170 ($330) plus tax. The Millennium Mayfair is a converted eighteenth-century mansion on the same leafy square as the US embassy, not far from Hyde Park. In the light of the events that were to unfold that day, the leaflet Dmitry Kovtun picked up from the check-in desk, describing the hotel as a 'welcoming, peaceful haven in the heart of London', now has an air of some poignancy about it.

Waiting for him at the hotel on the morning of 1 November was an old friend and colleague, Andrei Lugovoy. With the same muscular build and close-cropped grey hair as Kovtun, Lugovoy wore a look of professional wariness, his eyes sharp and mistrustful, darting constantly to and fro. He had flown to London from Moscow the previous evening, with his wife, two daughters and young son in tow, but he immediately told his wife he would be tied up with business matters for the whole of the day – she should occupy herself with the shops of Oxford Street and the galleries of nearby Bond Street. Kovtun, recently estranged from his German wife of eleven years, had no such problems.

The two men's greeting in the hotel foyer that morning was a brief, manly hug in the Russian manner. They seemed to understand each other almost instinctively, an easy sense of partnership and common purpose built on the experience of many years working together in frequently hazardous situations. They had known one another since childhood days; they had grown up in the same neighbourhood, in the same apartment block, and trained together at the elite Soviet Military Command Academy in Moscow in the mid-1980s. Kovtun and Lugovoy came from military backgrounds – their grandfathers had distinguished war records; their fathers served together in the Defence Ministry – so as teenagers in 1983 they had had little trouble getting into the academy. Its students were regarded as the chosen few, marked out for powerful careers and nicknamed the 'Kremlin cadets'. Both had excelled at their studies and training. When scouts from the security services came to the academy looking for promising recruits, Kovtun and Lugovoy were selected. Kovtun graduated in 1986, Lugovoy in 1987, and both went straight into the Kremlin Regiment of the KGB's Ninth Directorate, charged with the protection of senior state officials in the government and party.

There was a third soccer fan at breakfast at the Millennium Hotel that November morning. His name was Vyacheslav Soko-lenko, in his late thirties, three years younger than the other two, but also a graduate of the Moscow military academy and acquainted with Kovtun and Lugovoy for many years. Like them, he too had joined the KGB's Ninth Directorate and the three had served together until they all officially left the service in 1996. Afterwards, like so many former KGB agents, they had gone into the security business.

For three men looking forward to a night out at a big sporting event, the talk over the fried eggs, sausages and black tea was surprisingly restrained. Although the hotel staff serving breakfast in the plush, white-napkinned dining room were unable to make out the subject of the low, almost whispered Russian conversation, it is now clear that it centred largely on another Russian man who had been living in the British capital for exactly six years and whom Lugovoy – although not Kovtun and Sokolenko – had known for at least a decade. The man in question was Alexander Litvinenko.

3

THE INVESTIGATION BUSINESS

Because forensic examinations later determined that Alexander Litvinenko was almost certainly poisoned some time on 1 November 2006, the movements and actions of several people on that day became of considerable interest to the British police investigating his death. At one of the meetings he had that Wednesday, someone persuaded Litvinenko to eat or drink a quantity of polonium many times the amount required to kill him. To understand how he died I set out to retrace his steps, and from sources close to the events in question I have constructed a detailed picture of who did what and who went where. The names of Boris Berezovsky and a mysterious Italian wheeler-dealer, Mario Scaramella, will figure prominently, together with those Russians already named, and there is at times some conflict between the various versions of events. Some of the discrepancies may be the result of deliberate misinformation by some of the parties involved, and resolving them is crucial for the establishment of guilt and innocence in the crime that was committed.

According to Lugovoy, shortly after breakfast at the Millennium Hotel he had a conversation on his Moscow-registered mobile phone with Litvinenko. He says he cannot recall who phoned whom, or whether Litvinenko was speaking from home or on his mobile. He is clear, though, about the subject of their conversation: Litvinenko, he says, had contacted him several months earlier and suggested he and Kovtun might like to join him in a business venture.

Today, Lugovoy is coy about revealing too many details, but he says Litvinenko was involved in providing information and services to several British companies interested in investing in Russia. He will not name any of the companies, but he says at least two of them were 'well known, serious and respected'. When pressed, he will say only that their headquarters are located within walking distance of the Oxford Circus area of central London and adds rather dramatically, 'If I were to tell you their names, it would cause a sensation.'

Even allowing for the hyperbole, it is clear that Kovtun and Lugovoy do have extensive experience in the investigation business. Lugovoy describes himself as a security expert, and Kovtun says he is a business consultant. It seems plausible, therefore, that Litvinenko's interest in talking to the two men arose from his own activities providing information about market conditions in Russia – and about specific Russian companies – to Western firms.

Kovtun acknowledges that he is involved in such investigations, but he is reticent about revealing his other business affairs. It is known that Lugovoy is a partner in the Pershin drinks factory in the city of Ryazan, 120 miles south-east of Moscow, which produces mead, wine and *kvas*, a traditional Russian brew made from fermented bread. The Pershin factory, however, has attracted no attention from Western investors. What might be of more interest to them is the expertise of two former members of the KGB (and its successor organization, the FSB) in discreetly investigating the affairs of major Russian firms they are thinking of financing or buying. It is a widely accepted practice for large companies to employ investigation agencies to research their investment targets, and Litvinenko seems to have been acting as a go-between in this capacity. In Russia, where corruption and hidden criminality pervade the business world, the need for thorough investigation is all the more important.

As Litvinenko is now dead and his widow professes herself completely ignorant of his business dealings there is no one to challenge Lugovoy's version of the phone conversation that took place after breakfast that day. It may therefore be true that Litvinenko had been the instigator of the contacts with Lugovoy and Kovtun and that he was indeed seeking their help in digging the dirt on some Russian businesses.

It may equally be the case that contact had been instigated by Lugovoy and Kovtun, for an entirely different purpose.

What is clear is that as a result of their telephone conversation the three men agreed to meet later that day. According to Lugovoy, it was Litvinenko who was pushing the meeting, while Lugovoy and Kovtun were reluctant, citing a busy schedule of sightseeing, meals and some serious drinking before and after the evening game between Arsenal and their team, CSKA Moscow. Lugovoy is quite insistent they were not the ones who wanted the meeting and that Litvinenko told him during the phone call that he 'must see us today because he needed to tell us something'. Lugovoy says he replied, 'OK. But it can't be for long and it will have to be here at the hotel.' They agreed to meet at 4.30 p.m.

4

AN ANNIVERSARY OF THE PAST

Sasha had begun that cold, bright Wednesday morning in a mood of celebration. It was a special day for him and for his wife: it was six years ago to the day, on 1 November 2000, that they had arrived in England with their young son Anatoly. For most of that time they had been living comfortably – and mainly happily – in a spacious modern house in the respectable London suburb of Muswell Hill, the house that their patron, Boris Berezovsky, had bought for them. Sasha embraced Marina and congratulated her on the anniversary, but Marina could see his thoughts were elsewhere; he had that intense, excited look about him . . . buoyed up by some new project for the day that he, as usual, had told her nothing about. She could sense he had something on his mind, some meeting to go to or some new information to share with the world. But that was the way Sasha was: not nervous exactly, but always bubbling with nervous energy.

He was what the Russians call an *entuziast* – a man with a mission in life, with the physical energy to carry it out and the mental determination to see it through. Not an obsessive, she would later say, but not far from it. Marina read his articles attacking Vladimir Putin and the Kremlin regime; she worried that they had been growing more and more extreme, more and more provocative. She had asked him if it was really a good idea to be saying such things, but she didn't stop him. She knew her husband; she knew that when he had the bit between his teeth he would never let go. He would say, 'Yes, of course there is a danger. But I cannot act in any other way.' Marina feared for the family, but she supported Sasha's stand against the injustices he told her existed in Putin's Russia. 'When Sasha showed me his articles,' she would say, 'it didn't frighten me. I completely agreed with everything he said. Sometimes his articles were emotional. Sasha was very emotional.'

That Wednesday morning, Marina was hoping for a day free from the politics of fear and hatred. They always made the anniversary of their escape from Russia an occasion, enjoying a special meal together to reflect on their former life and the years since they had fled from it. Marina told Sasha she would be preparing his favourite chicken dish for when he came home that evening. Sasha was in a rush – but when was he not in a rush? He told Marina how much he was looking forward to their evening together, kissed her again and asked if she would drive him to the Tube station; he never drove in England – he'd never got round to converting his little red Russian licence into a British one. But Marina told him she needed to go to the food shops and had to buy a birthday present for a friend of Anatoly, so would he mind walking to the bus stop instead? Sasha cheerfully agreed; it was a dry, crisp morning that reminded him of early winter in Moscow. He wrapped a scarf round his neck. Marina watched him through the window as he ran down the street towards Muswell Hill Broadway to catch the number 134 bus into London ... just like a little boy, she thought to herself, in a hurry to play with his friends.

With the whirlwind that was Sasha safely packed off to his meetings and with Anatoly safely at school, Marina was looking forward to a few minutes at home before going out to the shops. Perhaps it was the anniversary that made her glance at the photos on the living-room wall: the picture of the two of them on their wedding day, looking so young and so in love; Sasha in his white shirt and new suit, and that tie she had bought him in the TsUM department store just near the Bolshoi. How handsome he looked as he gazed seriously and tenderly at his new bride. And there she was with that brushed-forward perm so fashionable in those days ... She unconsciously raised her hand to feel the short spiky hair she favoured now, dyed blond to complement her striking blue eyes, making her look younger than her forty-four years. In the photo

Marina was placing the wedding ring on her new husband's finger, cementing the union that would last until death would part them. The year was 1994 and they were thirty-two years old.

★

Both Marina and Alexander had been married before – he had two children from his first wife – but in the early years after their wedding they used to say they were like two teenagers together, always talking about the future, about the children they would have and the plans they would make. She had quickly fallen pregnant with Anatoly and the baby's birth brought Sasha great joy. He was always saying to her, 'Let's have another one, shall we?' Marina laughed when she thought about his bursts of enthusiasm. But he was a genuinely good husband to her, serious and loving; he never drank, unlike most Russian men, and he never beat her. He didn't smoke either, and he kept himself in peak physical condition. He told her he needed to stay fit for his job; in his line of business you never knew when you might need all the strength you are capable of. Litvinenko didn't tell Marina much about his line of business. Even before they married, she knew he was attached to the FSB, and she learned not to ask questions.

They had met at her thirty-first birthday party and she always said Sasha had been her very special present. At the time she was a dance teacher, slim, fit and attractive, and he was the rather mysterious friend of a friend. She knew he had been born in Voronezh and spent his early years in Nalchik, a pretty spa town in the mountainous Caucasus region of southern Russia, but his father, Walter, was a military man and the family had moved frequently to follow his postings. When Sasha was called up for military service, his family's connections got him posted to an officer training school – where he excelled – and after graduating he was posted to the elite Dzerzhinsky Division outside Moscow. He later told friends he'd had no idea the division was under the command of the KGB, although the fact that it bore the name of that organization's founder, Feliks Dzerzhinsky, may have been something of a clue. It was perhaps an early indication of a certain naivety that clung to Sasha throughout his life.

While serving in the army, he was temporarily attached to a counter-intelligence unit tasked with tracing the hundreds of thousands of illegal weapons that were causing havoc across the Soviet Union. Most of these had gone missing from Red Army stores, either stolen or sold by impoverished troops looking for a quick rouble. The buyers included criminal gangs, but many of the weapons were in the hands of ad hoc guerrilla armies fighting in the myriad ethnic conflicts of those years. Mikhail Gorbachev's loosening of the reins had unleashed age-old ethnic hatreds that had previously been kept in check by the heavy hand of Moscow. In places like Armenia, Azerbaijan, Nagorno Karabakh, Abkhazia and Ossetia, purloined Red Army bullets and bombs were fuelling increasingly bloody fighting and undermining the authority of the Kremlin. Litvinenko showed himself to be talented and able in the operations run by the unit, locating and seizing stolen weapons and breaking up rackets run by quartermasters and conscripts selling arms in huge quantities. He was given further work tracking weapons that had been sold onto the black market, including operations to electronically tag guns and trace their progress through the criminal groups that controlled the trade. It was Sasha's first encounter with the battle against organized crime and his record of success brought him a tangible reward: in 1988 he was invited to join the KGB's counter-intelligence service on a permanent basis. The KGB was starting to take him seriously and his career prospects were looking promising.

Shortly after marrying Marina, Sasha was sent to Chechnya. In 1995 Marina had baby Anatoly to look after and her husband had been sent to war. He was thirty-three and an officer in the KGB's special forces, the *Osobysty* as they were popularly known, with a conscious echo of Hitler's special forces, the SS. How could naive, idealistic Sasha be involved in that sort of thing? How could he be fighting the most terrible terrorists and killers the world had ever known? Russian television was making it clear to the viewing public that the Chechens were hardly human, citing the terrible cruelty and violence they inflicted on Russian civilians and soldiers. Marina sat at home in the apartment that was too big and too quiet without Sasha; she watched the TV news bulletins and feared for her husband's life.

When she heard from him, Sasha was reassuring. His phone calls were enthusiastic even. He said it was his duty to fight this war, to combat the enemy that threatened his homeland. The cause was just and he and his comrades were proud of what they were doing. When he had transferred from the army in 1988 the organization he joined was still the KGB; after the collapse of the Soviet Union in 1991 it had become the FSK; now it was the FSB. Whatever the initials, Sasha Litvinenko knew the security forces were doing honourable, vital work combating terror and keeping Russia safe.

In January 1996 his unit was moved up to the Chechen border close to the neighbouring republic of Dagestan. Chechen separatist guerrillas had been seizing hostages and threatening to massacre them unless Moscow withdrew from their country. Some of the terrorists – *bandity* as the Russians universally called them – had taken refuge in the town of Pervomaiskoe, just over the border in Dagestan. They had 120 hostages with them. Sasha sensed something big was about to happen. Along with his own FSB unit, there were troops from all parts of the Russian army: conscripts – *kontraktniki*, the enlisted men – police units and Interior Ministry troops, the OMON. The Russians surrounded Pervomaiskoe and besieged it for three days. Repeated attempts to storm the village were repulsed and sporadic negotiations with the Chechen fighters were leading nowhere. On the fourth day, Interior Minister Anatoly Kulikov and FSB Director Mikhail Barsukov were reported to have declared that the rebels had murdered all the hostages and to have ordered troops to open fire on the village with multiple rocket launchers. When they did so, Litvinenko and his colleagues realized immediately that, far from being dead, the hostages were very much alive and screaming to the Russians to stop the bombardment. Hundreds of Chechens and Dagestanis died under the Russian shells, including civilians and hostages. On the eighth day of the siege Litvinenko was with the Russian forces as they finally entered the village; it was littered with corpses and reduced to little more than rubble. The Dagestani authorities, who had previously been loyal to Moscow or at least neutral in the conflict, were outraged that Russian troops had wantonly destroyed one of their towns. The battle marked a small turning point in the attitude of the Russian public, who had hitherto been solidly behind the war.

It was, Sasha later claimed, a turning point for him too.

When he came back from Pervomaiskoe, he told friends he had been charged with transporting and interrogating a group of captured Chechen fighters, many of them injured from the battle. The fighters turned out to be young boys, all aged sixteen or seventeen. While questioning one of them, Litvinenko asked why he had joined the guerrillas at such a young age and the boy told him, 'I am not alone; the whole of my class enlisted straight after we graduated from school. We just knew we had to do it ... for our country.' Sasha told his friends that this was the moment which changed his mind about the war forever. The Litvinenkos were a military family and Sasha remembered the pride he had felt when his grandfather, a former fighter pilot, recounted tales of the same thing happening in Russia, of whole school classes joining up to fight the invading Germans in 1941. That was when he realized, he would say, that Russia wasn't fighting just some gangs, some *bandity* – it was fighting the whole Chechen population. 'After that,' he said, 'I knew it was completely useless. Our work was useless. And our cause was useless.'

Sasha's moving account of his activities in Chechnya and the epiphany he experienced there were later contradicted by some rather less savoury tales of his conduct. Stories were to circulate that Litvinenko had tortured Chechen prisoners in his charge and that at least one had died at his hands. He denounced the accusations as smears by his enemies, and no official complaint was made against him. Indeed, Akhmed Zakayev, who was then a leading figure in Chechnya's military command and fighting against Sasha and his comrades, never reproached him about his conduct there. Exiled to London and occupying the house alongside Litvinenko's in the years before Sasha's death, Zakayev led the Islamic prayers that wet December afternoon in Highgate Cemetery . . . two former adversaries united in friendship by a sea change in Sasha's political views that grew ever stronger after that day in Chechnya. Those views led him to his eventual obsessive hatred of the Kremlin, the FSB and the Russian state.

5

TRUST AND SECURITY

As Sasha Litvinenko kissed Marina and ran off to catch his bus on the morning of 1 November 2006 his thoughts turned quickly from anniversary dinners to more pressing concerns. After his brief telephone conversation with Andrei Lugovoy, he had been working on his strategy for their meeting and for the subsequent discussions he was planning. Litvinenko was pleased at the way things were going. He was in the process of concluding some business with the two visiting Russians, contracts that were potentially lucrative for all three of them. A few weeks earlier Litvinenko had taken Lugovoy to a meeting with an established British intelligence and security firm that was looking to provide its services to British and multinational companies operating in Russia. The name of the security firm was Erinys and their headquarters at 25 Grosvenor Street were virtually next door to the Millennium Hotel on Grosvenor Square. According to Lugovoy, he and Litvinenko had been in discussion with the firm on 'two or three occasions' over the preceding twelve months. Kovtun had been brought into the negotiations and all three of them had visited Erinys and another security firm by the name of Titon International, at the same address on Grosvenor Street, on 16 October. Kovtun says Litvinenko introduced them as consultants who could carry out security and intelligence-gathering operations for British companies in Russia, and that Litvinenko would take 20 per cent of their fee for doing so. It was a strictly business arrangement and, if it had worked out, they were planning to 'hand over the 20 per cent and say goodbye'. According to Lugovoy, Litvinenko's 'allowances' – the money he was paid by Boris Berezovsky – had been cut by two thirds to just £1,500 ($2,900) a month; he was in acute financial difficulties and 'very interested in money'.

Erinys describes itself as 'a British security company with an unparalleled reputation for delivering professional services under the most demanding of conditions to a client base representative of the world's leading corporations, and governments . . . With global experience in nationwide security projects, personal protection, training and site security, the Company has unique operational expertise in the petroleum, construction and mineral extraction industries.' The business was founded in 2002 by a South African apartheid-era official and a former British Guards officer with ties to the Iraqi politician Ahmed Chalabi, one of the sources of the pre-2003 claims that Iraq possessed weapons of mass destruction. These connections helped Erinys win a lucrative contract to guard Iraqi oil pipelines after the US–British occupation.

While neither Lugovoy nor Kovtun will say what sort of contract Erinys was discussing with them in the weeks before Litvinenko's death, Erinys has confirmed that it was at the time expanding its expertise in protecting oil and gas companies operating in 'difficult and unstable parts of the world'. Seen in this context, it is not difficult to understand Kovtun's assertion that naming the companies he and his partner were being asked to protect in Russia would 'create a sensation'.

Litvinenko's journey into London that morning was frustratingly slow. Traffic through the busy Archway and Camden Town bottlenecks was reduced to little more than a crawl. All the time he was turning over in his mind the risks and rewards of working with Lugovoy and Kovtun. Despite his natural naivety and enthusiasm, his KGB training had taught him to be cautious when it came to trusting people – in exile he knew he had to suspect everyone – but he had a positive feeling about these two guys. Like him, they were experienced FSB officers and they had a good knowledge of Russian security and intelligence matters. He had met Kovtun only two weeks earlier, but Sasha and Lugovoy had known each other in Moscow in 1996, although they had not been close. By coincidence, both of them had become inextricably connected with Boris Berezovsky, who in the mid to late 1990s was one of the most powerful men in Russia, the *éminence grise* behind the faltering presidency of Boris Yeltsin. After leaving the FSB in 1996, Lugovoy became head of security for Berezovsky's national television channel, ORT, and Litvinenko was thrown into friendship with Berezovsky by a series of dramatic, barely credible events that effectively set the course for the rest of his short life.

By the time the bus pulled into Tottenham Court Road in central London, Litvinenko had mulled over the past and decided he could trust Lugovoy and Kovtun implicitly.

6

THE ITALIAN JOB

But Sasha had another meeting to go to before seeing his Russian visitors. Another soccer fan was in London on 1 November 2006, although he appeared to have no interest whatsoever in the Arsenal–CSKA Moscow game. As a self-proclaimed friend and confidant of the billionaire former Italian prime minister Silvio Berlusconi, Mario Scaramella was a confirmed supporter of the club Berlusconi runs as his own plaything, AC Milan. But if the Arsenal match held no attractions for him, Scaramella nonetheless had a very clear reason for being in London: he had come to see Alexander Litvinenko and bring him an urgent warning about an imminent threat to his life.

Mario Scaramella is an ambiguous figure in the events surrounding the Litvinenko murder. Like much of what he claimed about himself, his story of connections with Silvio Berlusconi was a tissue of lies and inventions. At other times he has claimed to be a professor at Naples University, which says it has never heard of him, and an international expert on the world of espionage when he in fact applied twice to join the Italian secret service and was twice turned down. Two months after his trip to London he was arrested in Italy on the unrelated charge of slander and was being investigaged in relation to arms trafficking.

What can be said for certain about the events of 1 November is that Scaramella met Litvinenko at a London sushi bar and handed him a document. Because Scaramella was later thought to have shown traces of radiation poisoning, two theories immediately began to circulate: that he was the poisoner or that he was the collateral victim of a poisoning carried out by others. This is why the sequence of Litvinenko's meetings with Lugovy and Kovtun and with Scaramella would later become of paramount importance to the police inquiry.

In his account of their encounter that day Scaramella says that they met in Piccadilly Circus shortly after 3 p.m. and kissed each other three times on the cheek, an Italian greeting they adopted when they first met and continued with now even though relations between them had become somewhat less cordial. Then they walked to the nearby Itsu sushi bar for the meeting that was to raise so many questions in the subsequent police investigations. It was mid-afternoon and Sasha was hungry. He knew Marina would have a big meal for him when he got home, though, so he confined himself to the miso soup and some sushi.

Scaramella had been known to Alexander Litvinenko for some time. The two men had corresponded because Scaramella was a consultant to the Mitrokhin Commission, an investigating body set up by the Italian parliament on the orders of Silvio Berlusconi in 2001. Scaramella had obtained information about KGB and FSB activities from Litvinenko and fed it to the Italian parliamentary investigation, describing his informant as an unnamed but verifiable source. The avowed purpose of the Mitrokhin Commission was to examine and uncover the activities of Soviet and post-Soviet Russian spies in Italy. In fact, police phone taps are later said to have suggested that it was covertly being used by members of Berlusconi's Forza Italia party to try to smear his political opponents. In particular, Scaramella was interested in Litvinenko's alleged belief that Romano Prodi – Berlusconi's adversary, who was later to defeat him to become prime minister of Italy – was a KGB agent. It was a remarkable allegation, and even the usually forthcoming Litvinenko was a little reluctant to give it his full backing, but it was later to serve as another of the myriad suggested motives for his assassination.

Litvinenko had also put Scaramella in contact with other former Soviet agents, including Yevgeny Limarev, to whom Litvinenko had been introduced by Berezovsky in 2001. The son of a prominent KGB officer, Limarev had left Russia two years earlier after a career that he says provided him with good links to the hard-line forces –

known as the *siloviki* – now active in the government of President Putin. He settled in the mountainous Haute Savoie region of France and has subsequently offered his services as a consultant on ex-USSR politics and security, advertising on his own website and employing a press agent. Limarev claims to have maintained his contacts within the FSB, and over a period of months he provided Scaramella with information about Russia's secret services to be submitted to the Italian commission.

In October 2006 Scaramella received an email from Limarev warning about a new FSB plot to target enemies of Russia abroad. It said that Russian intelligence circles were 'speaking more and more about the necessity to use force' against several prominent critics of the Kremlin. Among those named in the document were Boris Berezovsky; Vladimir Bukovsky, the distinguished dissident who spent years in Soviet jails and now lives in Cambridge, England; Paolo Guzzanti, the chairman of the Mitrokhin Commission; and – most worryingly for him – Scaramella and Litvinenko themselves.

Scaramella had been due to meet Litvinenko on 10 November, but when he received the emailed warning insisted on bringing the meeting forward. He flew to London and told Litvinenko he needed to see him urgently.

The Piccadilly branch of Itsu, one of a chain with franchises throughout London, is small and modern, set behind a glass facade in an imposing Victorian building. Food and drink are partly served by waiting staff and partly selected by customers from a moving display. That afternoon the two men sat in the restaurant's lower room, where Scaramella drank mineral water and Litvinenko bought his sushi and miso soup, which he chose himself from the conveyor belt of dishes.

For Scaramella to have poisoned Litvinenko he would have had to find a way to contaminate this food, and that is what Sasha initially believed had happened to him. It would not have been easy to do this at Itsu because of the conveyor-belt system and the impossibility of knowing in advance which dish Litvinenko would choose. But the possibility remained that Scaramella had found a way to distract Sasha and administer the polonium while his attention was diverted or his back was turned.

Their meeting lasted for a little over half an hour. Scaramella produced the three pages of documents he had brought with him and gave Litvinenko copies to keep. The emails were from Limarev but quoted information he had himself received from one of his unnamed sources in Moscow. They detailed the charges the FSB was making against those named on the alleged hit list: that they were involved in efforts to blacken the name of the FSB; that they were close associates of the 'number one enemy of Russia ... Boris Berezovsky'; and that the Mitrokhin Commission was a provocative anti-Russian act. As always, the name of Berezovsky plays a central role in the fulminations of Vladimir Putin's Kremlin and it is due to contact with him that Litvinenko's name is included in the hit list.

This email contained a specific warning that the powerful association of fanatically loyal ex-KGB and ex-FSB officers known as Dignity and Honour was planning actions against Scaramella and Guzzanti. Two Russian agents were named as key figures in the impending operation: Valentin Velichko, the former KGB general who is president of Dignity and Honour, and forty-six-year-old Igor Vlasov, an alleged agent of the *spetsnaz* special forces, who was – claimed the email – already conducting reconnaissance missions on the intended targets. The name of Viktor Shebalin also appeared on the document, a name that will figure large in Litvinenko's story.

Scaramella's information was second hand and his descriptions of the assassin Litvinenko should be on his guard against ('black hair with slim build; walking with a slight limp but an expert in judo, with a good mastery of English and Portuguese') smacked a little of the stage villain. Litvinenko in any event was not impressed and evidently suspected the whole thing was another Kremlin attempt to scare its critics abroad. Scaramella claimed later that Sasha had laughed off the warning as incredible and 'more like a film plot'. Even allowing for the fact that Scaramella was by then one of the suspects in Litvinenko's poisoning and consequently had a vested interest in downplaying the importance of their meeting, it does seem clear that Sasha was sceptical. Soon after he was taken into hospital Sasha cited the banality of Scaramella's information as one reason why he suspected the Italian of being his poisoner: 'Mario didn't want anything; he gave me the email printouts. I said to myself, he could easily have sent these emails by computer. But instead he wanted to come and give them to me in person. Why? And why in such a hurry? He was very nervous.'

Sasha might or might not have been right to question Scaramella's motives in seeking the meeting with him that day. He might or might not have been right to dismiss the warnings of a Moscow-sponsored plot against his life. But there was one element of Scaramella's emails that Litvinenko did not dismiss.

On the last of the three pages handed to him that afternoon in the sushi bar, there was a paragraph that Sasha took very seriously indeed. In it, Limarev's Moscow source claimed he knew the name of the retired security forces agent, also linked to the Dignity and Honour association, who was believed to have planned the murder of the campaigning Russian journalist Anna Politkovskaya. Politkovskaya was an outspoken critic of President Putin, who had repeatedly drawn the Kremlin's wrath by exposing atrocities carried out by Russian forces in Chechnya. She had been killed in an execution-style shooting in her Moscow apartment building on 7 October. Politkovskaya was a friend of Sasha Litvinenko and he had been investigating her murder. The intensity with which he had been affected by her death is clear from the allegations he made in a passionate speech he gave at a meeting of a London journalists' club on 19 October:

'Someone has asked me who killed Anna Politkovskaya and I can give a direct answer: it was Vladimir Putin, President of Russia,' he said, speaking in clear, emphatic Russian, which was translated for the audience of anglophone journalists.

I have known Anna Politkovskaya for nearly three years. Every time she came to London, I would see her. She has been at my house; she knows my wife and my son. After publication of her book *Putin's Russia* she had increasing numbers of threats, which came directly from the Kremlin. At our last meeting, she asked me directly: Are they capable of killing me? and I answered: Yes, they are. I advised her to leave Russia at once. She told me that Putin had threatened her ... she was told the threat came personally from Putin. I make no secret of this. I am willing to testify in any court. I have absolutely no doubt that in Russia there is only one person who could order the murder of a journalist of the calibre of Anna Politkovskaya: that is Putin and no one other than him. Russia is completely controlled by the special services and I know how tight that control is. A journalist of Politkovskaya's standing could not be touched by anyone other than the president of the Russian Federation. Anna was a political enemy of theirs and that is the reason they killed her. Putin killed her. That is indisputable. We'll find out the full truth only when the regime in Russia changes.

In the light of Litvinenko's personal sorrow at Politkovskaya's murder and his vehement, unshakeable belief that Putin himself was behind the killing, it is little wonder that Scaramella's email excited his interest. Any indication, any proof, however tenuous, that the FSB or an FSB-related organization had a hand in the crime was just what he was looking for. He thanked Scaramella and – significantly in view of subsequent developments – shook his hand. It was late afternoon in London and a fine mist of rain was sparkling through the city lights; Sasha Litvinenko had somewhere he needed to get to in a hurry.

7

IN THE PINE BAR

Sasha was no fan of Mario Scaramella. Several years' experience had convinced him that the Italian was more of a self-publicist than a serious source of information; he certainly offered little in the way of business opportunities and the modest fees Litvinenko had received for providing intelligence to the Italian parliamentary commission had dried up long ago. But in the end Sasha was pleased he had gone to the meeting because Scaramella's information about who had killed Anna Politkovskaya was something that could be useful to him. And as always when he discovered something important, Sasha knew his duty was to take it immediately to Boris Berezovsky. When he shook Scaramella's hand that afternoon at the Itsu sushi bar, the place Litvinenko was hurrying off to was Berezovsky's office in a narrow street off the western end of Piccadilly close to Hyde Park Corner. He turned left out of the restaurant and jogged the quarter-mile to Down Street. He was there within five minutes.

Berezovsky himself was preoccupied and didn't rush out of his office to hear Sasha's news. For one thing he had had a busy day, for another Sasha Litvinenko had started to irritate him a little in recent weeks; his tirades against Putin and his allegations of professional and personal misconduct against the Russian president had gone a little far even for Berezovsky's taste. Berezovsky remembers the way he treated him that afternoon quite vividly, his evident sense of regret perhaps explaining his preoccupied air at Sasha's funeral.

> He came to my office – it was 1 November – he called me and said, 'Boris, I've got very important information about the Politkovskaya case' – because he was investigating it – 'and I want to give you some papers,' and I said, 'OK, Alexander. But I am in a hurry. Today I am leaving; and I've got a football game tonight

and so forth.' And he said, 'Boris, I'll come just for five minutes; I want to give you copies of these papers.' So I said, 'OK. Come.' He came to the office, but I didn't see him arrive. I only met him when he was already at the copier machine and he gave me these two or three pages, and I said, 'Look, Sasha, I don't have time. Please.' And then a friend of mine arrived and my assistant came up to me and I gave Sasha his papers back and I said, 'Sasha, I'll come back later and we'll read these papers together.' And he said, 'OK. You're wrong not to want to read it now. But OK.' I tell you, except for his family, for sure, his wife who knew him much better than me, I was the one who took him the most seriously of anyone. But even for me it sometimes seemed very far from the reality. OK, he was this kind of personality and unfortunately other people – even me – didn't take him seriously ... For sure he was not comfortable that people didn't take him seriously, in many cases. Even I – even I – who had the chance to recognize that he is correct – he saved my life – even, often when he presented me [with] some facts, I would say to him, 'Alexander, wait, please. Let's do this tomorrow, or after tomorrow, or a week later.' Even with the Politkovskaya papers.

It is clear there was some tension between Litvinenko and his long-time patron. Berezovsky had grown exasperated with his former protégé, and when Berezovsky's office was later found to have been heavily contaminated with polonium, suspicions arose that he may have been instrumental in Litvinenko's murder. Berezovsky reported that no food or drink was consumed at their meeting that day, and if Berezovsky was correct it is not easy to see how poison could have been administered. But Scotland Yard were on the case and they were not ruling Berezovsky out as a suspect. At the end of their encounter he had sent Sasha away without reading the papers he had brought from Scaramella, without reading the warning of a Kremlin hit list on which both his and Litvinenko's names figured prominently.

*

Litvinenko was disappointed by Berezovsky's reaction. He had hoped the information he had brought would impress his boss. Berezovsky had been cool with him recently and Sasha was constantly looking for ways to regain his favour, for ways to be useful to him in their common struggle against the Kremlin.

From Berezovsky's office Sasha set off for his 4.30 meeting with Lugovoy and Kovtun at the Millennium Hotel. The two Russians say they had had an unrelated meeting during the afternoon, but claim they got back a little earlier than expected, saw Litvinenko was not there and went to the hotel's Pine Bar for some drinks. They were drinking gin and, finding Western measures somewhat miserly, had ordered several of them. Shortly, Lugovoy got a call saying Litvinenko was in the hotel lobby. He went down to meet him and brought him to the bar. The three men talked for twenty to thirty minutes but did not eat anything and – Lugovoy vehemently insists – Litvinenko neither ate nor drank: 'I can assure you with 100 per cent certainty that he didn't order anything, and we didn't offer anything to him either. He ordered nothing; we poured no drinks for him.'

Lugovoy's claim could be literally true – Litvinenko might not have ordered anything and Lugovoy and Kovtun may not have poured him a drink – but the possibility remains that a drink was waiting on the table for him when he arrived in the bar. Talking later to Marina, Sasha described drinking tea and said it didn't taste good. It is also worth bearing in mind the very precise mechanics of a classic KGB assassination, in which the actual killing is carried out by a person not known to the victim – and possibly not known personally to the other members of the team. There are many ways in which Lugovoy could be telling the literal truth, but the undeniable fact is that the radiation trail leads just as clearly to the Pine Bar as it leads to Itsu and to Boris Berezovsky's West End office. All three locations were contaminated, and all those present at them were potential suspects.

The meeting in the Pine Bar ran its course smoothly: there was nothing serious discussed despite Lugovoy's claim that Litvinenko had said he had something important to tell them, and they arranged to meet again the following morning at ten o'clock. Lugovoy says he even reproached Litvinenko for insisting on a meeting which had turned out to be a waste of time: 'Sasha, we could have just spoken on the phone and fixed up to meet properly tomorrow.' But proceedings were brought to a more informal conclusion when Lugovoy's eight-year-old son ran into the bar and came to talk to them. The boy had been out shopping and sightseeing with his mother and two sisters and wanted to tell his father all about the marvellous toys he had seen in the shop windows. Litvinenko introduced himself to the youngster, there were a few minutes of chatting and joking, and they all went into the lobby, where they found Lugovoy's wife and two teenage daughters. Bearing in mind later revelations about their meeting, the unruffled bonhomie exhibited by Lugovoy and Kovtun was quite remarkable.

One element of their account closely scrutinized by the police is the claim that Lugovoy and Kovtun were alone with Litvinenko at the meeting. Vyacheslav Sokolenko, the third man in their party, was said to have been absent the whole time because he had gone sightseeing and shopping with Mrs Lugovaya and the children. Although he too is in the investigation and security business – he runs part of a security conglomerate called the Ninth Wave, apparently a reference to the Ninth Department of the KGB, where all three men served together, or to a maritime expression for the worst wave in a sequence – he is insistent that he had no interest in the business Litvinenko was offering to put their way.

Sokolenko will say little about his time in London. He says he never met Litvinenko, although he admits he may have exchanged greetings with him in the hotel lobby, had no part in any dealings with him and paid no attention to what was going on. His explanation is quite simply that he is a genuine soccer supporter – 'I'm a CSKA fan,' he says. 'It's my hobby. I went with them to Paris, and to Lisbon when they were playing in the final' – and that his only aim in coming to London was to see the game. 'I guess I must have been out with Andrei's wife and kids on an excursion when that meeting was taking place and we met up later in the hotel after it was already over. Then we went to the soccer game.' Everything Sokolenko says about that day is aimed at distancing himself from Litvinenko: 'The whole thing sounds like raving madness to me,' he says. 'I only found out [much later] that there'd even been a meeting with Litvinenko. I was miles away from all that. For me, it was football and nothing else.'

It is perhaps surprising, therefore, that the Arsenal stadium box office has no record of any ticket being issued in Sokolenko's name. This is of course far from conclusive proof that Sokolenko had come to London for any purpose other than watching the game; tickets are sometimes available at the stadium turnstile on the night of the match, or someone could have got the ticket for him. But it may be considered somewhat unusual to travel all the way from Moscow to London for a football match without a cast iron assurance in advance that you can get into the ground.

For the moment, though, nothing appeared untoward and the party of visiting Russians waved Sasha Litvinenko on his way out of the Pine Bar with a chorus of *Do svidaniya*s and fervent good wishes for a CSKA victory that evening.

Sasha was not going to the game and was looking for a ride home. He called the mobile phone of Akhmed Zakayev, his fellow Berezovsky acolyte and next-door neighbour in Muswell Hill. It was 5.15 p.m. and Litvinenko was pleased to learn that Zakayev was still in central London. They arranged to meet so Zakayev could drive them both back home. Sasha had copied the Scaramella papers on Berezovsky's photocopier and he read them out loud to Zakayev as the car crawled through the congestion of London's rush hour.

Berezovsky, meanwhile, completed his afternoon meetings and headed off to the Emirates stadium. Somewhere in the crowd, Lugovoy, Kovtun and – he says – the mysterious football fanatic Sokolenko were also present and cheering. The game itself was not a classic; Arsenal squandered a series of chances to score, with their star forward, the Frenchman Thierry Henry, missing from just twelve yards. The match finished 0–0, but for Arsenal the damage was only temporary: within a month they had new victories that put them top of the table; CSKA had faltered badly and were eliminated from the Champions League; and Sasha Litvinenko had lived an agonizing twenty-three days, suffering torments that doctors described as close to unbearable.

PART TWO

8

FIGHT FOR LIFE

In their subsequent investigations the British police determined that Alexander Litvinenko was fatally poisoned at some time on Wednesday 1 November. In the course of their inquiries they sought out and questioned everyone they could identify who met him that day, including Mario Scaramella, Andrei Lugovoy, Dmitry Kovtun, Vyacheslav Sokolenko, Boris Berezovsky and Akhmed Zakayev. Every one of them denied vehemently that he had had anything to do with Sasha's death, leaving the detectives from Scotland Yard with the task of determining who was telling the truth and who was lying; of discovering who had the means and the motive to murder a man who seemed to have accumulated enemies by the score.

On 2 November, the morning after the soccer game, Sasha Litvinenko was not in the best of spirits. At around 7.30 a.m., he picked up the bedside phone in his Muswell Hill house and dialled the number of a Moscow-registered mobile. It rang in the Millennium Hotel where Lugovoy and Kovtun were on their way down to breakfast. Lugovoy listened, said a few words and rang off. His face expressionless, he turned to his partner: 'It's him. He's feeling sick. He can't make the ten o'clock . . .' The two men walked in silence down the hotel corridor to the dining room, where they ate a good breakfast of sausages, ham and coffee. Alexander Litvinenko was eating nothing.

The previous night he had come home at 7 p.m. in a state of great excitement. He didn't show Marina the Scaramella email about the hit list with his name on it – he didn't want to alarm her, and anyway it was obviously all fabricated nonsense – but he did show her the message about the alleged killer of Anna Politkovskaya, jabbing the page with his index finger and repeating, 'I told them. I told them. I knew it was the FSB. Of course it was them. Of course it was.'

He had calmed down a little by the time dinner was ready. He changed out of his business suit into jeans and a casual shirt and asked for a drink of water. He told Marina her anniversary meal was wonderful, his favourite, and he ate it all. Afterwards, he watched the Russian TV news on the Internet and sat chatting with Marina. Eventually, at around 11 p.m., he told her he was tired and was going to have an early night; tomorrow was going to be a busy day with a string of business meetings beginning early in the morning. When Marina came to bed an hour or so later, Sasha said he was not feeling well. Within minutes he was vomiting heavily. Running back and forth with basins and wet towels, Marina was at a loss to understand. She and Sasha had eaten exactly the same food – the chicken was good quality, from the usual supermarket – and she was feeling fine. Marina reassured him: it was just something he'd eaten – maybe the miso soup or the sushi; he was going to be OK. But, inside, Marina had a feeling of growing panic. She had never seen anyone vomit so violently. The vomiting was coming every twenty minutes. She dissolved some magnesium tablets to try to purge his system, but even with his stomach empty Sasha continued to be racked by violent spasms. Eventually, he suggested she should move to the spare room to try to get some rest – she had to be up at 6 a.m. to take Anatoly to school – and Marina agreed. She got to sleep around 2 a.m. When she got up at six, she found Sasha still awake and gripped by pain. He took her hand and said, 'You know, Marina, it's strange. These are exactly the symptoms we learned about at military school: they're the symptoms of a chemical weapons attack.' Marina looked at him in horror. 'What do you mean, Sasha?'

He winced. 'It looks like they've poisoned me.'

For the rest of that Thursday morning Alexander Litvinenko lay in bed, his body turning first hot and then very cold. It seemed as if all the strength had been drained out of him; he told Marina he had never been so bad in his whole life. By the afternoon he felt he couldn't go on. It was as if his body was being turned inside out, as if he couldn't breathe – he kept asking for the window to be opened wider, even though his body temperature was becoming alarmingly low – and his lungs were filled with burning pain.

The following day Marina bought more medicine to try to settle his stomach, which was so upset he could take neither food nor, alarmingly, any liquid. She rang a Russian doctor they knew and he promised to come the next morning. But that night Sasha began vomiting again and he told Marina to ring for an ambulance. It arrived at 2 a.m. and took him to Barnet General Hospital in a neighbouring London suburb. In the Accident and Emergency department paramedics examined his stomach and throat and suggested he had picked up a stomach infection. They asked Marina how she was treating him. She said she was trying to get him to drink water and the medic said that was the best thing to do. They could take him into the hospital, he said, but really all they could do was give him water, so maybe it would be better if the ambulance took him home again? Sasha's temperature was below normal – around 35°C – and he showed no signs of the usual fever that accompanies infections. Later, Marina would look back on this moment and wonder if things might have been different if she had pointed out the inconsistency and demanded they make further tests. Today, though, she says she doesn't blame any of the medical staff, and she was later told that once Sasha had ingested the fatal substance he was already doomed.

In the hospital that night he was still fighting. He told the doctors about the racking pain in his guts but they said it was because the stomach was empty and contracting. In the early hours of the morning they sent him home. For the remaining days of his life Sasha would not have a single hour without pain.

9

THE EMISSARIES DEPART

On the morning of Friday 3 November, two days after they had met Alexander Litvinenko in the Pine Bar of the Millennium Hotel, Andrei Lugovoy, Dmitry Kovtun and Vyacheslav Sokolenko were on their way to London's Heathrow Airport. Their British Airways flight to Moscow – number BA874 – was due to depart at 12.25. The three men, together with Lugovoy's wife and three children, had been in London for less than three days. They had excess baggage at the check-in – whatever their purpose in coming to London, Russians always enjoy the shopping – but the clerk was in a good mood and waved their bags through. By mid-evening, they were back home in Moscow, 1,500 miles away from the hullabaloo that was about to break out in London.

BA874 was still in the air when Sasha Litvinenko was finally admitted to hospital.

The Russian doctor who had promised to come and see him had turned up at the Litvinenkos' home and was shocked by what he saw. He knew Litvinenko as a fit, healthy man: a non-drinker, non-smoker who could run five miles barely breaking sweat. The man he saw now was a shadow. He could hardly get to his feet; walking was agony; even the slightest pressure on his stomach was unbearable. The doctor confirmed the diagnosis of a serious stomach infection with acute inflammation and ordered him to be taken immediately to hospital. He had lost eighteen pounds in just a few days and his skin was turning yellow. The doctors at Barnet General Hospital suggested the presence of a virulent bacterium in his intestines, but acknowledged that this would normally cause diarrhoea rather than vomiting. They treated him with powerful antibiotics but to little effect. Then they noticed his blood analyses were indicating a catastrophic fall in white blood cell counts. Litvinenko's immune system was collapsing. The doctors conferred, but the plain fact was that no one in the hospital had seen a case like this before and nobody had a proper explanation for what was happening to him.

During those first days at Barnet Hospital Marina Litvinenko went to see her husband every day. Boris Berezovsky and his people did not. Litvinenko had phoned them to say he had been poisoned, but in recent months they had become a little exasperated with Sasha and his wild allegations – Berezovsky admitted as much when he expressed his regret for not taking him seriously over the Scaramella papers on 1 November. Marina later said, 'They just wouldn't believe he had been poisoned. They thought he was fantasizing again.' 'Fantasizing again' – it is a phrase that says a lot about the way his patrons had come to think of Sasha Litvinenko. Berezovsky did little except tell Marina not to worry and reassure her that the doctors had things under control.

Marina, however, was getting desperate. With the doctors repeating that they had no explanation for her husband's symptoms, she was increasingly alarmed that no tests appeared to have been carried out for poison in his system. After forty-eight hours in hospital, Sasha's throat was becoming painfully inflamed and swallowing was a problem for him. When Marina asked the medical staff about this, they said it was the likely effect of the antibiotics. By Sunday 5 November Litvinenko's throat was swollen to the point that he had difficulty speaking. Marina had brought some warm tea in a Thermos flask; he could not swallow it, but he asked her to leave it by his bedside 'for when he was feeling better'. According to Marina, he knew by this stage that he was fighting for his life, but he continued to believe he would survive.

The following day, Monday 6 November, the doctors began feeding Litvinenko through a tube. When she came to see him that morning, Marina was shocked to discover that he could barely talk – his voice was reduced to a hoarse whisper – and she panicked. She went to the reception desk of the ward and shouted, 'What are you doing? When I went home yesterday, at least my husband could speak! Now look at him!' The doctors were quick to explain that they were examining other explanations for his condition, including the possibility of hepatitis or Aids. Tests for both were carried out over the next few days, but proved negative.

Marina speaks of her horror when some days later she was stroking Sasha's head – because of the initial diagnosis of a viral infection, all his visitors were made to wear surgical gloves – and found his hair was falling out in handfuls. When she looked, she saw his pillow and pyjamas were covered in clumps of hair. Once again the doctors had no explanation, saying only that it seemed to be the result of the collapse in his immune system.

Ten days after falling ill, Alexander Litvinenko was in a critical and deteriorating condition. He was convinced he had been poisoned and frustrated that few people seemed to be taking him seriously. On Saturday 11 November he decided to air his story on the BBC Russian Service, a radio station that had interviewed him several times in the past. After decades of providing uncensored information to listeners in the repressive Soviet Union, the Russian Service continued to be widely, if perhaps unfairly, regarded as sympathetic to critics of the Kremlin. In any event, if Litvinenko thought talking to the BBC would gain widespread publicity for his case, he was right. Despite his swollen tongue and severely inflamed throat, he was able to summon enough strength to be interviewed by telephone from his hospital bed. In the interview, which was taped and broadcast in Russian, his voice is feeble but he is coherent and firm in his convictions about what had happened to him.

> BBC: Hello, how are you?
>   AL: I am listening.
> BBC: The Russian press is reporting that there has been an
>   attempt to poison you. Is this information correct?
>   AL: Look, after a serious poisoning I am still in very bad shape.
>   I feel bad and I am staying at one of London's clinics.

BBC: Do you think what happened is connected to a particular event? There are reports that there was a plan to give you some documents about the murder of the Russian journalist Anna Politkovskaya and that after that you felt sick?

AL: I was contacted by a certain person, he suggested a meeting, and the meeting happened on 1 November at a London restaurant. He gave me some papers which contain the name of a person who might be connected to the murder of Anna Politkovskaya. That's it. After several hours I felt sick with symptoms of poisoning.

BBC: Could you tell us where this happened? In what area of London?

AL: In the centre, in central London.

BBC: Whereabouts?

AL: I don't want to name the restaurant. Police are investigating this right now – let them work without distraction.

BBC: Was it Westminster or Chelsea?

AL: I told you, police are investigating. Let them work quietly.

BBC: I understand.

AL: When I feel better, when I am back home, I will pass these papers to *Novaya Gazeta* [the newspaper Politkovskaya had worked for in Moscow] . . . to police and to *Novaya Gazeta*, that's all.

BBC: But to your mind these two events are connected?

AL: I don't know whether they are connected. I guess you can make your own conclusion on this.

BBC: But the name which is quoted in the Russian press, does it make sense?

AL: It does.

BBC: And the documents, are they solid; can you trust them?

AL: The documents are in English. I didn't even manage to study them properly because when I was home I felt sick in just a few hours.

BBC: Many thanks. Take care. Get well soon.

Two things are immediately clear from Litvinenko's interview with the BBC Russian Service. First, he was in no doubt that he had been poisoned; second, he immediately suspected Scaramella. The interviewer's question about the 'name which is quoted in the Russian press' is a reference to items that appeared the previous day on several anti-Kremlin websites, which named the Italian as having met Litvinenko on the day of his poisoning. The fact that Litvinenko did not even mention his meeting with Lugovoy and Kovtun is a reflection of the trust he had in their good faith. His conviction that it could not have been his Russian visitors who had poisoned him endured until just a few days before his death. It was based on the fact that he and Lugovoy had served together in the FSB, that Lugovoy had left the organization in the same sort of acrimonious circumstances as himself, and that Lugovoy had become a trusted friend and partner of Boris Berezovsky, the very man who had been looking after Sasha and his family for many years.

In retrospect, Sasha's faith in his Russian acquaintances may seem tragically naive and his reliance on the Berezovsky connection like a fatal error. When we come to investigate the hidden reality behind the stories of those involved in the last days of Sasha Litvinenko's life, it will become abundantly evident that in many cases all is not what it seems.

10

TOXIC SHOCK

Such speculation, though, is for later. For the moment Marina was still fighting to save her husband's life. Because of his plunging blood count and dramatic hair loss, Sasha had been examined by the hospital's cancer specialist. He told Marina he could see similarities to the symptoms he was used to in patients undergoing chemotherapy, and said hair loss such as Sasha's usually occurred on the twelfth day following treatment. Marina thought for a moment and replied, 'Doctor, this is the twelfth day since he started vomiting.' It was the clue the medics had been waiting for. That same day samples of Sasha's blood were sent for tests to determine whether they contained evidence of chemical toxins similar to those used in chemotherapy.

At last, the poison claim was being taken more seriously. But as well as pointing the doctors in the right direction, it was a development which served to ignite the ferocious political propaganda battle, with claims and counter-claims of who did what to whom, that was to surround Sasha Litvinenko for the remaining days of his life.

First into the fray was the Berezovsky camp. Despite their initial silence Berezovsky and his acolytes were now suddenly vocal in proclaiming their convictions about the perpetrator of the alleged poisoning. Their public comments were exactly what might be expected from the Kremlin's self-avowed 'enemy number one'; Sasha's predicament was a gift that could be easily exploited. 'It's not complicated to say who fights against him,' said Berezovsky after a visit to the hospital. 'He's Putin's enemy. He started to criticize him and he had lots of fears.' Berezovsky's aide, Alex Goldfarb was a little more sophisticated: 'Nobody's saying that Putin personally ordered it . . . though it's very likely.'

There was no immediate reaction from Vladimir Putin, but Russian politicians sympathetic to the president were quick to give their version. Gennady Gudkov, a member of parliament and former FSB colonel, was quoted by the Russian news agency as saying, 'My advice to Litvinenko is: stay off the moonshine vodka. Berezovsky's a talented puppet master, but he's not going to make this performance work.'

Sasha himself was strangely heartened by the controversy now surrounding his case. He had spent the last eight years of his life seeking out ways to blacken the name of Vladimir Putin, and his poisoning gave him the greatest chance to do so he had ever had. It is clear from what his wife says about this period of his illness that Litvinenko was still expecting to recover, and, had he done so, his status as an anti-Kremlin martyr would have been assured. In a way, it was an opportunity for him, as well as a threat. If Berezovsky was exploiting Sasha's predicament, he was doing so with Sasha's blessing. In the hospital he was trying hard to make light of the situation, showing off his newly bald head and asking Marina, 'Do you think I look like Buddha?' He was unfailingly affable with the hospital staff, always apologizing for putting them to the trouble of changing and washing him, and the nurses became genuinely fond of their exotic Russian guest.

The day after Litvinenko's broadcast on the BBC Russian Service, two developments gave the case a sudden impetus. From now on Sasha's private tragedy was to become a very public business and events began to unfold at a dizzying pace.

First, the results of the blood tests came back positive: there was a – so far unidentified – chemical toxin in the patient's system, although tests for radiation inside his body were categorically, and confusingly, negative. Later the same day the toxin was provisionally identified as the metal thallium. A compound of thallium added to drinks causes hair loss, damage to peripheral nerves and – if untreated – eventual death. The good news was that thallium has an effective antidote, Prussian blue, which is fed to the sufferer, absorbs the thallium in his body and passes out in the stool. The fact that the KGB had been known to use thallium against its enemies seemed only to confirm the suppositions about the origin of the attempt on Litvinenko's life.

The second development was that the British police began for the first time to take an interest in the case, coming to his bedside to conduct the first of many interviews, which were to continue virtually to the day of his death.

With the story now beginning to appear in the British media – and with the name of Mario Scaramella being widely quoted as a suspect – the Italian decided he should defend himself before he was convicted in the court of public opinion. In a series of interviews Scaramella denied he had played any part in the poisoning, or had any motive to do so. He even suggested alternative suspects the media might like to investigate, such as organized crime bosses in Russia who may have borne a grudge against the former FSB crime buster. 'We know very well who are the enemies of Litvinenko,' he told several newspapers. 'The work he did for years was to underline the links among the Russian mafia and some high-level corrupt officers in the Russian government. I can only imagine that the people who he worked against . . . may be interested to attack him.'

The Kremlin too was now starting to get in on the act, dismissing Berezovsky's allegations against President Putin as 'sheer nonsense'. Unusually, the normally tight-lipped FSB saw fit to issue a formal denial that it was involved, breaking a decades-old tradition of never commenting on its activities outside Russia, alleged or real.

It was clear that the propaganda battle ignited by the case was going to be widespread and furious, and that it was going to reach the highest levels of international relations. It had brought into the open a vicious war between people like Litvinenko and a powerful president who has managed to neutralize virtually all opposition to his authority in Russia itself, but has driven his most dangerous enemies into a London exile where they are plotting his overthrow by fair means or foul. If Western public opinion had previously been ignorant of this war being fought on the streets of London and other cities, ignorance was no longer going to be an option.

11

'I LOVE YOU SO MUCH'

The boost to Sasha and Marina's hopes that followed the provisional diagnosis of thallium was short-lived. On 17 November, with his condition continuing to deteriorate, Litvinenko was transferred to the brand new University College Hospital (UCH) in the centre of London. After showing only sporadic interest for the first part of his illness, the British police were now springing into action. Sasha's private room in the hospital was put under twenty-four-hour armed guard and detectives were at his bedside for most of his waking hours. Given his condition, they were amazed by his determination to continue with evidence-taking sessions, lasting three to four hours at a time, until they had every piece of information down to the last detail. By now he was receiving a constant supply of very strong painkillers, but the doctors knew he was suffering greatly. The sores that had inflamed his throat had spread to many of his internal organs, including the oesophagus, stomach and intestines, and as a result he found it hard to swallow the crystals in the liquid antidote that had been prescribed for the presumed thallium poisoning.

When he was first transferred to UCH Litvinenko could still stand and even walk a little, but by Monday 20 November he had become so weak that the decision was taken to move him to the intensive care unit on the hospital's third floor. Here he was connected to a series of drips and, propped up on a bank of pillows, was unable to move from his bed. It was on this day that the photographs which have become the enduring public image of the dying KGB/FSB man were taken. They show him with no hair and looking painfully thin, his green pyjama jacket opened to reveal the electrodes on his pale, naked chest. But his blue eyes are looking straight into the camera with a mixture of pride, defiance and astonishing tranquillity. It is as if Sasha Litvinenko were saying, 'I may be stricken; I may be dying; but I know what I am dying for and I know the cause is a good one . . .'

The same day that Litvinenko went into intensive care, Scotland Yard announced its Counter Terrorism Command SO15 was taking over the investigation into what had made him sick. In an announcement they said they were treating the case as a suspected 'deliberate poisoning' but were awaiting confirmation of toxicology tests. In Moscow the Kremlin issued another statement scornfully dismissing allegations that the Russian authorities had poisoned Litvinenko because of his criticism of their policies. 'Litvinenko is just not the kind of person for whose sake we would spoil bilateral relations,' a spokesman for the Foreign Intelligence Service told foreign journalists.

★

When Marina first saw her husband connected to the intensive care apparatus, she says she suddenly realized the end might be close. For Sasha's sake she put the thought out of her mind, listened to his plans for the future and discussed with him who could be used as a bone marrow donor if the doctors' suggestion of a possible transplant were to become necessary. But on Tuesday 21 November there was another, agonizing blow: the UCH doctors announced they were stopping the administration of Prussian blue, the antidote they had prescribed for the presumed thallium poisoning. Now they were saying the provisional diagnosis had been incorrect; they were back to square one, with no clear idea of what the poison really was. They could see from Sasha's symptoms that he was being attacked by some sort of radiation, but their tests for gamma rays had been consistently negative. Finally they decided to send samples of the patient's urine to Britain's Atomic Weapons Research Establishment at Aldermaston, which has testing and analysis equipment that is much more sophisticated than any hospital.

The following day, Wednesday 22, saw an acceleration in Sasha's decline. When he asked the doctors what his chances were, they replied, 'Where there's life there's hope,' and the official UCH bulletins for that day were still labelling his condition as 'grave but stable'. His blood counts, though, were alarmingly low, his immune system virtually non-existent. There had still been no progress in identifying his poison and consequently no hope of finding an antidote. The only reassurance the doctors could offer Marina was that Sasha would be connected to machines to monitor the functioning of his vital organs – heart, lungs, liver, kidneys – so that any danger signals would be picked up quickly and in time to treat them effectively. She told the doctors her husband had had regular physical check-ups right through his FSB career and they had always shown him to have an exceptionally strong heart.

That night, in the early hours of Thursday 23 November, his heart stopped. With the help of reanimation equipment and an emergency dose of nitroglycerine, the medical staff were able to start it beating again, but his condition was now critical. Throughout that Thursday Sasha was slipping in and out of consciousness and the end seemed close. Marina sat with him from early morning to late in the evening and saw a terrible deterioration in his condition: 'Suddenly I saw he was tired. Before that, he'd been a strong fighter. This time I saw he'd almost given up.' In the evening, when Sasha's father Walter was due to take over the bedside vigil, she leaned over her husband and whispered in his ear, 'Are you OK? Shall I go home?' He opened his eyes and said the first words he had uttered all day: 'Marina, I love you so much.' With tears welling in her eyes, Marina squeezed his hand and whispered, 'Thank you.'

At about 8 p.m., with Sasha once again unconscious, she asked the nurse if it was safe for her to go – was there a chance that something might happen while she was away? But the nurse reassured her: he would be on a life support machine to stabilize his condition; he was sedated and in no immediate danger.

Twenty minutes after Marina arrived home in Muswell Hill, the telephone rang. It was the hospital telling her to come back at once.

Despite the panic the phone call threw her into, she had the presence of mind to ask twelve-year-old Anatoly if he would like to come with her. It was perhaps a premonition that it was time to say goodbye; Anatoly had seen his father only a couple of times in hospital and not since the previous Monday. He put his coat on and mother and son climbed into the car. When they arrived, they were taken into a room and given the terrible news: Sasha's blood pressure had fallen suddenly and catastrophically, possibly as a result of the large dose of nitroglycerine they had to use to restart his heart the previous day. Once his blood pressure plummeted, there had been no way to save him.

Just after 10 p.m., Marina and Anatoly were told they could go in to say a private farewell to the dead man. When they entered his room, they saw Sasha had been disconnected from the life support machine. Freed from all the medical paraphernalia, he looked strangely peaceful.

Three hours earlier the laboratory results from Aldermaston had confirmed that Litvinenko had died from a lethal dose of the isotope polonium 210. His urine was full of radiation, but not the gamma rays the doctors had been looking for; polonium emits alpha particles that can be detected only by sophisticated testing. It was no wonder that the medical staff treating him had struggled to find the cause of his illness. The scientists at Aldermaston sent an urgent warning that Litvinenko's body would be highly and dangerously radioactive. The warning, though, had not reached the ward sister. She told Marina and Anatoly they could hold him and kiss him without the need for gloves or masks.

12

'THE BASTARDS GOT ME'

The death of Alexander Litvinenko brought one man's suffering to an end. But the discovery that he had been poisoned with polonium 210 was causing considerable panic in the normally serene corridors of Britain's Health Protection Agency. At 6 p.m., three hours before Sasha died, the HPA received a phone call from the scientists at Aldermaston; they told the agency about their discovery and suggested it should be thinking about possible measures to protect the public. Ominously, they said there was reason to believe that anyone who had been in contact with the patient could have been exposed to dangerous radiation from his body.

Radiation experts from the HPA were dispatched to University College Hospital with instructions to assess all nurses, doctors, cleaners and other staff and, if necessary, institute isolation procedures for individuals or areas of the building that tested positive. They were met in the intensive care ward by policemen wearing all-in-one CBRN (chemical, biological, radiological and nuclear) suits against contamination. Very late that night Marina got a phone call from the police to warn her that a CBRN squad was on its way to her home in Muswell Hill. On top of her mourning for Sasha, her life was about to be disrupted by a continuing radiation alert.

> When we got home after Sasha's death, we were really shaken up. The police rang to say they were coming round to us straight away. I thought they wanted to question me, so I asked if it could wait till the next day. I was feeling really bad. But they told me, 'When we tell you why we are coming, then you will understand.' They arrived at 3 a.m. They said, 'Get some things together and step outside the house.' And I said, 'For three weeks, no one paid any attention to us and now such a hurry?' They just said, 'We've

never seen anything like this before, so even we don't know what we're up against or what effects this could be having.' That's when they told us it was polonium . . .

It was the start of a radiation hunt that would soon spread to many areas of central and suburban London and eventually extend across the globe. Over the coming weeks the polonium trail would be followed and examined, not only for the sake of public health and safety, but ultimately as a vital clue in the hunt for the murderers.

At 11 p.m. that Thursday evening, Jim Down, a spokesman for University College Hospital, appeared on the steps outside the building's main entrance. He had a statement to make that the waiting group of reporters had been expecting for several days.

We are sorry to announce that Alexander Litvinenko died at University College Hospital at 9.21 p.m. on 23 November 2006. He was seriously ill when he was admitted to UCH on Friday 17 November and the medical team at the hospital did everything possible to save his life. On Sunday evening he was transferred to the intensive care unit where he could be closely monitored and receive any critical support he needed. Every avenue was explored to establish the cause of his condition and the matter is now an ongoing investigation being dealt with by detectives from New Scotland Yard.

Within minutes, Jim Down's words were being wired to news agencies across the globe; his voice was heard on television and radio stations from New York to Beijing. With its secret agents, international vendettas and radioactive poison, the Litvinenko case had caught the imagination of millions raised on lurid spy thrillers and exotic stories of revenge and murder. Commentators were falling over themselves to proclaim that any author writing such a work of fiction would be laughed out of court, but such consider-ations were no bar to the screeds of speculation and fantasy that were about to be unleashed in the pages of the world's press. Suddenly, every journalist who had ever read a John le Carré novel, every columnist who had been on a ten-day holiday to Moscow, was chipping in with theories that strove to outdo each other in their ingenious, exaggerated or simply invented explanations. Journalists love to see themselves as experts and above all they prize exclusivity; the spate of 'exclusives' in the British and American press and the stories claiming to have the 'real truth' about the case were endless.

For the politicians, news of Litvinenko's death was less of a jamboree. The British prime minister, Tony Blair, had been trying hard to cultivate good relations with Moscow; with Britain heavily dependent on Russia for oil and gas supplies, there was no way he could afford not to. But Litvinenko's death presented him with a dilemma: the presumed murder on British soil of a British citizen – Sasha's UK citizenship came through on 12 October while he was at Westminster Abbey attending a memorial service for Anna Politkovskaya – was not something he could sweep under the carpet with a few platitudes and expressions of regret. If the Russian secret services were shown to have had a hand in the matter – and everyone was immediately assuming they had – then London would have to ask some pretty awkward questions. At the very least, Scotland Yard would have to be given carte blanche to investigate the case and that could make things tricky for Blair. If the police uncovered the hand of Moscow, it would spell disaster for relations with his hitherto friend Vladimir Putin; but if he told the police to go easy, he would incur the usual annoying accusations of political expediency and kowtowing to powerful allies – and he'd already had quite enough of those over George Bush and Iraq.

While thinking caps were being donned at Downing Street, other interested parties were preparing for action. The announcement on the steps of University College Hospital that Thursday evening was the starting gun for a very public and acrimonious struggle. Within hours, Sasha's death had become the main subject of interest to all the warring parties in the conflict between the Kremlin and its critics at home and abroad. In the context of the war which had been raging between Putin and his allies on one side and Boris Berezovsky and the dispossessed oligarchs on the other, it was inevitable that the murder of an outspoken critic of Vladimir Putin would be seized upon as grist to the propaganda of both camps.

*

Before we consider the sordid unfolding of this unseemly battle over a dead man's memory – and before we turn to the assessment of who really did kill Sasha Litvinenko – it is worth examining the eyewitness testimony of someone who knew him well and was with him in his final days. Marina Litvinenko was of course closest to her husband and best understood what he was going through, but she was hardly an objective observer and herself says she took little interest in his political and business dealings: 'I don't know what his business was. I just know about our family life.' Andrei Nekrasov is a Russian film-maker who had known Litvinenko for over four years. He is not a totally impartial witness – he is sympathetic to the anti-Kremlin camp and has made a film which has angered the authorities in Moscow – but he was with Sasha and heard his last thoughts in the days before he died. Speaking shortly afterwards, he told me that Litvinenko was genuinely convinced it was the FSB who had targeted him and that ultimately he had dropped his suspicions about Scaramella. He did, though, confirm the picture of Litvinenko as a fanatical and sometimes irrational polemicist that I had heard from other sources, including, indirectly, Boris Berezovsky himself.

'I first met Litvinenko in 2002,' Nekrasov told me. 'After I met him, I spent days and even weeks talking to him. I liked him. I don't know what it is, but a lot of people just simply didn't have the time for him. But I somehow thought it was wrong to ignore him. I think he had a lot to say. But it was just his manner that slightly put people off; he was slightly obsessive, very enthusiastic, very intense, too intense. So people would walk away from it; they would find it even suspicious.'

The view of Litvinenko as a fantasist, or at least an overly obsessive zealot in the anti-Putin cause, was widespread. The list of his accusations against the Kremlin included some that were plainly ridiculous: over the years he had alleged that al-Qaeda number two Ayman al-Zawahiri was trained by the FSB in the period before the World Trade Center bombings in New York, that the Kremlin played a role in the July 2005 bombings of London Underground trains and buses, that the FSB was responsible for staging the 2002 Moscow theatre massacre, and that Italian Prime Minister Romano Prodi was a long-time KGB agent. In July 2006 he had written an article on a Chechen website accusing Putin of having regular sex with underage boys, the evidence seemingly being that he had been filmed playfully kissing a toddler during his election campaign.

Despite these wild excesses, however, Litvinenko – as we will discover – was the source of some genuinely credible and damaging revelations about the behaviour of the Russian government and the FSB, revelations that may have played a role in his eventual assassination. According to Andrei Nekrasov, Litvinenko felt strongly that he was not given the credence he deserved in life, and only in death did he feel the world was beginning to take him seriously.

> Seeing Sasha in hospital was a terrible experience. When I saw him, he was almost apologizing to me for the state he was in and the way he looked. He was a tough, hard man, a typical Russian man; he wasn't one of your intellectual types who are prone to complaining about things. He always wanted to be strong; he looked after his body a lot and didn't drink or smoke. But it was heart-rending: the first thing he said when I walked in was, 'Andrei! Look at me!' He knew I would be shocked by his appearance, so by way of greeting me he said, 'That's what it takes to be believed . . . I suppose this is the cost of telling the truth . . .' and he gestured to his withered and wasted body. I thought that was very together. He wasn't just disintegrating; he knew what he was dying for. And that, in my eyes, made him a much more profound person than I may unfortunately have taken him for

previously. I liked him but I never thought he was, you know . . . But now here already there was a touch of greatness about him. If you are dying for what you say and believe, and you are conscious of that, it's not something that's given to everyone. He was very clear about that. He was clear what he was dying for.

Nekrasov also saw a more vulnerable side of Litvinenko in those last days of his life. Sasha may have been an anti-Putin fanatic, but while he seemed to welcome a martyr's death, he was nonetheless scared of it.

At other moments he was saying, 'I don't want to die; I don't want those guys to dance on my grave.' He said that on the first day I saw him, on the Monday. On the Tuesday things were deteriorating very fast and he was already saying, 'They got me.' He felt he was losing the battle. And he knew he was going. He meant not just that they had poisoned him, but that the poison would mean his death. And when he said 'they', he called them *gady*, bastards. It was clear that he meant the FSB. 'The bastards got me, but they won't get everybody.' And the question, 'Why now?' It's proof that the timing of these operations can happen literally at any time. The way he talked about it in the last days was very much *oni vse-taki menya dostali*, 'they got me all the same' . . . even though it is all these years later. They don't forget. He said to his father that *dlinnaya ruka Moskvy*, the 'long arm of Moscow', reached out and got him. In Russian it also means that they wanted to do it long before, but now they got him at last . . .

Nekrasov was present at some of the sessions at which Litvinenko gave evidence to the police and marvelled at his stamina in providing the evidence they needed. But within a short space of time, he began to lose the will to fight.

He didn't want me to film him or even to give an interview. He didn't want to be seen in such a weakened state. Even in that famous photograph he still looks very proud. It got much worse, of course, afterwards. On the Sunday he looked like on the photograph. But by the evening he looked different already. It was so rapid, you could almost see him deteriorate by the hour. His face became more and more drawn and like a skull; his cheeks were sinking all the time deeper and deeper. You see it in cancer patients, but it's spread over weeks or months; but with Sasha it was a matter of hours. He was different on Tuesday from Monday morning. I saw him for the last time when he was already unconscious on the ventilator and he never recovered. It's something that will stay with me forever.

Nekrasov is close to Boris Berezovsky's circle of anti-Putin exiles. He says they were surprised it was Litvinenko who was targeted and alarmed that his murder was intended as a crude warning to all of them:

Sasha, of all people! Out of that little group, Boris Berezovsky and Akhmed Zakayev, the little circle of friends – and Politkovskaya was part of it; she didn't live here but she'd come and visit – and Vanessa Redgrave, he was the most physical and cheerful and healthy, so on that account too it was a shock . . . Also because he never went to Russia, unlike Politkovskaya; he even told me, 'Don't go there' . . . So in many senses we thought he was the least likely of the candidates, the longest way away from real danger. Everybody thought Zakayev was the most in danger, because he was officially described as a terrorist and so forth by the Kremlin and with that new law being passed by the Russian parliament to allow the elimination of enemies of the state at home or abroad, it seemed to apply directly to him; and the law would allow them to claim it was legal and if Israel does similar things and the Americans do too, to eliminate their terrorists abroad and kidnap people and so forth . . . that's why we thought that Zakayev was in real danger as a target. We never expected it to be Sasha.

On the main state-run Russian television channel news of Litvinenko's death was greeted with rather less sympathy. Mikhail Leontiev, the celebrity presenter of the seminal *Itogi* programme, tends to reflect the opinions of his masters in the Kremlin and spares no tears for its enemies. His on-air remarks were scathing about Litvinenko himself: 'It wasn't the Kremlin who did this, because it had nothing to gain from killing Litvinenko . . . If the Kremlin wanted to exterminate its opponents, think about it: Stalin had Trotsky knocked off, not Trotsky's chauffeur, not Trotsky's dog. Why bother killing Trotsky's dog when your enemy is Trotsky? Killing Litvinenko was no use to anyone. Litvinenko isn't Trotsky. I'm sorry, but Litvinenko is Trotsky's dog . . .'

To the Russian television audience the meaning of Leontiev's remarks was crystal clear: Litvinenko was a nobody, a dog, not even worth the price of a bullet, but Litvinenko's master, like Trotsky, would certainly be worth knocking off. And Litvinenko's master, as everyone knew, was Boris Berezovsky . . .

13

PR AND PROPAGANDA

The day after her husband's death, Marina was trying to come to terms with what she had lost. The thought that more could have been done to save him – by both herself and the doctors – gave her no peace. All she could do was recall the words of the medical experts that the polonium dose was many, many times higher than that needed to kill a man and that once Sasha had swallowed it, there was no medical means in the world to save him.

Eventually, Marina says she reached a state of acceptance where she could let go of the regrets and remember the Sasha she had known and loved. 'In the end, I know there was nothing that could have made things different. So I don't hold anything against the doctors. The only person I blame is the killer. And don't forget: he didn't just kill Sasha, he did it with such spiteful cruelty that he made him suffer terrible torments. Such a thing could only have been dreamt up by the most perverted sadist you can imagine.'

Marina's sorrow at the loss of her husband was touching and straightforward, but other people and organizations were gearing up to make use of his memory for their own purposes, to claim his story for their own political cause. Within days, the battle resembled the commercial scramble for image rights that surrounds famous actors and sports stars.

The first shot was fired by the Berezovsky camp. It transpired that the iconic photograph of Sasha on his deathbed released on 20 November had been taken and released to the world by Bell Pottinger, the Mayfair-based public relations firm that had found fame as Margaret Thatcher's image maker during her years as British prime minister. She had ennobled the firm's founder, Tim Bell, who as Lord Bell was now orchestrating the PR strategy of Berezovsky and Co. As the bulk of the British media began to reproduce the anti-Kremlin rhetoric that Bell Pottinger was putting out about the Litvinenko case, the *Financial Times* sounded the first note of caution:

> [Lord Bell's] role as a spokesman in the Litvinenko case reflects the fact that for the past four years he has represented Boris Berezovsky, the exiled Russian billionaire and friend of the former Russian spy. He also confirmed to the *FT* that he had been offering advice on media handling on a pro bono basis to relatives of Litvinenko and Alex Goldfarb, the former Russian spy's spokesman, during his dying days in a London hospital. His comments had been preceded by copious coverage in the British media portraying Litvinenko as a reformed former KGB agent turned political dissident allegedly poisoned by agents of President Putin as part of a wider conspiracy of politically motivated assassinations. That suggestion has been vigorously denied by the Kremlin. From a purely PR perspective, such scenes appeared a coup. It brought the bulk of the British media on to the side of Mr Berezovsky and the Litvinenko family.

As for the Kremlin's contentions that Berezovsky was more likely to have been behind the murder than any agents of Moscow, the *FT* says 'these were dismissed by Lord Bell in his "characteristically unruffled ... prompt and co-operative" manner. "It was inevitable that the Kremlin should try and blame Boris for this, they are always trying to blame him for something. But the idea that Boris did this to embarrass Putin is potty," Lord Bell said, insisting that anyone who knew his client would know he was incapable of killing anyone.'

On the day after Sasha's death, Friday 24 November, Bell Pottinger called a meeting in Berezovsky's Down Street offices to coordinate the PR handling of the Litvinenko story. Demonstrating that Tim Bell had lost nothing of his fabled talent for guiding the media, the meeting pulled off a PR coup that must have had Berezovsky in fits of delight, and Vladimir Putin in fits of rage.

According to the Berezovsky camp, by Tuesday 21 November Alexander Litvinenko had accepted he was going to die and wanted to leave a political testament to the world. It was to be a *J'accuse* letter and a warning about dangerous men not dissimilar to Lenin's famous deathbed warning against Stalin. That night he asked for Alex Goldfarb, Berezovsky's lieutenant, to come to his bedside. Sasha had known Goldfarb for a long time; Alex had arranged the escape route for Sasha and Marina's flight from Russia in November 2000. According to the subsequent Berezovsky PR, Sasha squeezed Alex's hand and told him he had something important to tell him: he had a statement that Alex should note down and release to the press in the event of his death. In the presence of a lawyer Goldfarb took out his pen and wrote down Sasha's words:

> I would like to thank many people. My doctors, nurses and hospital staff who are doing all they can for me; the British police who are pursuing my case with vigour and professionalism and are watching over me and my family. I would like to thank the British government for taking me under their care. I am honoured to be a British citizen.
>
> I would like to thank the British public for their messages of support and for the interest they have shown in my plight. I thank my wife, Marina, who has stood by me. My love for her and our son knows no bounds.
>
> As I lie here I can hear the beating of the wings of the angel of death at my back. I may be able to give him the slip but my legs do not run as fast as I would like. I think, therefore, that this may be the time to say one or two things to the person responsible for my present condition. You may succeed in silencing me but that silence comes at a price. You have shown yourself to be as barbaric and ruthless as your most hostile critics have claimed. You have shown yourself to have no respect for life, liberty or any civilized value. You have shown yourself to be unworthy of your office, to be unworthy of the trust of civilized men and women. You may succeed in silencing one man but the howl of protest

from around the world will reverberate, Mr Putin, in your ears for the rest of your life. May God forgive you for what you have done, not only to me but to beloved Russia and its people.

Two days later Sasha died.

On 24 November Alex Goldfarb appeared on British television to read out the statement. The BBC credited him as a 'friend of Alexander Litvinenko' but that was misleading. It gave the impression that Goldfarb was a neutral in the war between Putin and the London Russians, that he could be trusted as an impartial witness with no agenda other than that of a grieving friend. But as we have seen Goldfarb is a member of the anti-Putin opposition and a lieutenant of that movement's leader, Boris Berezovsky.

Because of this, questions were quickly raised about the authenticity of Litvinenko's supposed testament and about the credibility of the man who had presented it to the world. A Kremlin spokesman asked pointedly, 'Why should I trust this? A man who was about to die unexpectedly, writing a letter in the last moment of his life? He was unable to speak; he was extremely poisoned; he was very sick ... Was it written by him or by someone else who was a good orchestrator of that story?' Russian Defence Minister Sergei Ivanov was even more scathing, according to the Reuters report: 'Why should we care about what he may or may not have written on his deathbed? Litvinenko was a man of little intellect. He had an unreliable character ... He was never an intelligence agent and knew nothing that would be of interest to foreign intelligence services. The FSB took him on when we had a recruitment problem and he was fired for incompetence and his bad reputation. Litvinenko was a nobody who meant nothing to us.'

The story of Litvinenko's testament and the way it was produced begs many questions. The words attributed to Sasha are eloquent, polished and moving in their cold fury. But are they really his words? He allegedly speaks, for instance, about hearing 'the beating of the wings of the angel of death at my back'. It is true that Sasha could have a florid turn of phrase – you can hear it in some of his Russian radio interviews – but he spoke very little English and there is no equivalent expression in Russian. The phrase sounds fake or, at the very least, an embellishment. And if Sasha's words were being improved by judicious editing, how credible is the document as a whole? The Berezovsky camp claims the statement was composed in Russian and then translated into English, which could explain some of the stylistic issues, but the original has never been produced and doubts have been expressed over its existence.

When the statement was allegedly dictated by Litvinenko, he was already critically sick and close to the end. In the words of one of the nurses who treated him at that time, and who communicated with me through a mutual acquaintance, Sasha was heavily sedated for the last couple of days of his life; the medical staff had, she said, 'switched him off'. At the very least, Litvinenko was drifting in and out of consciousness. Yet the language of his testament is complex, balanced and powerful. Questions over its authenticity would dog the PR campaign being waged on behalf of the Berezovsky camp.

While there is little doubt that the statement reflected Litvinenko's belief that Putin was behind his death and his desire to have that belief broadcast to the world, the questions over its provenance and the manner of its exploitation are an important indication that investigators into the case should hesitate to trust anything or anyone. The man behind the Litvinenko 'testament', Alex Goldfarb, is an intriguing player in the Berezovsky camp, a foot soldier in the anti-Putin opposition that has become so vocal. As with all the vested interests striving to impose their version of the Litvinenko story on the media and public opinion, it is vital to consider exactly how much credence should be attached to the testimony of witnesses who are pursuing personal or political agendas.

It cannot be stated too often that the maelstrom of claims and counter-claims in this case originate in a world where things are not always what they seem.

The day I first met Alex Goldfarb, 31 March 2003, we had a

leisurely drink at a London pavement café. As the conversation unfolded, he told me the colourful story of his life. His grandfather, he said, had been the KGB station chief in San Francisco from 1941 to 1945 and had helped run the Soviet spies infiltrated into the US nuclear bomb programme. He had known Oppenheimer and been friendly with Charlie Chaplin and other Hollywood figures later to be accused of pro-communist sympathies by Senator Joe McCarthy. After his return to Moscow, his grandfather was shocked to find himself arrested by Stalin's NKVD as part of the so-called Doctors' Plot. The ailing, paranoid dictator was convinced that Jewish doctors were trying to poison him; Goldfarb, who was a Jew, seems to have been rounded up almost by default and was eventually saved from hanging only by Stalin's death in March 1953.

His son, Alex's father, was soured by the experience. He fell out of love with the system which had nearly exterminated his parents and turned to the underground political opposition. In the 1970s he distributed dissident pamphlets, trying to alert the West to the repression and anti-Semitism Moscow continued to practise. Later the KGB attempted to blackmail him into implicating an American journalist, Nick Danilov, as a spy; he refused and was arrested. Eventually, the Kremlin swapped him, the poet Irina Ratushinskaya and the dissident Yuri Orlov for a Soviet agent arrested in New York. They flew out of Russia on the private plane of Armand Hammer, the octogenarian American Sovietophile and former companion of Lenin.

Alex Goldfarb, a child of the 1950s, was drawn into dissidence too. Trained as a microbiologist he worked on the USSR's infectious diseases programme, winning national recognition for his research. But his political views were a matter of public knowledge. He collaborated with Sakharov and Nathan Sharansky on a political manifesto which questioned the very basis of Soviet power. Thanks to the high profile of his fellow protestors, Goldfarb was not arrested but given the chance to emigrate. He took it. In 1975 he flew to the United States and returned to the study of virology at New York

University. His expertise brought him to the attention of the billionaire George Soros, who engaged him to head a programme he was setting up to combat TB worldwide. Goldfarb quickly rose through the ranks in the Soros Foundation and played a key role in his boss's dealings with post-Soviet Russia, including some of the massive privatizations of the 1990s. Billion-dollar deals were common as Boris Yeltsin took the advice of Western economists and plunged Russia head first into capitalism by privatizing many state companies and resources. Soros profited from Yeltsin's lunatic fire sales, but so did native Russians like Roman Abramovich, Mikhail Khodorkovsky and – more than anyone – Boris Berezovsky. As soon as Berezovsky came across Goldfarb, he knew he had to have him on his team.

A genial, Americanized Russian Jewish intellectual with seemingly endless anecdotes, jokes and quips for every occasion, Alex Goldfarb is today firmly on Berezovsky's books and committed to the struggle to oust Vladimir Putin. There is a twinkle in his eye. He is inventive and blessed with a quick imagination. When I got to know him better, he confided that he wanted to be an author and showed me the manuscript of a novel he had written. It was about a plot by the FSB and a hard-line Russian president to engineer war in Chechnya by blowing up Moscow apartment blocks and blaming it on Chechen separatists. In Goldfarb's novel a Moscow businessman and sworn enemy of the president learns about the plot, but the FSB frames him for the bombings. He escapes and 'survives incredible odds to get his story out, only to discover that the world doesn't want to know the truth'. Incredible? Maybe. With such an imagination, no wonder some were asking who actually wrote Sasha's last statement.

14

A NUCLEAR TERROR

Other people were speaking about Sasha that first day after his death. Walter Litvinenko, who had helped care for his son during the last two days of his life, was on the steps of the hospital, blinking under the glare of the cameras. A little overweight but with the residual military bearing of an army career and smartly cropped grey hair, he was fighting back both rage and tears. 'A terrible thing happened yesterday. My son died yesterday and he was killed by a little tiny nuclear bomb. It was so little that you could not see it. But the people who killed him have big nuclear bombs and missiles and those people should not be trusted. He was very courageous when he met his death and I am proud of my son. He was a very honest and good man and we loved him very much. Now he is not with us.'

It was the first public reference to the nuclear theme – a slight distortion of course, because radioactive material had been used to poison rather than blow up its target – but it was a shot across the bows of Western politicians. If this was indeed the world's first act of international nuclear terrorism, it was going to be headache time for those like Tony Blair and George Bush who were seeking to contain the threat of nuclear proliferation. If these killers had gained access to radioactive material, how many others had done the same, how many dirty bombs and poisonings were already being prepared? Walter Litvinenko pointed the finger at the Kremlin:

This regime is a mortal danger to the world. Sasha fought this regime. He understood it, and this regime got him and he is not with us any longer ... If we let this go, if we go about our business as usual, this regime will get to all of us. Marina and Sasha were the most wonderful couple. They loved each other so much. They were so happy here in London, but the long hand of Moscow got them here on this soil. I feel extremely sorry for Marina, who has lost a wonderful, wonderful husband, as I have lost a wonderful son. If this regime falls, and I think it will fall, because a regime with no morality and conscience is doomed, then the street where Alexander was born in the city of Voronezh will be named after him ... He will always be in our hearts and in the hearts of the Russian people.

Pictures of the grieving, angry father were fed to news agencies and TV stations around the world. Vladimir Putin, in Helsinki for an EU–Russia summit, could hardly fail to take note. He conveyed his condolences to 'those close to Mr Litvinenko' and said, rather grudgingly, that 'the death of a person is always a tragedy'. But he was evidently well prepared for accusatory questions when he appeared at the final press conference. He categorically denied any Kremlin involvement and questioned whether there had even been a crime at all. 'The medical statement of the British physicians doesn't say that this was the result of violence. This was not a violent death. So there are no grounds for speculation of this kind.' Putin called Litvinenko's deathbed statement a 'political provocation' and questioned why it had not been published before his death, when he could still be challenged about it. 'Mr Litvinenko is not Lazarus. I think these tragic events are being used for political provocations. The Russian authorities will offer any help needed for the British investigation. And I hope the British authorities will not contribute to the instigation of political scandals.' Meanwhile, Sergei Yastrzhembsky, Putin's aide for EU relations, sounded the opening note in the Kremlin's fightback against the Berezovsky camp with the first suggestion that Sasha's death may have been a deliberate and cynical piece of mischief by the president's enemies. 'I am hardly someone who believes in conspiracy theories,' he told journalists, 'but in this case I think that we are witnessing a well-rehearsed plan by Russia's enemies to discredit Russia and its leader.'

In London Tony Blair was fighting fires on all fronts. Aware of its importance to both security in the UK and international relations with Russia, he had asked to be kept personally informed of developments in the Litvinenko case. By the middle of the afternoon, he was beginning to wish he hadn't. The Health Protection Agency had been in touch with the news that traces of alpha radiation – the characteristic signal of polonium – had been found first in Litvinenko's north London home and now in the Itsu sushi bar on Piccadilly. The house had been sealed and the dead man's widow and son moved. Similar measures were being implemented at the restaurant but, said the HPA, this was a public place which had been frequented by hundreds, possibly thousands of people since the radiation had been left there. If the level of contamination proved to be high, then the prime minister might like to consider a public screening programme to trace possible victims. To cap it all, the agency was now dispatching investigators to the Millennium Hotel and several other unnamed premises in the central London area.

The prospect of a major public health scare was looming. At the same time the Foreign Office was asking for an urgent meeting and the foreign secretary, Margaret Beckett, was due in Downing Street to update the prime minister. The Litvinenko case had already caused one acrimonious discussion between cabinet ministers after Beckett informed them that she had received an official complaint from the Russian Foreign Ministry over the way London was handling the affair. In particular, she said, Moscow was angry that Sasha's deathbed statement had received such widespread media coverage while Putin was in the public eye at the Helsinki summit. The Russians had, she said, apparently failed to understand that Litvinenko was under police supervision rather than in custody for any crime and that the British government could not in any event control what is and what is not carried by the media.

Blair had told the cabinet meeting that he viewed the UK's long-term relationship with Moscow as the key issue to bear in mind in the current climate, which some ministers had interpreted as a sign that he wished to minimize fallout from the affair and perhaps restrict the police investigation into the presumed murder. One minister, Peter Hain, objected strongly to any suggestion that London should go soft on Russia and pointed out that Vladimir Putin's human rights record was far from perfect: under his leadership, he said, there had been 'huge attacks' on liberty and democracy and some 'extremely murky murders'; in view of the Litvinenko case, it was going to be 'tricky' to maintain good relations with the Kremlin.

Alarmed by the vehemence of Hain's remarks, several ministers including Blair were at pains to point out that Britain relies heavily on Russian oil and gas; one senior minister expressed 'alarm' that supplies might be disrupted and described the Russians as 'too important for us to fall out with them over this'. John Reid, the ultra-loyal Blairite home secretary, was said to have cautioned his colleagues against 'making assumptions' about who was to blame for the murder, pointing out that Litvinenko had been 'involved with' organized crime during his time in Russia – presumably one way of referring to his KGB duties combating mafia-style operations.

Blair concluded the session by announcing that he was calling a meeting of Britain's emergency response committee, COBRA, to assess the implications of the Litvinenko affair. The committee, which meets at times of national crisis and which had last convened over the alleged plane hijack plot of August 2006, includes the heads of British Military Intelligence, MI5, the police and the civil contigencies secretariat, as well as senior cabinet ministers. It would convene the following day, Saturday, and report back to him on Monday morning.

Later that afternoon, Scotland Yard notified Downing Street that Deputy Assistant Commissioner Peter Clarke, head of the Counter Terrorist Command SO15, would be personally leading the inquiry into the murder. He would be asking the British counter-intelligence service MI5 to hand over all its files on Litvinenko in order to conduct a thorough investigation of his activities and contacts since he arrived in Britain, as well as tracing his career in the FSB before he arrived. If Downing Street had been hoping the police could be persuaded to go easy on their inquiries in the name of British–Russian relations, they were going to be disappointed.

Peter Clarke spent that weekend reading MI5's Litvinenko file at home. A member of his team says Clarke was 'flabbergasted' by the extent of the dead man's activities, both in Russia and since his arrival in the UK, which could have provided a motive for his murder. Scotland Yard has Russia specialists permanently on its staff – since the collapse of the Soviet Union in 1991, Russian mafia-style gangs have flooded into many west European countries including Britain – but even they were taken aback by the number of potential enemies Litvinenko seemed to have made.

PART THREE

15

THE LITVINENKO FILE I

Without access to the MI5 files, it was impossible to say exactly what activities DAC Clarke had highlighted in Sasha's past, or what possible motives he had identified from them. I had to start from scratch. Like Peter Clarke, my purpose was to uncover not only the mechanics of how Alexander Litvinenko was poisoned, but also who might have had such a pressing reason for wanting him dead and was prepared to go to such lengths to eliminate him in so cruel and public a fashion. From the use of polonium and the intricate planning and careful choreography, I was already convinced that an organized and powerful group with access to the most secret weapons in the FSB's armoury stood behind the killing. The riddle seemed to be: Who were they and what were their motives? The answers had the potential to trigger a diplomatic time bomb.

By speaking to close friends and colleagues of the dead man, to those who knew him best during his KGB/FSB career and his subsequent defection to the Berezovsky camp, I set out to piece together a detailed portrait of the remarkable path he had travelled, the dramatic events which changed his life forever, and the shady deeds he was himself involved in before he fled to London. All this, I hoped, would lead me to Sasha's killer or killers and to the men who had ordered his assassination.

As I conducted my research into Sasha's background, I too was amazed by what I discovered about the life he led, the risks he took and the enemies he made with such ease and apparent insouciance. What I found out about Litvinenko's past both astounded me and threw up so many potential reasons for his murder that I ended my research more surprised he survived as long as he did than that he eventually fell victim to the assassins who sought him out in London.

We have already touched on Alexander Litvinenko's early life, his conscription into the army and his time in Chechnya; we considered his recruitment to the KGB and his activities fighting the organized trade in stolen weapons in the old Soviet Union and the new Russia of the early 1990s. We left him in 1996 after his experiences at the battle of Pervomaiskoe had raised his first inklings of doubt about his commanders in the FSB and the government of Russia.

Until Pervomaiskoe Sasha had been a loyal, committed member of Russia's security forces. As the son and grandson of military men, he was proud to serve in the KGB and its successor the FSB. His attitude was simply that the work he did was necessary for the protection of Russia and that his superiors knew best: if they told him to do something, he did it ... including, at times, some unsavoury acts.

In November 2006, with the controversy surrounding his death intensifying, alleged crimes from Litvinenko's past were being aired, quite vocally, by men who now found themselves on the side of the Kremlin and its campaign to blacken Sasha's reputation. Among them was Litvinenko's former FSB commander in Chechnya, Lieu-tenant Colonel Alexander Gusak. Gusak spoke to several Russian newspapers about Sasha's conduct at Pervomaiskoe and his account bears little resemblance to the almost saintly, Pauline conversion Litvinenko described to his family and friends. Gusak said that, during the security forces' attacks on the Chechen militants who had captured the village, he asked Litvinenko to transport a wounded Chechen fighter to a screening and interrogation point. 'We had captured several militants that day. I spotted Litvinenko and instructed him to take one of the militants to the filtration point. That evening, when I wanted to question the Chechen,' Gusak said, 'they told me that Litvinenko had apparently tortured him to death ... Litvinenko liked to make the prisoners scream. That young prisoner did not scream. So Litvinenko stuck a finger in his wound.' According to Gusak, the incident was 'widely known' among the

FSB troops and to the Chechens themselves, so it may easily have been the motive for Litvinenko's poisoning, Gusak claimed, even throwing in a little hint that the Americans might have been involved for good measure: 'The Chechens have blood vengeance . . . and they could have got the polonium 210 from special services sources. Whose special services is another question . . .'

Asked about Litvinenko's character, Gusak said he was a good agent and investigator, but excessively talkative, unrestrained and nosy. In addition, he was a coward. During the fiercest of the fighting in Pervomaiskoe, Gusak said, 'I turned round and saw that Litvinenko was lying down. At first I thought he had been wounded. But when I came up to him I saw that he was clearly scared out of his wits. This was the reason he was subsequently withdrawn from front-line operations to staff work.'

Lieutenant Colonel Gusak, however, is not a disinterested witness. As we will see in a later chapter, he was intimately linked with the most dramatic public event of Litvinenko's life before he left Russia, and the role Gusak played in that event was by all accounts not a neutral one. Gusak's testimony is not necessarily inaccurate; it is indisputable that the FSB committed many atrocities in Chechnya and Litvinenko was after all a member of the feared *Osobysty*. But the fact that the story came out just as Moscow was seeking dirt to use against Sasha suggests Gusak was – willingly or unwillingly – playing a part in the Kremlin's game.

While Gusak's evidence may be tainted by the propaganda purpose it was put to, even Sasha's friends say he was almost certainly involved in some killings. His long-time colleague the historian Yuri Felshtinksy told me,

> It is understandable that if an FSB unit is sent to Chechnya with special powers, then they were probably sent there for a reason. I don't want to speculate exactly what they were doing there but I am quite sure that since they all received promotion and medals, then they probably were killing people as well. Litvinenko never

said this in so many words, not even 'This was a war, so we were killing people'; you would not get it from him. But I think we have to agree that they probably were involved in killings one way or another.

The film-maker Andrei Nekrasov, who was very close to Sasha in the last years of his life, gave me the same answer:

You don't have to infer that I believed everything he said – I'm not his widow, he was a friend – but precisely because I believed him then and still believe, I can say he was not an angel and he's not . . . He'd been through a lot – the war in Chechnya which he did, and all those gangster wars; and fighting organized crime in the 90s sometimes involved being . . . You know, they recruited agents from the milieu, basically criminals and you tried to make them work for yourself. So he was very familiar with all that milieu and that was his life. I dare say people do get . . . You can't come unscathed out of all that . . . and I dare say he was too.

Even away from the fury and passion of Chechnya, there are persistent stories about Sasha's life that cast doubt on his widow's idealized portrait of him as a kindly, sensitive paragon of virtue. Litvinenko spent a considerable amount of time working in the FSB's operations against organized crime gangs and – just as in Chechnya – there are suggestions of some less than tender behaviour on his part. Sasha himself allegedly told a British newspaper that part of his work involved the recruitment of contract killers to carry out FSB hits, and that the methods of doing so could be quite brutal. 'If somebody was the victim of a crime, like his daughter was raped,' Sasha is reported as saying, 'you would offer to let them take revenge on the perpetrator . . . This was how we recruited killers.' There were allegations too that Sasha didn't hesitate to do some of the dirty work himself. In one case he is reported to have carried out the execution of a loan shark with whom a senior FSB colleague had got into serious debt, eventually ascribing the killing to the ongoing operation against terrorists.

According to his widow, Sasha's work involved the pursuit of gangs who made money from kidnapping the sons and daughters of rich families. One such gang, from the former republic of Abkhazia, became notorious. Abkhazia was resisting annexation by neighbouring Georgia and the kidnappers were raising funds for the independence struggle by seizing and ransoming prominent Georgians in Moscow. Sasha helped to free the son of one such family and earned their undying gratitude.

16

THE LITVINENKO FILE II

Gradually, Litvinenko moved from anti-terrorist work to full-time cooperation with the Moscow police organized crime squad. Once again, he distinguished himself by his obsessive dedication, unflagging loyalty and relentless energy. Even his widow says that beneath his 'boyish exterior' she glimpsed an underlying *zhestokost*, literally cruelty but in this context more suggestive of ruthlessness. Sasha's friend, the distinguished and respected dissident Vladimir Bukovsky, describes him as one of the Three Musketeers, always eager for action, always keen to impress. 'He was like a hunting dog,' says Bukovsky. 'When he took a scent, he would rush off and you could never stop him. He was enthusiastic, keen, almost obsessive. That's why he was a good detective: his great determination.'

It appears that Litvinenko's qualities were noticed where it matters. According to his later account, in the winter of 1996 he was approached by a senior FSB officer who told him a new unit was being created to spearhead the battle against organized crime. The name of the unit, the Directorate for the Analysis and Suppression of the Activities of Criminal Organizations, or URPO, barely hinted at the reality. URPO was to be composed of hand-picked officers who would be given special powers to wipe out the country's top crime bosses. Their target was the men who ran the syndicates in drugs, extortion, kidnapping, blackmail and people-trafficking which were plundering Russia and terrorizing its population. To tackle such a powerful enemy, the FSB boss said, the unit would be granted immunity from the law: virtually any means would be acceptable, as long as they achieved the required results. He looked Sasha in the eye and told him he had been selected to be one of the unit's senior figures. Now that he knew the truth about URPO, he was of course at liberty to decline the invitation, but the FSB hierarchy would be honoured if he would accept.

Sasha's reaction to the invitation was pride. In 1996 he was still the old Litvinenko at heart – loyal, unthinking and dedicated to the system he was engaged to serve. He told Marina it was a great honour to be selected; he seems to have had no qualms about the nature of the work he would be doing; his self-esteem had been pleasantly boosted.

Andrei Nekrasov told me that Sasha was reticent about discussing what he had done in his prior career that made his bosses think he would be suitable for such ruthless work.

> It was a super-elite outfit. It had strong overtones of a unit that was charged to pursue, threaten, blackmail and possibly kill. That unit, to be completely frank, was composed of people that the leadership thought were capable of pulling off quite violent operations and blindly obeying orders, without ever disclosing . . . just doing the jobs and never talking about them. Those were the prerequisites for that unit. And later on Sasha actually said that the bosses had formed that unit with exactly those criminal intentions. And I asked him: So why did they pick you? and his answer was that one of his subordinates had used his firearm – lawfully, to neutralize a criminal, but not to kill him . . . shot him masterfully in the legs and so forth – and Litvinenko knew about this, and about another similar case of a subordinate carrying out such an act . . . and he defended them in a court case over the legality of using firearms or something similar – he defended them and effectively got them off the hook. So it was a combination of those incidents and his own reputation as a tough guy that got him selected for the special department.

It is an explanation that sounds like Litvinenko was being a little economical with the truth about his own ruthlessness, but he was keen to stress to Andrei Nekrasov that compared to some of the other founder members of URPO, he was a model of propriety.

He certainly said that others in the department had been considerably tougher than him in the past, including his immediate superior, Mr Gusak. They were all recruited at the same time and then Gusak was made the boss. He was the guy who recently made the claims about Sasha torturing a Chechen prisoner ... Well, Gusak had been involved in really tough operations, rounding up criminals and businessmen – in Russia, the distinction is not always very clear – and there were certainly some deaths. So Sasha hinted that all the guys who were invited to join were tough guys, but at the time he thought they were fundamentally good people.

When URPO started its activities in early 1997 it was clear that its members were expected to make full use of the special powers – and immunity from the law – granted to them. Most of the recruits had served together in Chechnya, where questions of legality and human rights rarely impeded FSB operations. Now the same *bespredel* (lawlessness within the state) was going to be unleashed in Moscow. Litvinenko would later describe URPO as the 'bureau of non-judicial executions', responsible for illegal punishments and blackmail of businessmen, politicians and other public figures. 'The Department's job was to "neutralize sources of danger to the state". In other words, extra-judicial executions. In theory, it was all fine: there's a vicious criminal; you can't get him with lawful methods, but you can get him with a bullet. The problem is that the system itself started to decide who to define as sources of danger. It meant the special services got a free hand to shoot who they wanted.'

The director of the FSB at the time, Nikolai Kovalyov, says Litvinenko himself was a prime mover in making URPO what it was. 'Litvinenko and Co. supported the creation of so-called White Death Brigades – in plain language, hit squads. Their reasoning was that it was impossible to combat organized crime in Russia with legal methods, so illegal methods would have to be used. That is to say, murders . . .'

Vladimir Bukovsky told me that Sasha baulked at some of the

most outrageous abuses, but raised no objection to what he saw going on around him.

> They were used to murder some influential figures in the under-ground, in the underworld, among the organized crime. Sasha and some of his colleagues were very much against that. He didn't take part; it was not compulsory; someone else would do it if you did not. But then he and his colleagues were asked to murder a businessman. Sasha objected. He said, I will not do that; if anyone else wants to do it, then let them, but I won't . . . Within a year, he had discovered that things weren't so clean and honest as he had thought. He discovered that most of the organized crime groups they were investigating had links within their own building! In the next offices!

In late 1997, following an internal power struggle, URPO was put under the control of a senior FSB colonel by the name of Yevgeny Khokholkov. Unfortunately for Litvinenko, Khokholkov was a man with whom he had crossed swords in the past. A few years earlier Sasha had been detailed to investigate a drugs and extortion racket which some members of the FSB had been running with a criminal gang. Such was the atmosphere of the times and so deeply was corruption ingrained in the system that few people batted an eyelid at the thought of Russia's law enforcement agencies collaborating with organized criminals. But Litvinenko claims to have carried out the investigation with his usual zeal and made some inconvenient discoveries. In particular, he alleged that he found a videotape of Khokholkov and leading mafia bosses discussing how they would divide the Russian drugs market between them. At the time Litvinenko was still working with the Moscow police and was frustrated when the case against Khokholkov was dropped. It was another blow to Sasha's faith in the system and, he claims, opened his eyes to the corruption and double-dealing which permeated the Russian state. 'I had never felt more betrayed,' he would say much later. 'I was knee-deep in the dirty system.'

Of more immediate concern, however, was the fact that Khokholkov had been given command of URPO and was in effect
Litvinenko's boss. The two men were destined to clash. Marina
Litvinenko remembers her husband's reaction at the time but was
evidently unaware of the details behind it.

> Sasha's problems seemed to start all of a sudden. He had been
> working on some case and they came and told him to drop it;
> he'd been digging too deep and in places where he should not
> have been digging. He started getting disillusioned. He wanted to
> work in a system where cases got seen through to the end. But the
> URPO unit was just a place of *bespredel*, lawlessness. Its bosses
> had acquired the right to carry out murders, in Russia or abroad.
> They could order their men to rob people and beat them up –
> completely unpunished.

It is clear that Litvinenko was losing his faith in the system. It is
also clear that he hated his boss Khokholkov. But throughout the
whole of this time he retained a touching faith – bordering on hero
worship – in one influential figure in the FSB pantheon: former
colonel and now significant political figure Vladimir Putin. Andrei
Nekrasov told me that Sasha had an obsessive fascination with the
man he would later turn so violently against.

> Litvinenko was always comparing himself to Putin, you know. It
> was a little love–hate ... or hate–love. There was hate and
> fascination. He disliked him profoundly for being immoral, for
> doing everything 'by the book' ... like looking away when some-
> thing wrong was happening or even countenancing criminal activ-
> ities. Nothing like that could have happened without the
> knowledge of Putin, who was the director of the FSB. That was
> one thing. But this moral thing was quite important to him too.
> He was very like Putin. He was ten years younger of course, but
> their careers were very similar, almost parallel: they were both
> lieutenant colonels; they were not recruits; they both volunteered
> for the force. Like Putin, Sasha thought he was doing a good thing,
> serving the country.

And yet, just a few years later, Litvinenko was devoting his whole life to accusing and insulting the man he had formerly held so high. When, after his flight to the West, Sasha railed against Vladimir Putin and accused him of bestial crimes including murder and paedophilia, was his fury perhaps driven by the memory of the love he had once borne the man, a love that had been spurned and rebuffed?

17

THE LITVINENKO FILE III

By the end of 1997 Litvinenko's disenchantment with his job and his animosity towards Khokholkov were at their peak. Sasha was disgruntled and spoiling for a fight; the cue for hostilities was not long in coming. The most dramatic and important events of Alexander Litvinenko's career in Russia were about to unfold, events that would change the course of his life.

A regular part of Sasha's duties in URPO was the physical intimidation of criminals, but since parts of the FSB were deeply involved in illegal activities, the definition of a criminal was becoming more and more elastic. By 1997 it had come close to meaning anyone the URPO bosses defined as a criminal, and that included anybody who threatened the FSB's own criminal interests, whether rival gang bosses, innocent businessmen or those who sought to uncover the truth about corruption in the heart of the security services.

Mikhail Trepashkin belonged to the last category. He was a lieutenant colonel in the FSB who had been running an investigation into allegations that high-ranking officers were involved in illegal arms sales, extortion and murder. Trepashkin claimed he had found proof that could convict several important men, but when he took it to his superiors he says he was told to drop the case; too many vested interests were connected to the crime ring he had uncovered and too many FSB people stood to lose out.

Trepashkin, though, was a stubborn man and told his bosses he would not let the matter drop. 'So I was removed from the case,' he later reported. 'When I said I would challenge this order, they told me I would be fired.' But Trepashkin was a trained and able lawyer and he brought a legal challenge against his immediate superior, an

FSB colonel called Nikolai Patrushev. Shortly afterwards three men came round to his apartment block, ambushed him in the stairwell, gave him a violent working over and confiscated his FSB badge. Yet Trepashkin would not be dissuaded. He spent the years after he was fired from the FSB fighting cases of alleged corruption in the Russian security forces with some measure of success. In 2003 he was arrested. He is currently in a Russian prison camp; Nikolai Patrushev, the man he challenged, is currently director of the FSB.

Mikhail Trepashkin is an important character in the story of Sasha Litvinenko, but their relationship began inauspiciously. Litvinenko was one of the three men who went to beat him up that night. There was little Trepashkin could do to avoid the professional kicking from Sasha and his colleagues – Trepashkin is not a strong man and the others certainly were – but he did manage to talk to them. He begged Sasha to give him the opportunity to explain what he had found out about FSB corruption, and Sasha agreed to meet him later in secret. The moment was charged with drama: the man who could easily have killed him was now prepared to listen to Trepashkin's case.

Marina Litvinenko says Trepashkin helped convince Sasha that things were badly wrong in the FSB and that someone had to do something about it. Sasha looked at the files Trepashkin had collected and came to the conclusion that he was right. The two men became friends and remained so until Litvinenko's death. With Trepashkin's encouragement and moral support, Sasha began to question the orders he was receiving from his URPO bosses. Angry with both Khokholkov and the FSB, Litvinenko was now looking for an excuse to pick a fight. He didn't have long to wait. On 27 December 1997 Sasha said he and four other URPO officers were called into Khokholkov's office and told they had been selected for a special mission: they were going to assassinate Boris Berezovsky . . .

18

THE TIPPING POINT

The alleged order to kill Boris Berezovsky threw Sasha and his comrades into a panic. It was not that they had never carried out such operations – killing people was an accepted part of their job. It was not even that they were horrified by the thought of murdering a politician – members of the Duma and opponents of the Kremlin had met similar fates in the past. The problem was that Berezovsky at that time was probably the most powerful man in Russia. And they knew it.

Berezovsky's official title, deputy head of the national security council, was merely for public consumption, a pretext to explain his constant presence in the corridors of Boris Yeltsin's Kremlin; his real power lay in the influence he wielded behind the scenes. The previous year, 1996, Berezovsky and a group of like-minded billionaires had rescued Yeltsin from certain defeat in the presidential elections in June. I covered the campaign as the BBC's Moscow correspondent and saw the miracle of a president resurrected from single-digit poll ratings to romp home in a two-legged election which was not even rigged – or at least not *very* rigged. Yeltsin owed his survival to the oligarchs who had given him unlimited money, expertise and blanket media support – they owned all the newspapers, TV and radio stations – and had helped him defeat a resurgent Communist Party that looked odds on to recapture power. In return for saving his bacon, Yeltsin had rewarded them with the keys to Russia's economy, auctioning off major state companies at knock-down prices and protecting them from rivals at home and abroad. Boris Berezovsky got his share of the wealth – he once boasted that he and six other financiers controlled 50 per cent of the whole Russian economy – but wealth was not enough for him;

his real interest was the acquisition of power. In the years after 1996 he exerted such influence over the weak, ailing and chronically drunk president that he was widely regarded as making Yeltsin's decisions for him. By the time Sasha Litvinenko was ordered to kill him, everyone knew that Berezovsky was the Kremlin's grey cardinal and a man not to be trifled with.

Litvinenko and his buddies later portrayed their response to the challenge as an act of principled revolt against a corrupt system. It wasn't. It was a calculated political gambit and a pragmatic attempt to protect their own skins. But it changed all their lives forever.

At first, the five men were terrified by what they had been asked to do. Litvinenko spent the remaining days of 1997 and the first month of 1998 in a stupor of indecision, wavering between his usual response to an FSB order – obeying it – and a deep-seated fear of what might ensue if he did so. Marina recalls the emotional turmoil he went through over the New Year period.

> I remember that December vividly because Sasha was so gloomy and so upset. Every time I suggested he come along to one of the concerts we were putting on, he just said, 'Marina, I can't think about concerts right now. I know so many things – and I can't tell you about them.' He used to come home in a terrible state and I'd say to him, 'Just put it out of your mind.' But he said, 'I can't do. Maybe after work we can go for a walk for an hour and maybe I'll feel better.' He just took all those things to heart. He couldn't escape from the pressure he was under at work.

Writing about it years later, Litvinenko gave a rather heroic cast to the dilemma he was in at that time and was mindful to paint the FSB's nominated victim as a champion of honesty and propriety:

> No one explained why we were asked to kill him. There was no need to; Berezovsky was the leading oligarch, a billionaire businessman, and his Liberal Russia Party was standing up to the corruption at the heart of the FSB and of our own unit, URPO. He was a threat to us.

Litvinenko maintained that as soon as he received the order to kill Berezovsky, he followed the dictates of his conscience and went to warn him about the plot. In fact, Sasha and his comrades took nearly two months to make up their minds: from 27 December 1997 when the command was given, to February 1998 when they took the first steps towards blowing the whistle.

For those two months, like the good security officers they were, the FSB men were carefully teasing out who was behind the proposed assassination, talking to contacts and sources, trying to discover if its backers were themselves powerful people and whether it would be in their own interests to go along with it. They were in short covering their backs, and who would blame them for doing so? Litvinenko and his four colleagues had been thrust into a power struggle at the highest levels of the Russian state, where the stakes were literally life and death. They knew a bad call could mean an end to their careers and, quite possibly, their lives.

The first problem for them was that there was no written order to carry out the killing. It had been given to them orally at a meeting with Khokholkov and his deputy, Captain Alexander Kamishnikov, so was deniable. What Sasha needed to know was whether the order originated from the highest levels of the FSB command, in which case it probably came with the blessing of a senior minister or even the president himself. If powerful forces were behind the hit, it might make sense for them to agree to do it. But if it originated solely from Khokholkov and his cronies, scared their illegal rackets were under threat, carrying out the order would leave Sasha and his comrades dangerously exposed. With no protection in high places, they would almost certainly be identified as the perpetrators and handed over to face the music. Marina Litvinenko recalls the moment they reached their decision.

> They got to a point where they decided that the initiative to eliminate Berezovsky had come from their own boss, from within their own division – it was a division that had a reputation for

doing its own thing – and that the top people in the FSB didn't know about it. So they drew up a report on the matter and took it to the director of the FSB, who was Kovalyov at the time. He listened to what they had to say and called in the man who had given them the order. Confronted by them, the man denied everything of course. He just denied anything of the sort had ever happened. And all those who had come to report the affair were taken off their duties and put under investigation.

If we assume that Sasha was telling the truth about the order to kill Berezovsky, several important things emerge from his account of the affair. The first is that he had the clout to reach the top man in the FSB. His standing in URPO clearly made him a credible and sufficiently senior officer to be taken seriously, so the stories he was later to recount about his operational experiences were not the product of some low-ranking Walter Mitty. The second, more worrying, inference to be drawn is that URPO was quite evidently a law unto itself, a body within an organization that could take decisions as important as the assassination of a major public figure. Murders could be ordered at colonel and lieutenant colonel level; the FSB command need never know. And third, there was clearly a well-established process of deniability in place: major decisions were taken in cosy chats on sofas in private offices with no minutes and no paper trail. Both of the last two elements will be of crucial importance when we come to examine the decision-making process behind Litvinenko's own assassination nearly a decade later.

Back in January 1998 Sasha and his partners were wondering if they had done the right thing. They had avoided carrying the can for an unsanctioned and disavowed murder, but they had disobeyed an order, informed on their superior and – worst of all – had not been believed: their charges had been dismissed as 'frivolous'. For Litvinenko there was the added, deeply galling spectacle of the hateful Khokholkov continuing in his post while he and his colleagues were being investigated for serious misconduct. The danger of Khokholkov seeking to avenge himself on his unruly subordinates was a clear and imminent threat.

Suspended and sent home on gardening leave while his fate was being decided at URPO headquarters, Sasha knew he was in a race against time. If he didn't make a move, Khokholkov most certainly would . . . and Khokholkov's options ranged from having Sasha fired to the ultimate sanction; URPO was not squeamish about the targets it picked for its death squads.

For the next few days Sasha could neither sleep at night nor find peace by day. He paced endlessly through the apartment in the high-rise block where he, Marina and little Anatoly were living, waiting constantly for the knock at the door. Litvinenko had been instructed not to communicate with his four suspended fellow officers while investigations were being carried out but he knew – and they knew – that they had to coordinate their moves; any disunity or hesitation could be fatal.

In the middle of February 1998 the five men met at a secret rendezvous, discussed their plight and concluded that they were being thrown to the wolves. They could no longer expect justice from their own organization; their only chance was to jump ship and seek protection from their proposed victim. They went to Boris Berezovsky and told him the whole story.

19

THE BEREZOVSKY CONNECTION

Litvinenko would later suggest the approach to Berezovsky was an existential moment of revolt against corruption and dishonesty, a moment of bravery in standing up for honour and integrity. It is a good story, a heroic story, but it is not the whole truth. Even those closest to Sasha acknowledge that he and his colleagues were acting to protect themselves from the looming threat of retribution. Vladimir Bukovsky:

> Yes, he was brave, of course he was brave. But he and others in the department were very scared for their own futures and that's why they all took such a collective step. Berezovsky at that time was a member of the government – deputy secretary of the security council. So he was official, not just a rich man or whatever. He was official and also very close to Yeltsin's family. So the whole department got scared. And they understood that, OK, they might murder Berezovsky . . . but then they would be quietly killed one by one themselves. So it was really self-protection.

It was self-protection and also a good tactical move. Sasha and his comrades could see there was a power struggle going on in the Kremlin for both the ear of Boris Yeltsin and the succession when Yeltsin reached the end of his term – or the end of his seemingly charmed life: he had already suffered two serious heart attacks. In February 1998 it looked as if Boris Berezovsky and his supporters were winning the battle and could be very powerful patrons for a group of ambitious FSB officers looking to further their careers. What better way to win Berezovsky's patronage than by snitching about a dastardly plot to kill him?

And this is where Sasha Litvinenko held a very strong card – a trump card, if ever there was one. Through a series of interconnected circumstances Sasha was already known to Berezovsky, and Berezovsky had every reason to listen to him and believe what Sasha had to say.

The acquaintance between Litvinenko and Berezovsky went back some four years to 1994, when Berezovsky was just a tycoon worth several hundred million dollars from his monopoly on Russia's car distribution network, Logovaz. On 7 June 1994 there really was an attempt on Berezovsky's life – most probably by business rivals he had got the better of over some deal or other – and he had been lucky to escape. A bomb had been detonated next to his armoured Mercedes; his driver, Mikhail Kiryanov, had been decapitated and his bodyguard, Dmitry Vasiliev, lost an eye. Berezovsky himself emerged with burns and minor injuries. The FSB was called in to investigate the attack and the officer put in charge of the case was . . . Alexander Litvinenko.

Litvinenko and Berezovsky were to work closely together during the course of the investigation; they became friends, and the experience was to give Sasha a strong claim to Berezovsky's trust. Speaking of the incident today – gesticulating with a hand still scarred from the bomb – Berezovsky says he was at first wary of the FSB man sent to question him, but soon grew to like him.

> I met him about the time in 1994 that they tried to kill me . . . and exactly at that time Alexander presented himself and said he was asked to investigate this case. It was the time when the Soviet Union had collapsed and our old mentality was collapsing and the FSB was pretty much the same as the KGB and I could not imagine that one man from the KGB was really sincere to help me. And it was really a shock for me that he really genuinely tried to find out who had made this attempt to kill me. It was very unusual. And particularly when he asked me about my vision of business in Russia . . . and my vision for the country. It was almost crazy that this simple guy from FSB was really trying to understand – not only to understand, because quite often he also gave his

vision of events. At first I didn't take it all that seriously. I thought maybe it was an FSB game to try to get close to me and so on. But step by step I recognized that he was absolutely sincere.

The relationship between the two men was cemented the following year, when, Berezovsky says, Litvinenko saved his life.

In the spring of 1995 – the first of March – a very famous Russian journalist, Listyev, was killed. Several months before that I had appointed Listyev to the position of general manager of the leading Russian TV channel. And they started a big police investigation into what had happened. And it was a real attempt to put me in problems . . . not only in problems, I started to feel strong pressure to make out that I am behind this murder and so forth. I felt that it was something special organized against me . . . and I remember well this evening in Moscow when the police came and practically seized me . . . Alexander at that time was in the office and he stepped beside me and he said, 'If you now take Berezovsky, I will kill you, because you have no right to do that' . . . And he was right: the police did not have any documents and so forth . . . and they were absolutely shocked . . . and he took out his gun, yes, and demonstrated his gun! And the police officer was very surprised and asked, 'Who are you?' And Alexander presented him his document and said he was an FSB officer and he was 100 per cent sure I was not involved and he would not allow them to take me away because he thought they would kill me. There were some events before that when the police tried to put some criminal people around me and tried to create the story that through these people I was trying to kill this journalist. It was a special operation – I don't want to go into all the details – but a set-up . . . Alexander really saved my life, there was no doubt about it.

After their initial contacts in 1994 and 1995, Berezovsky and Litvinenko remained close. It was widely rumoured but never proven that Berezovsky had taken Sasha onto his payroll as an informant within the FSB. Berezovsky's critics allege that Litvinenko was an agent provocateur for his patron, feeding him inside information and seeking out ways to weaken or incriminate his enemies in the security services. Some accused them of deliberately engineering the scandal over the alleged assassination plot, but again no proof was produced. The pact between the two men would endure through the twists and turns of Sasha's remaining few years in Russia and the tragedy of his subsequent exile.

So when Litvinenko was fighting for survival after his refusal to kill Berezovsky in 1998, he knew at the very least that he would get a sympathetic hearing from the man himself. Berezovsky recalls the moment Sasha came to tell him about the plot.

> Three years later, in '98, one day he came to me and said that he was ordered to kill me; he was ordered by his boss in the FSB. Initially I thought it was just a joke, because everybody know that I had good relations with Alexander, so how was it possible to give him an order to kill me if they knew that we have good relations? But he said, 'Boris, not only just me was present at this meeting; there were four other officers present at this meeting. And they may confirm that they really got order to kill.' They were special agents. And the boss told them that I am a big problem, that I am a big enemy of the FSB, that I tried to convict them and I tried to influence the president to crush their organiz- ation . . . so the best way is just to kill him!

20

TURNING THE TABLES

On the one hand Sasha's story was a terrible blow for Berezovsky. He was not a naive man and had been the target of an assassination attempt in the past, but to hear that the state security service is plotting to murder you is undeniably shocking news, all the more so in the Russia of the 1990s, where life was cheap, contract killings were a real and accepted part of daily life and most of them went unremarked, uninvestigated and unpunished.

On the other hand it was also an opportunity, and Berezovsky is the ultimate opportunist. His star was high in February 1998, but he was already picking up worrying signs that it might be waning. He knew his ascent to power in Boris Yeltsin's administration had ruffled many feathers and made a lot of enemies. The Kremlin corridors were awash with power struggles and intrigue, much of it aimed at him. Berezovsky was regarded as an economic liberal and a dove on the war with Chechnya. Ranged against him were the old-style hard-liners, the power ministers in Defence, the Interior Ministry and the FSB, who were constantly lobbying the president to be tougher, more authoritarian, more like the old way of doing things. Both sides would seize any chance to do down their opponents, and when Litvinenko came to him with his tale of an assassination plot, Berezovsky spotted its potential at once.

His first move was to ask Sasha to bring his fellow officers – or as many of them who would dare to come – to a meeting in his office, where they would make a videotape of their allegations. It was a wise precaution. If he was going to make a scandal out of Litvinenko's story, and if he was going to use that scandal in a very public political power battle, Berezovsky needed to have something tangible to back up the case he was making.

After some weeks of negotiations and hesitation, Sasha and two comrades turned up at Berezovsky's office. The video of the meeting shows three men sitting on one side of a long table in a rather imposing room with a high ceiling and ornate doors. Berezovsky is seen lighting some candles on the table. He then ostentatiously closes the doors and goes to sit just out of frame. The grainy footage, badly focused and drained of colour, is shot from a camera that seems to have been placed at the end of the table where the men are sitting. It is unclear if the men actually know they are being filmed: the video resembles the secret filming of a hidden camera, but at one moment one of them looks fleetingly and surreptitiously into the lens.

Litvinenko is one of the men at the table and he is heard saying to Berezovsky, 'Four other KGB officers heard this order and they can confirm this. Let them tell you so it's first hand, so nobody can say I made it up.' Then a second man, clearly one of Sasha's FSB colleagues, is heard quoting the order they received from their URPO boss: 'He said to us, "If there was an order to knock someone off" – sorry, to kill; he said to kill – "could you fix it?"' Berezovsky's voice then asks, 'To kill me?' and the agent replies, 'Yes, of course you. It would hardly be me, would it? . . . It happened a few times. Last time it went on for twenty minutes. He said to me, "You do things like that, don't you?" That's what he asked me.' The third man at the table then chips in to underline what his colleague has been saying: 'He [the boss] asked Sasha, "Could you do it?" He asked him, and then there was a long pause.' On the videotape Sasha himself confirms that he was indeed asked to do the deed: 'It should be considered a terrorist act, but when it's the deputy chief of one of the big FSB departments who says this to his lieutenant colonel, I take it as an order.'

While the name of the instigator of the plot does not appear on this portion of the video, it is clear from other contexts that the men are accusing their FSB line manager Yevgeny Khokholkov and his deputy Alexander Kamishnikov. In another portion of videotape, which is date-stamped April 1998, an unnamed FSB man later identified as the URPO commander, Alexander Gusak, is shown confirming that he had been summoned to a face-to-face meeting with Khokholkov where he was asked if he would kill Berezovsky. On the tape Gusak says, 'I replied that if it was properly sanctioned and had the right stamps – that is, the stamp of the prosecutor's office and the stamp of our own organization – and it had the right materials to back it up, I would be ready to kill Berezovsky and anyone else.'

Over the next few weeks Berezovsky took the incriminating videotape to several influential people, including a rising star in the Kremlin leadership. The name of that man was Vladimir Putin.

★

There is no record of Berezovsky's negotiations with Putin over the Litvinenko tape and neither man will talk publicly about them, but it is undeniable that at that moment the two of them were on cordial terms and that Berezovsky considered Putin a political ally.

In the context of the time this makes sense. Berezovsky felt threatened by the vested interests of the power ministries, including the FSB. For him, Sasha's story was a chance to undermine his enemies in that organization; to get the FSB restructured and reformed; to introduce a new mentality and, crucially, a new leadership. Putin would have seen himself as a potential beneficiary of Berezovsky's efforts. He was a young promising official with an FSB background and a glittering future; he was not tarred by the old-style, hard-line mentality of the apparat and could easily fit the bill of the 'new men' Berezovsky was likely to favour. To cap it all, Berezovsky and Putin were buddies at the time, regularly visiting each other's houses and even taking skiing holidays together. They were in the same political camp and shared the same reformist ideals. From all the evidence it is not unreasonable to conclude that Berezovsky felt he had Putin's backing for the steps he was about to take over the Litvinenko affair.

Sasha himself was not privy to the negotiations his patron was undertaking. From his perspective the first priority was to get his position and that of his four comrades secure against the vengeful Khokholkov. And on that score Berezovsky showed he had the clout to deliver. Sasha recorded his own account of the following few weeks: 'Behind the scenes, Berezovsky was pulling levers in the Kremlin and he persuaded Boris Yeltsin to turn on our department. Within a few weeks, our secret directorate [URPO] was disbanded, Colonel Khokholkov was transferred and FSB Director Kovalyov was fired.'

The shake-up happened on Saturday 25 July 1998, and Boris Yeltsin explained it by saying the FSB was being remodelled to concentrate on ensuring Russia's economic security rather than the cloak-and-dagger activities it had traditionally been associated with. Everyone knew the hidden hand behind the move was that of another Boris – Berezovsky.

It was a good result for Litvinenko and he celebrated, first with his comrades and later that evening with Marina. His tormentor had been removed, he had cemented his relationship with Berezovsky, and it looked like the FSB was indeed about to be cleaned up. Berezovsky himself appeared to have gained ground in the Kremlin and further developments seemed to confirm the extent of his influence. Boris Yeltsin announced that the next director of the FSB, replacing the disgraced Kovalyov, would be Vladimir Putin, a forty-five-year-old former FSB colonel who had retired from the service a decade earlier for a political career and was now working inside the Kremlin administration.

Government sources were soon spreading the word that Putin's appointment meant the FSB was being upgraded. 'The fact that the FSB will now be headed by a man who earlier held the post of first deputy head of the presidential administration is a reflection of the FSB's new status,' reported the Novosti News Agency. 'The service has not been led at such a level since the days of Yuri Andropov.' It appeared to be a victory for both Berezovsky and Litvinenko. Putin had been their confidant in the machinations that got him appointed; he was promising a clean sweep to clear out the FSB corruption Sasha had been so vocal in denouncing and he was widely considered to be much closer to Berezovsky than his predecessor – almost, in the language of those days, 'Berezovsky's man'. Only history would show how wide of the mark both these assumptions would be.

21

THE PUTIN FACTOR

Having provided the ammunition for Berezovsky's coup in the FSB and having helped secure the rise of Vladimir Putin, Litvinenko was confidently expecting to be involved in the campaign to clear out the organization's old guard. Berezovsky, for his part, was intent on getting Litvinenko and Putin to work together on his behalf. Sasha recalls their first meeting: 'I met him soon after his appointment. I was still technically suspended, but one day Berezovsky called me. "Alexander, could you go to Putin and tell him everything that you have told me? And everything that you have not. He is new at the service and would benefit from an insider's view."'

Litvinenko was nervous before the meeting with Putin. He wanted to impress his new boss and stayed up all night compiling a dossier of evidence to back up his allegations of what some FSB bosses had been up to – the illegal businesses, the protection rackets, the intimidation and the killings. He had collected all the information Putin would need to put things right.

> I arrived with two colleagues, but Putin wanted to see me alone. It must be incredibly tough for him, I thought. We had been of the same rank, and I imagined myself in his shoes – a mid-level agent suddenly put in charge of some hundred seasoned generals with all their vested interests, connections and dirty secrets. I did not know how to salute him without causing embarrassment. Should I say 'Comrade Colonel' as was required by the code? But he pre-empted me and got up from his desk and shook my hand. He seemed even shorter than on TV.

Speaking many years later with the benefit of hindsight, Litvinenko is scathing about Putin – he had by then spent half a decade attacking him for all manner of alleged crimes – and seems eager to forget the admiration he once felt for him.

> I felt he was not sincere. He avoided eye contact and behaved as if he were not the director but an actor playing a role. He looked at my chart, appeared to study it and asked a couple of random questions. I knew he could not have grasped the details in the brief glance he had given it. 'Shall I leave the chart?' I asked. 'No. No, thank you. You keep it. It's your work.' I gave him another list I had compiled and told him, 'These officers are clean. I know for sure that you can rely on them in the war on corruption. There are honest people in the system,' I said. 'We could bring the situation under control.' He nodded as though he was in full agreement. He kept my files, said we would keep in touch and took my home number.

Litvinenko waited in vain by the telephone; Putin never called.

The purpose of Sasha's files on who could be trusted and who could not was quite clearly to persuade Putin to fire some FSB bosses – those that Berezovsky perceived as enemies – and promote some others whom Berezovsky regarded as allies. It would be naive to think that Litvinenko and Berezovsky had not discussed this presentation to Putin; they were ostentatiously serving notice that they had helped get him appointed and now expected him to pay them back by installing new, friendly faces in all the positions of power. If things worked out according to plan, the FSB would become a Berezovsky fiefdom and remain loyal to him in the power battles that were looming over the succession to Boris Yeltsin. The stakes riding on Litvinenko's exploitation of the alleged assassination order could not have been higher.

After two months of silence, it began to look like the new director was in no hurry to investigate the Berezovsky plot and that Sasha's dossier of who should be fired and who promoted was not being followed up. Litvinenko was bemused, offended and annoyed. When Berezovsky called him to his office to ask what was going on,

Sasha told his patron there were two possible explanations: either Putin was genuinely trying to get something done and was being stymied by the hard-liners, or he had no intention of rocking the boat and was planning to collaborate with the apparat. If it was the former Berezovsky could still have faith in the man he helped bring to power, but if it was the latter it would suggest Putin had no intention of being Berezovsky's man and was ungratefully striking out on his own.

Berezovsky was in a dilemma. He had invested time and political capital in getting the new FSB boss installed and felt he was due his legitimate reward. On the other hand he did not want a confrontation with Putin which would risk destroying the goodwill between them. Berezovsky's hesitation was the first sign that Putin had attained a position of sufficient power for the big players in the Kremlin to tread warily around him. Putin himself was undoubtedly weighing up the warring factions with an eye to deciding where his best interests lay. The Berezovsky camp was just one among several. Putin owed him a debt of gratitude, that was true, but gratitude was small beer compared to the need to look after number one. Vladimir Putin was already looking ahead to the power struggles that would determine Russia's fate in the post-Yeltsin era.

22

GOING PUBLIC

By November 1998, with no sign of action by Putin, Berezovsky told Litvinenko that things had to be brought to a head. He had given the matter serious thought and had found what he said was a means of forcing Putin's hand without alienating him: Litvinenko and his colleagues would have to go public with their revelations in a nationally televised press conference. Sasha was taken aback. FSB agents just didn't do that sort of thing, and what would be the consequences for him and his friends if things went wrong? It would invite the wrath and revenge of those they were denouncing in the FSB.

According to Litvinenko, Berezovsky was unmoved. He had everything planned for Tuesday 17 November. The press would be invited to the event, which would be given wide exposure in the media and broadcast on Russian television. Impact was everything and Berezovsky could guarantee it: as well as owning some important newspapers he was crucially the proprietor of the most widely watched national TV station, ORT, which would show the press conference and subsequent interviews. Sasha's task was to ensure he came across as convincing in front of the TV cameras and to get his colleagues to do the same.

The exchanges between Berezovsky and the FSB men over the next few days were understandably fraught. By going public, the agents would be risking everything. They and their families would be in danger. Marina Litvinenko told Sasha she was scared: 'How can this be happening, Sasha? It's putting your family at risk. Who knows how it will all end?' But Sasha was now decided: 'If I don't do it, who else will?' His mind was made up and Marina says he was not in the mood to change it. 'He would have done things his way, whatever I said. I knew this was a serious undertaking and I knew I could have distanced myself from it. But I decided to stand by my husband. Sasha was not just my husband, he was my friend. Even though he often couldn't tell me what was going on, he knew I would always support him. And I could always rely on him to look after me.'

But some of the agents who had been solicited to take part in the Berezovsky murder plot were scared. Some initially refused to appear. There were demands and counter-demands. Berezovsky told them they had come too far to turn back now. The agents asked Berezovsky for assurances they would be protected. Then they demanded money to compensate them for the risk they were taking. In the aftermath of the press conference rumours circulated that vast sums had been paid over – $100,000 for Litvinenko and smaller sums for the others was mentioned – but no proof was ever forthcoming and they all denied it. What they did insist on was that Berezovsky should allow them to appear in some sort of disguise.

All those involved were aware of the impact the press conference would have and of the anger it would cause in the Kremlin. In the days leading up to 17 November no one slept at home for fear of being arrested; Berezovsky provided them with a series of safe houses to throw the Kremlin off their tracks. The evening before the scheduled press conference was tense. Berezovsky summoned Sasha and his colleagues to his offices on Novokuznetskaya Street. They arrived one by one at the grey-stuccoed building that had once been the family mansion of the noble Smirnov family. Inside, they were served drinks in Berezovsky's club, the Logovaz Salon, with its decor of early-nineteenth-century elegance and the latest in modern Russian chic: lavishly gilded walls, ornate decorations and a giant illuminated aquarium in one wall. Then they were taken into Berezovsky's private office for some last-minute coaching in the statements they would be making.

The historian Yuri Felshtinksy, who would collaborate with

Litvinenko right up to the time of his poisoning in London, gave me a first-hand account of what went on that night.

> It was the day before the press conference. That evening I sat with the group of officers who were going to participate in it, in Berezovsky's office in Moscow. We were discussing what they would say and do. The text for the press conference was prepared that night. I helped to edit it for them, but for a field officer Litvinenko actually had very good writing skills. I wouldn't say he was scared before the press conference; he was always very nervous when important things were involved. He wasn't calm; he was never a calm person. He wouldn't quietly sit and think; he was a man of action. He would become a little bit hysterical, not because he was nervous but probably he thought this was the best way to reach a person; if he was calm and quiet, he thought this was not the best way to reach a person, to communicate to a person. If he's hysterical and talks a lot, he thought he could communicate and make people take notice; it was his way to get attention.

The following day, in front of the television cameras and the world's press at the headquarters of Russia's Interfax news agency, Litvinenko did not come across as hysterical. His accusations against the FSB and certain named officers within it were bitingly clear. Reading from the prepared text in a voice that showed signs of strain but did not crack, he made a series of allegations that were explosive in their ferocity: 'The FSB is being used by certain officials solely for their private purposes; instead of its original constitutional aim of providing security for the state and citizens, it is now being used for settling scores and carrying out private, political and criminal orders for payment. Sometimes the FSB is being used simply for the purpose of making money.' Litvinenko accused his superiors of extortion, kidnappings and murder. He spoke of the order to kill Berezovsky, and said that when he refused his bosses accused him of 'betraying the patriots of the motherland who wish to kill the Jew who has robbed half this country'.

Then, in a not very coded personal message to Putin, Litvinenko spelt out exactly what the Berezovsky camp was expecting him to do to clear the debt he owed them: 'We hope and trust that the FSB will summon the courage to cleanse itself of those persons who, having attained the positions of generals and who embody state security, sabotage the gains of recent years and pervert the constitutional mission of the FSB, abusing their offices and issuing illegal orders to commit terrorist acts.'

Litvinenko was clearly the key figure at the press conference. He did not wear a disguise and his name was given to the journalists who were present.

The five officers with him were not so brave: one wore a black ski mask revealing only his eyes and mouth and the others dark glasses. Although there has been some dispute over the identity of those who accompanied Sasha that day, I now believe I know their names, names that would recur with ominous regularity in both Litvinenko's future life and the investigation of his eventual death. They included Colonel Viktor Shebalin, who sat next to Sasha on the podium that day making an exaggerated show of his friendship and support; Major Andrei Ponkin, who was the only other man to speak; and Colonel Alexander Gusak, the field commander of URPO and the man who was later to accuse Litvinenko of war crimes in Chechnya. All of them had served together in Chechnya. Sasha Litvinenko was convinced there was an unbreakable bond of friendship and trust between them.

Mikhail Trepashkin, no longer a member of the FSB since his beating by Sasha and his pals and now concentrating on his work as a lawyer pursuing FSB abuses through the courts, was also there, both as a whistle-blower and former victim.

In response to questions Andrei Ponkin elaborated on Litvinenko's opening statement. He said he had personally been ordered to kidnap and if necessary kill the brother of a Moscow-based businessman of Chechen origin. Umar Dzhabrailov had close contacts to the mayor of Moscow, Yuri Luzhkov, and there were strong suggestions of a political or business feud behind the alleged order, with URPO being enlisted to help out one of the warring factions. Ponkin said he had asked his boss to put the order in writing, but his request had been refused. He also alleged that he and others had been instructed to kill Mikhail Trepashkin because he was stirring up trouble with his legal work against the FSB. Finally, he said he had reason to believe the FSB had been involved in the 1995 murder of Vladislav Listyev, the popular television personality and journalist. As we have seen, Berezovsky says the FSB tried to frame him for Listyev's killing and claims Litvinenko 'saved his life' when they came to arrest him.

It is evident from the recording of the November press conference that Berezovsky was still trying to offer Putin a deal. In every one of the allegations of criminal behaviour that Litvinenko and his colleagues made that afternoon they were always careful to stress that the misdeeds had happened before July 1998. In other words, they were not alleging any illegal activities since Putin had become director. It was a clear signal to Putin that he could still fire the men Berezovsky and Litvinenko had fingered without any opprobrium attaching to him – he could still pay the debt of gratitude they were demanding from him and he could still be an ally of the Berezovsky camp. No bridges had yet been burned, but the message was clear: this was Putin's last chance to do the right thing.

23

CHALLENGING PUTIN

Vladimir Putin's response to the challenge thrown down to him at the press conference was cautious. Caution is in his nature, but on this occasion caution was dictated also by the precariousness of his own position. On 17 November 1998 he had been FSB director for less than four months. He was still feeling his way, testing his support and seeking alliances to consolidate his power base. He was undoubtedly moving to lessen his dependence on Boris Berezovsky – to escape from the stranglehold he knew the oligarch was trying to exert on him – but he still could not be sure that he was strong enough to cast him off altogether. And maybe he would need Berezovsky in the future . . .

As a result, Putin's public statements were neutral and very carefully balanced. The accusations about the plot to kill Berezovsky and all the other alleged crimes had been referred to the military prosecutor, he said, and no one would be protected by his rank. But at the same time he complained that Berezovsky was trying to bring 'a certain pressure' on the investigation by going public, which was not helpful. There was just one flash of temper. In a televised interview on the affair Putin showed his patience was wearing thin: he called on Berezovsky to 'do his job' and suggested he should not be poking his nose into other people's affairs. But he was quick to add, 'I have known Boris Berezovsky for many years and I respect him.'

An FSB spokesman, Colonel Alexander Zdanovich, was less diplomatic, accusing 'all parties' of trying to use the FSB for their own aims. 'We've never been in anybody's pocket and we never will be,' he said. The alleged assassination order was dismissed with a formulation worthy of George Orwell: an illegal FSB order was impossible, said the spokesman, and if there were one, no one would obey it!

For Litvinenko and his colleagues the period immediately after the press conference was filled with fear and apprehension. Berezovsky had told them he would be doing his best to protect them but that he couldn't guarantee they wouldn't be arrested. Marina says it was a time of silent terror, with the constant threat of danger hanging over them. Sasha told her she must prepare for the worst: 'They could easily throw me in jail or kill me in some alleyway.' Marina pleaded, 'Sasha, how can you say these things?' but he was determined to look the truth in the face: 'Marina, I am telling you what might happen; you have to deal with this,' and he expressed no regrets about what he had done. Marina says they knew their phones were being tapped and that the authorities were carrying out surveillance on them. But a day went by and Sasha was not arrested. Then another . . . and another . . . Marina was beginning to hope the worst was over.

In the Kremlin, however, there was no talk of forgiveness. Putin had been infuriated by the press conference and knew he was being set up. He sensed Berezovsky was trying to back him into a corner and was determined to resist at all costs. But Putin also knew he could not move immediately to attack Litvinenko and his protector however much he might have wished to. For one thing, the accusations against the FSB had struck a chord with the public and had received much approval in the media. For another, Putin knew Berezovsky was still a powerful figure; a frontal assault on him now would be a dangerous, possibly fatal mistake. Indeed, Berezovsky showed his power two days later by getting Boris Yeltsin – the president was still very much under Berezovsky's spell – to ring Putin and instruct him to take Litvinenko's accusations seriously. The FSB director was ordered to send the case to the procurator and submit a report on the whole affair by 20 December.

Putin went through the motions of investigating Litvinenko's allegations, even inviting Berezovsky to take part in the process.

Today, Berezovsky is scornful of the conclusions that investigation reached and believes there was never any real attempt to find the truth.

> And what is important is that these officers . . . repeated absolutely the same things that they had told me. And after that, with them, I went to the deputy head of the presidential administration and they opened a case against the FSB people. And there was an absolutely strange result: the result was that we got a paper [acknowledging] that it really was commanded to kill me by this general . . . but that actually it was just a joke! And it was this official paper that I used in this country when I was asking for political asylum. And, as I understand, the judge in London was absolutely shocked when he saw this paper saying that it was commanded to kill Boris Berezovsky but it 'was just a joke'.

At the same time as he was stringing Berezovsky along with the pretence of an official investigation, Putin was taking more serious steps behind the scenes. His real priority was to discredit the oligarch and his whistle-blowers, and to do that he had to undermine the solidarity of the URPO officers who had appeared at the press conference, to divide the group and isolate its leaders. In the days after 17 November all of them were interviewed by interrogators from the FSB's Internal Affairs Directorate, the USB, ostensibly with the aim of collecting information about the illegal activities they had identified and announced to the world so that the matter could be properly investigated by the military prosecutor. But the actual purpose of the interviews was more sinister. Several if not all of the rebel officers were quizzed at length about their motives in going public. Some were threatened, others offered inducements. The goal as far as the interrogators were concerned was to see who might be persuaded to back down, who might change sides, who might come back to the FSB fold and who might be willing to work as a double agent, informing on the dangerous Berezovsky. Putin was desperate to infiltrate the Berezovsky–Litvinenko operation. He knew a showdown was looming and he wanted to have his spies in place before it was too late.

For the five URPO officers who had appeared with Litvinenko before the media the USB interrogations were immensely difficult. It was made forcefully clear to them that they had transgressed against the code of the FSB and that their behaviour had brought shame on the service and the motherland. The displeasure of their superiors who had been implicated in the allegations they had made was unmistakable, and they were left in no doubt that their careers were at an end. Under the strain of questioning they began to regret the decision to speak out with Litvinenko and several of them blamed him for tricking or bullying them into taking part. Some told the investigators that Berezovsky and Litvinenko had manipulated them into appearing at the press conference. The USB then offered the officers a choice: they could wave goodbye to their careers and face the prospect of prison, or they could recant and agree to work against the 'traitors' who had led them astray.

The question of exactly which of Litvinenko's comrades succumbed to Putin's blandishments has remained a subject of controversy, but it is crucial to understanding the future relationship between Litvinenko and the FSB. It is a vital piece of information for anyone seeking to unravel the events which were to lead to his death.

Marina Litvinenko claims that at least one of the men was already working as a double agent for the Kremlin even before 17 November. 'You know, Shebalin was the man who went into that press conference as a provocateur working for the FSB . . .' Yuri Felshtinsky concurs: 'Shebalin really did return to the FSB. He was a colonel and he came back to work for the FSB.' In addition, Felshtinsky has strong suspicions about another member of the group, Andrei Ponkin. Felshtinsky was sitting close to the podium at the press conference and says he observed the men's behaviour. 'Ponkin *officially* did not go back to work for the FSB again. But I think he was actually working for the FSB the whole time, right through the episode of the press conference. At the press conference his behaviour was strange – he was trying to be close to Litvinenko; he was calling Litvinenko's name very often – and later we thought that at times he was trying to control Litvinenko, to spy on him, to know where he is and who he is meeting and so on.'

Felshtinsky believes the threats and inducements of the Internal Affairs interrogators achieved their aim with three of Litvinenko's supposed allies – Shebalin, Ponkin and Gusak. He believes that all three of these men 'came back' into the FSB fold and later took roles of varying importance in Putin's war against Berezovsky and Litvinenko.

> Yes. You have to remember: there are several levels of 'coming back' to the FSB. Overall, there is a saying that no one leaves the FSB and it is true, unfortunately. So it's not a question of whether they went back; it's just a question of what level they went back at. What do they do for them? Are they an active officer, in the reserve, used as agents for occasional operations? Here are different levels of involvement and we outsiders do not know even what the difference is.

Berezovsky concurs that the hold of the FSB over its former employees is unbreakable: 'I just want to tell you my experience with people from this organization. To understand them, you need to know that there is an entrance to the club of the KGB, but there is no exit from this club. And they make sure that people must never step out of that club. It is the unwritten rule . . .'

For the future of Sasha Litvinenko, the unwritten rule of FSB loyalty would be of crucial importance: of the men who stood by his side to denounce the FSB, more than one repented. From that day on they would have every incentive to silence the increasingly irritating voice of the man who they claimed had tricked them into putting their lives and careers on the line. They would have reason to take an active part in a campaign that was ultimately to have fatal consequences.

24

REPENTANCE AND REPRISALS

The phoney war against Alexander Litvinenko lasted for a few weeks. All those who had taken part in the press conference remained suspended from their duties, but disciplinary action was not officially begun against them. There was an incident in which Sasha was physically attacked on the streets of Moscow, but neither he nor Berezovsky could provide conclusive proof that it was connected with the FSB. Meanwhile, Putin announced that URPO was being dismantled because of its 'unprofessional work'. Astoundingly, it looked as though Litvinenko was going to get away with it.

Andrei Nekrasov says the Kremlin's hesitation during those weeks was a function of the covert power struggles which were just beginning to reach boiling point.

> To be absolutely honest, things were different at that time than they are today. To be objective, Sasha did have some support, because the channel he broadcast on belonged to Boris Berezovsky. So it was under the auspices and protection of those people. In 1998 even though most of the things Sasha revealed were true, including those very dangerous people running the FSB, the atmosphere in society was very different. You could still . . . I don't know if he had this illusion, but certainly many of us had the illusion, or feeling, that there were still pockets of society that were free and you can resort to their support and appeal to natural justice . . . It wasn't yet that authoritarianism was total; it was still Yeltsin . . . That's an important point. Sasha's action was courageous then, but today it would be much more difficult . . . it would be suicidal.

Shortly afterwards, Putin began to show his hand. His resentment at the way the FSB had been put to public shame had kindled the desire for revenge. He had been challenged overtly and publicly;

from now on he would have every reason to work towards an equally public demonstration that such acts would not be allowed to stand. Years later he was to exact terrible vengeance against the oil giant Mikhail Khodorkovsky, who had challenged his authority; Litvinenko's actions seemed likely to provoke the same response.

Litvinenko was called to the Internal Affairs Department and told he was being fired. When he got home, he contacted the others who had appeared at the press conference and each of them said that he too had been called in and given the same message. The URPO officers had fought together in Chechnya; they had served in the toughest, most ruthless unit of the FSB. Sasha told Berezovsky he was certain of their integrity and their loyalty to him personally. But Berezovsky was a realist and warned Litvinenko that the Kremlin would do everything possible to make them betray him. Andrei Nekrasov says that, following the FSB interrogations, Litvinenko was aware that some if not all of his former comrades were almost certainly working as double agents.

> Litvinenko thought all those with him that day were his comrades – he once said to me, 'We were all in danger; if anything happens to us, you know whom to blame.' It was not just himself in danger – he called it a rebellion, actually, of the whole department. There were about eight people in the whole department and all of them, Sasha said, rebelled to some different degree. That's how he presented it. He thought all his comrades were with him. But afterwards, most of them went back to the FSB, if not directly, in some shape or form . . . and for some reason, from being friends they became haters of Sasha. The suspicion was that one of them, at least, may just have been pretending to rebel and pretending to be Sasha's comrade in arms. Some people say that one of them may have been behind his murder . . .

The loss of his FSB job at the end of 1998 left Litvinenko badly exposed and, he claimed, short of money. When Marina asked him about the rumours that Berezovsky had paid large sums to those who had taken part in the press conference, she says that Sasha replied, 'Marina, if I had taken money from him, how could I have stayed friends with him? There is no way.'

Berezovsky himself had a new job by this time: earlier in the year Boris Yeltsin had appointed him executive secretary of the Confederation of Independent States, the trade and cooperation organization that replaced the old USSR when the former Soviet republics became independent in 1991. As a sign of his gratitude to Litvinenko Berezovsky gave him a job on his staff with the title counsellor for security issues.

But by early 1999 Berezovsky's star was beginning to wane. His influence over Boris Yeltsin had been slipping badly as other aides and advisers moved in to supplant him. It was widely believed that the decision to appoint him to the CIS job had been forced on Yeltsin by rival courtiers who knew it would keep Berezovsky conveniently out of Moscow for long periods and weaken his hold on the president – the headquarters of the CIS were in Minsk in Belarus and there were eleven other former republics for him to keep an eye on too. Litvinenko may have attached himself firmly to Berezovsky, but it was looking increasingly as if Berezovsky was sliding down the greasy pole of Kremlin politics.

A crisis was reached in March 1999, while Berezovsky was away on CIS business with Sasha loyally at his side. Back in Moscow Yeltsin's prime minister, Yevgeny Primakov, a man who embodied the values of hard-line communism, made no secret that he was plotting his downfall. Primakov had no time for the economic liberalism and free-market capitalism that Berezovsky stood for; neither did he like Berezovsky's conciliatory stance on Chechnya. On 4 March, with Berezovsky's plane in the air over Ukraine, Primakov prevailed on Yeltsin to announce his rival's immediate dismissal. Yuri Felshtinsky was on board the plane and remembers the panic when the news came through on the radio.

We had been travelling through the CIS states with Berezovsky who at that time was CIS secretary. We'd been away from Moscow for a week or more, and by the time we were on our way back, we heard that Berezovsky had been fired. We were flying back to Moscow and we just didn't know what awaited us there. There was talk that Berezovsky was going to be arrested at the airport. We discussed whether we should divert the plane to Minsk . . . I remember Sasha Litvinenko arguing strongly, telling Berezovsky, 'You must avoid going to Moscow because you will be arrested.' But Berezovsky said, 'You go to Minsk if you like, but I'm going to Moscow.' Since we were all on the same plane, and since Berezovsky was the boss, there was only one conclusion . . . When we arrived in Moscow, Berezovsky was not arrested. But it became clear very quickly that he was losing all his power.

For Litvinenko, Berezovsky's fall from grace was a disaster. He had thrown in his lot with him and burned his boats with the FSB. Yuri Felshtinsky says his world was falling apart.

Litvinenko had been playing a political game and he had lost. His only insurance, the only person he was sure of in his struggle against the FSB, was Boris Berezovsky. As long as Berezovsky was powerful, no one would touch Litvinenko, that was clear. But as soon as Berezovsky started to lose power, it became clear that Litvinenko's position was badly weakened. He knew he might soon be arrested. Indeed, I remember he would tell me that: 'I think they might arrest me' . . . And of course they did so, in March of 1999.

25

ARREST

Litvinenko was arrested at 3 p.m. on 25 March 1999. Marina says she can remember the day perfectly because she, Sasha and four-year-old Anatoly were due to go on a family outing, but their car would not start. She and Anatoly set off on foot and Sasha waited behind with the car. Later that evening his former FSB colleagues came to her and said he was in jail.

Litvinenko was taken to Moscow's Lefortovo Prison, an old tsarist pile later used by the NKVD and the KGB to house their political prisoners. Moscow's urban grapevine had long carried the rumour that the prison was home to an outsized meat grinder in which the bodies of victims were ground to a pulp and flushed into the city's sewers. Marina was filled with foreboding, but Sasha's friends reassured her that the fact his arrest had been announced meant he was alive and would be treated according to the law.

The next day Marina engaged a lawyer to plead for bail, but his efforts were in vain: the court decided that Litvinenko might present a danger to the public and could not be trusted not to flee abroad. It was several days before charges were brought against him, and when they were it was clear that the prosecutors had dredged through Sasha's FSB service record for any episode of alleged misconduct they could find. Sasha's father Walter scathingly dismissed them as trumped-up pretexts to convict an innocent man: 'They lodged six charges against him, but four were dropped. It was obvious that these charges were fabricated. They found a couple of quite ridiculous things. He was accused of pilfering some cans of food and of slapping someone in the face.'

But for the interrogators the validity or otherwise of the charges made little difference. One of them explained to Sasha that the technique was just to throw everything at him until something stuck: 'We've got a list. There are nine things on it. We'll try the first one and if that doesn't work, then we'll try the next one, and then the next one and so on.' In fact, that was exactly what happened over the next two years, with three separate prosecutions being brought against Litvinenko, one being opened after another. The key thing was for the Kremlin to keep him in jail indefinitely.

Speaking much later about the circumstances of his arrest, Litvinenko says he is convinced it was ordered personally by Vladimir Putin. 'Putin was the director of the FSB and he personally ran the Internal Affairs Directorate, the USB. My arrest simply could not have happened without his approval.'

Since Sasha's interrogators knew he was an FSB man himself, they didn't even try to disguise what was going on. One of them said to him, 'You know why you're really in here, don't you? It's got nothing to do with all that stuff on the charge sheet, mate. It's because you went on the telly [*potomu chto ty na telek khodil*]. That's what you're in here for.' Litvinenko's real crime was that he had made public allegations about things going on in the security forces, and the security forces did not like that at all.

Yuri Felshtinsky makes the telling point that had the authorities wanted to find real crimes Litvinenko had committed, they could most likely have done so. But these misdeeds had been carried out with the state's connivance and they had to resort to other, minor misdemeanours. 'Maybe he did kill many people, in Chechnya, but they couldn't arrest him for that because those killings were all ordered by his superiors. So instead they arrested him for trumped-up petty crimes.' Felshtinsky goes on to say that the FSB's initial pressure on Litvinenko was to persuade him to cut a deal with the Kremlin, in the same way that his former colleagues seem to have done.

All of them were approached by the FSB and told, 'OK, look, you guys. You were playing this game with Berezovsky, but, look, he lost. So now it's time not to deepen the conflict; it's time to forget about releasing information about the FSB to the public. Let's deal with this quietly; why don't you come back?' And I believe that's when people like Shebalin and Gusak said, 'OK, I'm coming back.' Probably even Ponkin. But, you see, Litvinenko refused to come back.

It was a brave, somewhat puzzling refusal by a man with a young wife and child to think about, especially brave in view of the threats Felshtinsky says the interrogators made against him.

When he refused to come back . . . the FSB told him, 'Look. Now you must know the end of the story. The end of the story is that you are going to be killed, or you are going to be put in prison and killed in prison. But you know our organization: there is no other way. You are going to be killed.'

It is fascinating but probably futile to speculate exactly why Litvinenko turned down the chance to make peace with the Kremlin. It could be that Berezovsky had made him a more attractive offer; it could be that Sasha was just a very stubborn man, that his obsessive character made it impossible for him to back down. Or could it possibly be because of the hurt pride we saw in him earlier, the feeling that he had made an overture to Vladimir Putin, that he had offered his help and friendship, but that Putin had rebuffed him? Felshtinsky says Berezovsky and Litvinenko certainly thought Putin was part of their team before the press conference so his rejection of them afterwards was a cruel blow.

Don't forget Putin was head of FSB and was considered by everybody to be Berezovsky's friend. They went to the press conference with a friend of Berezovsky, Putin, in charge of the FSB; so they had reason to believe that actually it was kind of approved by the top man, the director of the FSB. And even Berezovsky was thinking there was an understanding with Putin, that it was kind of approved. That was the problem: Litvinenko thought the FSB really was going to be reformed by Putin, with the help of his press conference, into a different kind of organization, and that he, Litvinenko, would play a big role in it.

In fact, it is clear that Putin was leading Litvinenko up the garden path and had been plotting for some time to renounce Berezovsky and all his works, including Alexander Litvinenko. But he did give Sasha one final chance to kiss and make up, to accept the interrogators' offer to repent. Andrei Nekrasov says Litvinenko's proud refusal was an ultimately fatal decision: 'That's where his troubles stemmed from. From that time forward he was considered to be a traitor . . . a pariah. All his troubles – maybe even including his death – stemmed from that. It was a terribly brave thing to do.'

26

TRIAL

Litvinenko's day in court came eight months later, in November 1999. He was driven from Lefortovo Prison to the Central Moscow Military Courthouse, where he was charged with 'abuse of power', beating up an arrested terror suspect two years earlier in the town of Kostroma. To seasoned FSB men the whole affair had an air of the ridiculous about it; very few of them could think of times when arrested terror suspects were *not* beaten up. But the court was solemnly presented with evidence from eyewitnesses (most of them FSB officers) of how Sasha had dragged the suspect, twenty-two-year-old Vyacheslav Babkin, an alleged bomb maker, from his car and used excessive force to restrain and handcuff him. Litvinenko was then said to have fabricated forensic evidence to frame Babkin as a terrorist, but his testimony was discovered to be false and the accused acquitted.

One FSB officer who was present at Babkin's interrogation on 25 June 1997 said he had seen Sasha pull a polythene bag over the man's head and slap him 'with full force' on the ears. This allegedly happened three times, until Babkin signed a detailed confession. As corroboration, the prosecution produced a grainy video recording of an interrogation session, showing a blond-haired FSB officer dressed in combat fatigues and seen from the side, carrying out acts similar to those mentioned on the charge sheet. On the tape the FSB man is squatting in front of a crouching prisoner, punching him in the face and demanding information. The interrogator is wearing a military cap and I certainly could not identify him with any confidence as being Sasha Litvinenko. He is, however, surrounded by several standing men who do appear to be URPO agents. As soon as the video was shown, two officers who had at one time served with Litvinenko recognized it: it was a film they had had in their offices and they knew the man in it was not Sasha. They found the original of the tape, which had other footage showing it was not Litvinenko beating up the detainee. According to Sasha's father, they were about to produce the tape in court and get the charges overturned, but the FSB came to Litvinenko in his cell and threatened him and his family: 'And that's when the FSB came to him and said, "You have a son. If you produce that video in court, you should be very afraid for your son."'

The threats against his family made a big impression on Sasha; he had served in the FSB and had seen what they were capable of. It was clear, though, that the case against Litvinenko was weak and the military court was struggling to convict him. With an acquittal looking likely, Litvinenko's family was informed that the verdict would be pronounced on the afternoon of Tuesday 16 November. Marina was in court that day and says she knew something was amiss as soon as she arrived. As well as the judges and the usual legal teams, a delegation from the military prosecutor's office was seated at the front of the court. After a review of the case, the judge rose to pronounce his verdict, which – to her great relief and surprise – cleared Sasha of all the charges. But that was just the start of things.

Marina says that as soon as the judge finished speaking, the court was transformed into something out of a film set. Before Sasha could leave the dock, a team of crack *spetsnaz* troops – Russia's equivalent of the British SAS or the US Delta Force – stormed into the room and surrounded the prisoner. The men were wearing full camouflage uniforms with black ski masks over their faces and carrying automatic weapons. The military prosecutor rose to his feet and announced that Mr Litvinenko would not be released because new charges were going to be filed against him and applications for bail would not be considered. A free man for less than ten minutes, Sasha was marched out of the building and back to prison; it was clear the authorities were intent on keeping him there.

This time, Litvinenko was thrown into Moscow's Butyrsky Prison and held under conditions of high security. Marina says it was almost impossible to visit him for the next two months and she feared for his safety. In December their lawyer succeeded in getting the court to hear an appeal against Sasha's continued imprisonment. The grounds for the appeal were quite simple: he had been acquitted eight weeks earlier and, despite promising new charges, the prosecutor had simply re-presented the old ones. Marina says the events of that second day in court restored her faith in at least one part of the Russian legal system, because the judge at the military tribunal had quite clearly had enough of the FSB's machinations. He encircled the courtroom with security men and gave them instructions to defend the building against any intrusion by the *spetsnaz*. Then he stood to announce that he had once again found Litvinenko innocent of the charges against him and urged him and his family to leave the court as quickly as possible. Marina says, 'We just grabbed him in our arms and carried him off because we were so afraid of what might happen next.'

In fact, nothing happened. There were clearly some acrimonious recriminations going on within the FSB and – it was later revealed – new charges were being prepared against him, but for the moment Sasha was free. For the next few months the Litvinenkos were put under surveillance and their car was followed by a team of FSB men. After a while Sasha was getting on so well with them that he would tell them before all his journeys where he was going so they didn't have to go chasing through Moscow looking for him. He and Marina even invited them to share their family meals.

But the fraternization and the waiting came to an end in the summer of 2000, when it was announced that a new trial would be held. This time it would not be in Moscow, but in the town of Naro-Fominsk forty miles south of the capital, where proceedings would be secret and no information given to the media. Litvinenko was not rearrested but was brought back in for daily questioning sessions to be harangued by FSB interrogators. 'Who gave you the right to hang out our dirty laundry in public?' they yelled at him, and threatened retribution not just against himself but against his family. 'If they find you not guilty this time, it's not you we'll be talking to; we'll sort things out with your wife and your kid. You don't think you'll get away, do you? You're a traitor to the system and you're going to be punished.' Litvinenko knew he was approaching the endgame. 'I can't say I wasn't scared. Only a madman would not be scared. I knew I had rebelled against the system. I knew they'd stop at nothing.' His friend Yuri Felshtinksy made an unofficial approach to an FSB general on Sasha's behalf, asking if a deal could perhaps be done for the Litvinenkos to slip quietly out of Russia and into exile abroad. The general replied, 'I can honestly tell you there is no way for that man to leave Russia alive. And if ever I meet him again, I will personally kill him with my two hands.'

That, says Marina, is when Sasha made up his mind to flee.

27

FLIGHT

Getting out of Russia was a problem. For one thing, Litvinenko had had to surrender his passport to the police as soon the first set of charges was brought against him over a year earlier and it had never been returned. And there were worrying developments on the political scene which would make Sasha's task even more difficult.

On New Year's Eve 1999 Boris Yeltsin, appearing on national television for his usual New Year message, had shocked the country by announcing he was resigning. In an emotional and not always coherent speech, the man who had ruled Russia for eight and a half years gave no reason for his dramatic step, except to say that the dawn of the new millennium meant Russia needed new leadership. 'Russia must enter the new millennium with new politicians,' said a drawn-looking President, seemingly not far from tears, 'with new faces, with new, smart, strong, energetic people. And we who have been in power for many years already, we must go. I beg your forgiveness for having failed to jump in one leap from the grey, stagnant, totalitarian past to the clear, rich and civilized future,' he said. 'I want to beg forgiveness for your dreams that never came true. I am leaving. I've done what I could.'

There was no doubt who Yeltsin had in mind when he spoke of those new, strong, energetic politicians; Vladimir Putin had been appointed prime minister the previous August and had firmly established himself as heir apparent to the presidency.

The circumstances of Putin's appointment had been controversial and Berezovsky had played an ambiguous role in it which we will consider when we come to assess the events that set these two titans on their final collision course. For the moment, though, Putin was the force to be reckoned with. Shortly after his address Yeltsin gave Putin his presidential pen and medals, symbolizing his new status as the Kremlin's anointed. Yeltsin also turned over to him the case which contains the codes to launch Russia's nuclear weapons and endorsed him as 'a strong man who is well worthy of being our president'.

From 1 January 2000 Putin had become the acting president of Russia and he was making the most of it. On New Year's Day he had convened emergency sessions of the Russian cabinet and Security Council to smooth over the transition and grant Yeltsin immunity against prosecution on growing allegations of corruption. He was seen on national television assuring the Russian people that he was in complete control. 'At no minute will there be a vacuum of power in the country,' he boasted. And then he was in Chechnya, for a morale-boosting visit to the troops. 'Russia thanks you,' he told officers and soldiers. Already backed by the military because of his hard line on Chechnya, Putin bolstered his position further by telling the troops and the country that the military not politicians would decide on the pace and conduct of the war.

Three months later, unsurprisingly, he won a decisive victory in the presidential elections of 26 March.

As Putin's star rose, Boris Berezovsky was falling dramatically from grace. Since his dismissal as CIS secretary his power and influence had been in steep decline, so when Sasha came to him in the summer of 2000 to tell him about the new FSB prosecution against him, Berezovsky could do little about this except shrug his shoulders. The days when he could pick up the phone to the president and tell him what to do were long gone. Beneath the garish aquarium in Berezovsky's gilded salon they drank coffee and mulled over the predicament they were in. Several coffees later they were in an extraordinarily gloomy mood, agreeing they were in a corner and that Vladimir Putin was to blame. By the fifth coffee they had decided: Sasha had to get out of Russia or he would rot in jail for the rest of his life. And on that score at least Berezovsky could do something. It was 1 p.m. in Moscow when he picked up the telephone, 4 a.m. in New York. The voice on the other end of the line was sleepy and a little grumpy; Alex Goldfarb was in bed in Manhattan a million miles away from the afternoon sunshine in Moscow. Goldfarb had been Berezovsky's lieutenant since the mid-1990s and was always ready to carry out his boss's requests. This was a tough one, but Goldfarb was confident he could do it. As his boss spoke, he listened and took notes. Ten minutes later Berezovsky put down the phone, turned to Sasha and said, 'Go pack your bags.'

Speaking today, Berezovsky says he was under a moral obligation to help Litvinenko escape from Russia in 2000. If he had not done so, Sasha would inevitably have fallen victim to the 'bandit rules' of the FSB.

> Alexander was exactly the sort of person to whom these bandit rules were applied . . . I wasn't the only one who could understand why he needed to run away from Russia, because what he had done was a very unusual step. After this investigation of the order to kill me the FSB created a case against Alexander and they put him in jail. Absolutely false case, alleging that when he was questioning a suspect, he used power in a special way. It was completely, completely false. I knew Sasha and I knew what sort of man he was. And they put him in jail and the court took a decision to release him and they arrested him in court and opened another case against him and – I don't know, maybe three months after that – he decided to leave Russia. And he asked for my help and I gave him every possible help to do so.

Marina remembers the next few weeks with a mixture of wonder and incomprehension. Sasha had come home from his meeting with Berezovsky to tell her he would shortly have to go off to Nalchik to visit his father and sell the family apartment there. Marina assumed her husband was making provision in case the worst came to the worst and he was sent to jail when his case came to trial. Sasha never told her anything about his dealings and this time was no exception. The next she heard from him was a message from

Nalchik, via a friend, that she should buy a new, unregistered mobile phone to communicate with him. When she rang, Sasha said, 'Buy a ticket, Marina. One for you and one for Anatoly. Buy a package holiday to any country you like, but don't tell a soul what you are doing or where you are going.' When Sasha spoke like that Marina was used to doing what he said. She bought the tickets – a two-week trip to Spain – but she says she never thought, right to the very last moment, that he was asking her to leave Russia forever. The only person Marina told about the Spanish trip was her mother; the story she told her friends and other relatives was that she was sick and would be out of touch for a couple of weeks. 'My son, he didn't know until the last day before leaving. I just took him to say we're going to the airport and he said, "Where, why, where are we going?" I told him, "We're going to Spain." "Mummy, why you didn't ask me? Maybe I don't like to go to Spain!" He was six years old; he had a lot of activities going on. I cancelled everything for him, for me. And we flew to Spain.'

Sasha rang them as their plane was in the air between Moscow and Madrid. He was fretting, worried. 'Marina, are you in the plane? Are you in the air?' He had been terrified they would be stopped at the Russian emigration control.

In Spain Marina really did get sick. She was in Malaga, alone with Anatoly, full of virus and full of anxiety. 'And all this time when we stayed in Spain I didn't know what was coming next. I was absolutely sure we were going back to Russia. And when it was maybe two days left, Sasha rang me. "You should go to the airport; somebody will meet you and you will fly where these people will tell you." Then he said, "Marina. It looks like we're not going home . . ."'

28

IN LIMBO

Marina remembers that telephone conversation as one of the hardest of her life. At first she could not understand what Sasha meant. He had never told her that they were fleeing from Russia and her first instinct was to resist. 'What do you mean, we're not going home? I can't do that,' she pleaded. But Sasha was in his unshakeable, determined mode. 'Marina, if you go back to Russia then I will be with you. But if I am in Russia, they will put me in jail again, maybe even kill me.' In the face of such a powerful argument Marina decided once more to stand by her man.

Sasha was in the former Soviet Republic of Georgia by this time, biding his time before making a hazardous escape across the Black Sea to Turkey. Berezovsky says he personally made the decision for Sasha to leave Russia and 'Sasha agreed with that.' According to later accounts, it was Berezovsky's people who procured the forged papers Sasha used for his trip and who made the arrangements for his journey to freedom. The person sent to collect Marina from Malaga and put her and little Anatoly on a flight east was also a Berezovsky hireling. Their destination was the seaside resort of Antalya on the Mediterranean coast of Turkey. For Marina and Anatoly, arriving in the sunny town surrounded by mountains, forests and ancient ruins was like a dream. She had not seen Sasha for nearly a month; she had left home with only the possessions she needed for a two-week holiday and now Alex Goldfarb had arrived to tell her she would not be going back again.

When Sasha got to Antalya, he was worn out and looked terrible. His first phone call was to Berezovsky, who greeted him with joy: 'Well done, Sasha. You got out!' Marina saw he had lost a lot of weight. She was immensely relieved the family was back together but fearful of what awaited them. Berezovsky had instructed Gold-farb to look after his protégés and he was generous in caring for their material needs: they stayed in a good hotel, ate well and soaked up the Turkish sun. But the nagging question of what to do about the future never left them. Sasha was struggling to stay calm and his nerves were shot.

Goldfarb's first suggestion – and Sasha seemed to agree with him – was that the Litvinenkos should ask for political asylum in the United States. The message from Berezovsky, currently in the French Riviera resort of Cap d'Antibes, was that things were getting compli-cated for him too, and he also was considering flight to the West.

After some days spent in fevered discussion of the options open to them, Goldfarb took Sasha to the US embassy in Ankara to ask for asylum. Goldfarb was himself an American citizen and says they just walked into the building and asked at the front desk to see an official. According to the account of the meeting he later gave to a *New York Times* reporter, the Americans took one look at the unlikely pair and told them to get lost. 'I brought him to the US embassy at the end of October in Ankara. We just walked in and said here's the FSB colonel . . . and they are not interested.' Marina says the embassy considered Sasha's case but explained it was too sensitive for them to take on – there were presidential elections pending in the US and they didn't want any sensational headlines rocking the boat.

In fact, the reasons for the US refusal of political asylum were much more ambiguous. As Litvinenko himself confided to Andrei Nekrasov, he was extensively interviewed by the CIA, who only then made the decision to turn him down.

> Sasha told me the USA was his first choice for asylum, not the UK. Even while he was still in Turkey after escaping from Russia, he asked for asylum in the US. He went to the US embassy in Ankara and they interviewed him – an intelligence officer, prob-ably CIA – and they told him, 'This will help you help us make a

case to grant you asylum. If you talk to us and tell us *everything you know*.' But then, having already debriefed him on all his KGB and FSB past, they said no. They were not pulling punches . . . They promised it first, but there was a strange twist of events. Sasha was pissed off. So the UK was a sort of second choice.

This account throws a different light on the events in Turkey. It is plausible that the Americans really didn't want difficult headlines in an election year, but might there not also be another credible explanation – that the CIA examined Litvinenko's story of how he fell out with Putin and the FSB and concluded he was not telling the truth?

The first duty of an intelligence officer, whatever country he is serving, is to be wary of infiltration, to spot potential double agents trying to pass themselves off as defectors. So might it not be that the CIA men in Ankara found Sasha's story just too good to be true? The CIA would almost certainly know that the other URPO officers at the famous press conference a year earlier had gone back to Putin's FSB (or had in reality never left it) so why would Litvinenko be any different? Maybe he was a double agent too? They would have listened to Litvinenko's barely credible story of how he, a serving FSB officer, had gone to an enemy of the Kremlin and told him about a government-sponsored plot to assassinate him. And they could have been forgiven for thinking that the whole thing just didn't add up.

The way things panned out in Ankara suggests the CIA were not convinced of Litvinenko's bona fides. But were their suspicions justified? Had the massively publicized press conference really been an elaborate charade to persuade the West they would be getting an important defector while all the time Litvinenko actually remained loyal to Moscow? If this were the case, it would suggest Litvinenko was not a whistle-blower at all and that he had continued to work for the FSB, just as at least some of the other participants in the press conference had.

The question that needs to be asked, therefore – and the CIA seems to have asked it – is whether Litvinenko was all the time playing an elaborate double game with Berezovsky. It is clear that Berezovsky's own reaction when Litvinenko first approached him with offers of help was to think he was probably an FSB infiltrator, an informer. 'At first I didn't take it seriously . . . I thought maybe it was an FSB game to try to get close to me and so on . . .' It is undeniable that it would have been very useful for the FSB to have an agent in Berezovsky's entourage, someone who could provide vital intelligence on a powerful enemy whom the Kremlin loathed and feared, whose efforts to stir up political opposition they regarded as a threat. Such a prize might have been worth the extraordinary lengths they went to. The Kremlin knew that only a compelling story, only a seismic event like the 1998 press conference, would convince Berezovsky of Litvinenko's bona fides; only such a public demonstration of Litvinenko's 'genuine' break with the FSB would allow him to infiltrate the Berezovsky camp.

So were the Americans right to mistrust Litvinenko and turn down his asylum application? Might they have been right to suspect he was still working for the FSB? The evidence is unclear and only the classified files of the CIA, the FSB and – possibly – Britain's MI5 can answer those questions with any certainty. What is clear is that the Kremlin has staged such elaborate cover for its double agents on many occasions in the past . . . and that one of them at least will play a role in our investigations of the Litvinenko murder.

29

TO LONDON

Having been turned down for political asylum by the Americans, Litvinenko and Goldfarb had to find a Plan B. Waiting for an ordinary US visa was a long process and they had little time to spare; Goldfarb feared the Turkish authorities might get wind of the defector in their midst and decide to curry favour with Moscow by sending him back home. So at the end of October 2000, Alex Goldfarb bought the Litvinenkos air tickets from Istanbul, via London, to Moscow. No visa was needed because their flight was scheduled to end in Russia, but the Litvinenkos had no intention of using the second leg of their tickets. When the plane landed at London's Heathrow Airport on the morning of 1 November 2000 they followed the yellow and black signs for 'International Transit' until they reached the central hub where onward flights are indicated. There Sasha told Marina to take a seat with young Anatoly and walked calmly up to a British police officer. In halting English he said, 'Good morning, sir. I am Russian security agent and I wish to claim political asylum.'

It was the start of a six-year stay in England that Litvinenko, Berezovsky and all their followers believed would end with a triumphant return to a post-Putin Russia.

Goldfarb's role in the Litvinenkos' defection was to cause him trouble in the future: for several months he was barred from entering the UK as he was considered to have aided and abetted an illegal immigrant. Even now an entry in the computer files of the US Immigration Service means he is regularly stopped and questioned every time he flies into New York.

As for Sasha, he was detained and interviewed by the British police and the Immigration and Nationality Directorate. After ten hours of questioning he was told he could remain in the country while his case was being reviewed; he and Marina would have to report to immigration officials on a regular basis, but otherwise they were free. Sasha was astonished when a senior police officer treated him with respect and sympathy ('I remembered how Russian policemen would treat you!') and said to him, 'Now you are on the territory of Great Britain and you are under the protection of the British government. If ever you feel you are being threatened in any way, you must immediately report it to the police. We will protect you.'

Luckily for Litvinenko but less fortunately for Boris Berezovsky, his patron had arrived in the West several weeks earlier and he too had requested asylum from the pursuing wrath of Vladimir Putin's Kremlin. In the months after Sasha fled from Moscow Berezovsky had been trying desperately to defend both his political power and business empire, signally failing on both counts. In early July Putin had moved from grudging toleration of the oligarchs who had wielded such clout under his predecessor to all-out attack. As we will see in a later chapter, Berezovsky had tried to fight but was eventually forced to accept the inevitable.

After the Litvinenkos were released from police custody, Goldfarb and Berezovsky took good care of them. Berezovsky, who was living in France at the time, came to London to see Sasha. The pleasantries of the reunion between the two men and their families were tempered by the circumstances they found themselves in, but there was genuine pleasure at finding old friends so far from home. Marina and Berezovsky's wife, Yelena, busied themselves preparing lunch while Sasha and Boris discussed politics and the best tactics to persuade the British to grant them political asylum. Over coffee and biscuits they drafted a statement for Sasha to release to the press, stressing the danger he would be in if he were sent back to Russia: 'My family and I fled from Russia as the result of permanent persecution on the part of the Russian special services. Threats have been made against the lives of my wife and child. I have repeatedly asked prosecution agencies to protect me and my family, but there was no reaction to my requests.' Few newspapers printed the story, but those that did speculated that the mystery Russian was likely to be granted leave to stay, if only because he claimed to possess information on who was behind the mysterious apartment bombings in Moscow the previous year that the Kremlin blamed on Chechen rebels.

If the British media was showing little interest in Alexander Litvinenko, the British authorities were showing even less. According to Viktor Suvorov, a Russian military intelligence agent who defected in 1978 and who knew Litvinenko, his offers to provide information about his past in the FSB were politely turned down. 'I raised the question: "Look, here's a man who has lots of information about organized crime." No one else had so much information, but no one questioned him about it, British, French, Americans. He had incredible knowledge.'

It was the start of a frustrating six years for Sasha Litvinenko, years in which he would repeatedly be rebuffed trying to make the world take notice of his allegations about the misdeeds of the Kremlin and its master.

In material terms Sasha and Marina had little to complain about. For their first few months in London Berezovsky found them a spacious, high-ceilinged apartment in a Victorian white-stucco terrace in the central Earls Court district. Later he bought them a modern red-brick house in the affluent suburb of Muswell Hill, although he kept the deeds to the property in his own name. In recognition of his past services and in return for his continuing work for the Berezovsky cause, Sasha was paid £5,000 ($9,800) a month. He was given few official duties to carry out for his patron, but was tremendously self-motivated in seeking out information and stories he thought would be useful in the anti-Putin propaganda campaign Berezovsky was now waging.

Berezovsky's explanation is that he helped Litvinenko because he owed him a debt of gratitude. 'I was more than happy to pay him,' he says, 'because he was very professional and he was helping me with the story I was starting already in this country. The story is very simple – I start to create political opposition to Putin, to his political regime. And Sasha was very helpful because when he went abroad, he took more than a hundred kilos of documents about the FSB's crime activities and it was very helpful for him and for me to help develop opposition against the existing regime.'

If it is true that Litvinenko brought with him a hundred kilos of compromising documents about the activities of the FSB – it is unlikely he personally carried them on his hurried flit through southern Russia and Georgia to Turkey, but it is quite possible that he smuggled them out in some other way – it is not hard to see that he would indeed be 'very helpful' to Berezovsky in his fight against Putin. It may even explain why Berezovsky himself 'took the decision that Sasha must leave Russia' back in the summer of 2000. But most of all it would have made Litvinenko mortal enemies among his old colleagues – among the former URPO men who had carried out crimes as part of their job description, and among the top brass of the security forces who condoned and encouraged such illegal behaviour.

Shortly after his arrival in the UK a court in Moscow tried Litvinenko in absentia. He was found guilty of the misuse of office and the illegal possession of firearms and ammunition, with all the charges dating back to his time in Kostroma in 1997. The judge in the case ruled that a voice-match analysis of the disputed video-tape showing the brutal interrogation of a prisoner had proved that the man dishing out the beating was indeed Litvinenko. For good measure, his former URPO colleague Viktor Shebalin confirmed it was him in testimony to the court. He could not see the man's face, he said, but he knew from the way he moved and talked that it was Litvinenko. There could no longer be any doubt that Shebalin was back in harness with the FSB. In all, thirty-five witnesses and six 'victims' who had allegedly suffered at Sasha's hands were called to testify. Litvinenko was given a suspended sentence of three and a half years. It was bad news for Sasha's relations with Moscow, but good news for his pending UK asylum appeal, which the prison sentence made all the more credible.

The Litvinenkos were getting used to life in London and Marina says her husband quickly grew to appreciate his adopted country.

> Almost every month he would ask me, 'Marina, are you happy here? Are you happy to be in England, to be in London?' And I told him, 'Sasha, it really doesn't matter for me because I can't compare; I've never been with you in Paris, or some other place.' Maybe he still had some contact from Russia with some people who he knew before, but it wasn't people who he felt could harm him, you know what I mean?

Marina should not have been so sure.

One of the first things Sasha did after arriving in London was to ring his former URPO comrades who were still in Moscow. As far as he was concerned, these were the men who had fought with him in Chechnya and had stood by him on the day of the infamous press conference two years earlier. Sasha felt he could trust them, and in their telephone conversations he spoke openly about his experiences and plans. His comrades listened attentively and expressed their understanding of his worries and homesickness. But two of them at least were back in the fold of the FSB and were making notes on Sasha's calls and running to inform their bosses of everything he had told them. Viktor Shebalin in particular was zealous in his efforts to vilify his former colleague, as he revealed in a self-serving report:

> Yes, he rang Ponkin from England to ask him what was going on back here in Moscow. And he was always ringing his so-called businessmen friends ... The night he ran off to England, Gusak called me and said, 'Did you hear? That freak's in England.' That's the word he used – that freak. 'He never thought about his family or his colleagues, did he? The only person he thought about was himself.'

Gusak himself says Litvinenko was constantly ringing him. When he did so, he would call Gusak's cellphone so the conversation could not be monitored by Russian security. Gusak says he found the calls highly suspicious. Far from dissociating himself from his FSB past, Litvinenko was reaching out from London, trying to re-establish contact. He invited Gusak to meet him outside Russia, first in England and then in Italy. 'I refused,' says Gusak, 'because judging from certain signs I understood that he was being controlled and was collaborating with the British special service.' Gusak says his suspicions were confirmed when British intelligence began to round up Russian citizens living in the UK who had been placed there by the FSB for covert operations. Litvinenko knew the names of these undercover FSB contacts, and Gusak believes it was he who betrayed them to MI5 in an effort to prove he had valuable information to offer. And no intelligence agency shows mercy to traitors who betray its agents . . .

PART FOUR

30

ABSENT FRIENDS

While Litvinenko was settling in to life in London, the FSB was encouraging his former URPO colleagues to dish the dirt on their departed friend. The 1998 press conference still rankled badly with Putin, who was by now president. Just a week after Sasha disembarked at Heathrow Airport, the Kremlin propaganda machine swung into action. A pro-Kremlin journalist named Alexander Khinshtein was summoned to FSB headquarters and told he was being given an exclusive. Khinshtein plays up his scoop. He doesn't mention that he was given the interview on a plate. 'You know, a journalist's work is like an iceberg: most of it goes on beneath the surface. Even now I can hardly believe that I managed to get that interview . . . the story of how I got it would make a book all on its own.'

The interview was with Viktor Shebalin, the lieutenant colonel who had sat next to Litvinenko on the press conference podium and made such a point of demonstrating his friendship and solidarity with him. In fact, far from being a triumph of investigative journalism, Khinshtein's 'scoop' is part of the time-honoured Soviet tradition of rewriting history. Shebalin's version of the events of 1998, as recounted in November 2000, bears little resemblance to how things seemed at the time. The whole episode, he says, all the accusations and all the controversy, was a put-up job, and the culprits behind it were Berezovsky and Litvinenko.

Shebalin is quoted as saying, 'As to whether we were asked to kill Berezovsky, it's a very complex and very simple question. No, there never was any assassination attempt. The whole thing was planned in advance by Litvinenko under the instructions of Berezovsky. It was, basically, a provocation. Now I understand that they were using us.' According to Shebalin, there was never really an order to kill Berezovsky.

'That day when we were all called into the URPO offices – me and Litvinenko and Ponkin and Latyshonok – the boss, Kamishnikov, just let slip, "That Berezovsky . . . it'd be a good idea to kill him." He was wrong to say it, of course. I think he was just very stressed, or it just slipped out in the heat of the moment.' From then on, Shebalin says Litvinenko was determined to turn a slip of the tongue into an international incident.

> Litvinenko was always boasting about how well he knew Berezovsky. He used to say, 'You know who I am friends with?' He worshipped Berezovsky . . . He used to use his connections with him to put pressure on his bosses and even the leadership of the FSB. Lots of people were afraid of Litvinenko; they thought he was an informer, feeding information to Berezovsky. He asked us to come along for a chat with Berezovsky . . . and then he threatened us that if we didn't tell him about Kamishnikov's remark, we would all be prosecuted.

According to Shebalin, Litvinenko was himself involved in criminal activities and being investigated by the FSB's Internal Affairs Directorate. By inveigling his comrades to take part in the snitch to Berezovsky, he was trying to amass material to scare them away from testifying against himself. Shebalin said the video recording of the meeting where they spoke to Berezovsky about the 'assassination order' was secretly filmed without their knowledge or permission, and Litvinenko used it to blackmail them into taking part in the press conference.

> Litvinenko was always pressurizing us, always threatening us. He used to scare us by saying we would all be arrested; that they would plant some drugs or guns on us; that the Interior Ministry was going to kill me personally. We felt like we were being driven into a corner. We couldn't get out of it. And then Litvinenko would say, 'Boris will look after you all . . . if you all do the right

thing, it will not be forgotten.' So we went along with it. I didn't want to go to that press conference. But I was in a terrible state. Litvinenko caused it; he never stopped threatening us.

Shebalin says he was shamed by his own actions. Litvinenko had tricked him and the others into a political conspiracy and then used it to blackmail them into carrying out further tasks on behalf of his master. 'Afterwards ... Berezovsky used to send us orders. For instance, he ordered us to gather as much dirt as we could about the prime minister, Primakov, about the Moscow mayor, Luzhkov, about his rival oligarch Gusinsky. I understood that I had been tricked.'

The purpose of Shebalin's testimony is clear: to exculpate the FSB of the crimes it had been accused of and to blacken the names of Berezovsky and Litvinenko. Having done the Kremlin's bidding on that, Shebalin goes on to make a very serious and deliberate threat against his old colleague.

Litvinenko was always a coward and a troublemaker. He was always intimidating prisoners, physically and mentally. That's why I broke with him and became his enemy. If I could turn back the clock, I would never have done those things with him. Now that he has run away, I consider him a traitor and directly linked with Berezovsky. I have a message for him: *Litvinenko, you had better come back and give yourself up. You have no other way out. If you are innocent, you have nothing to fear by coming back. But let me make it clear: we do not forgive traitors!*

31

IRREVOCABLE WAR

Sasha Litvinenko received word of Shebalin's threat just before Christmas 2000. He didn't want to spoil the holiday season so he didn't tell Marina about it, but he knew the warning was serious. It was the beginning of six years during which he would be constantly menaced by rumbling intimations of vengeance from Moscow. It was a recurring threat, and on more than one occasion it moved from words to actions. Litvinenko would spend the rest of his life being reminded that there was an unseen hand that might one day reach out and claim its prey.

In London, though, Sasha was growing used to life in a Western democracy. He began to take for granted the guarantees of safety and personal liberty that Britain had cherished for many centuries. He knew that Moscow had not forgiven him and that people there desired his death. But he came to feel that being part of the British way of life would somehow protect him. Vladimir Bukovsky, who was very close to Litvinenko in those years, says his faith bordered on the naive: 'He was like a younger brother to me. He was straightforward . . . he had some boyish notions of chivalry. He told me that when he got political asylum in England, he went to the Tower of London. He took his young son, who was seven years old at the time, and he showed him the crown. And he said, "Look and remember. This is the crown which protects us and keeps us safe."'

Marina too noticed how Sasha was beginning to relax after the years of stress and watchfulness. While other exiles were constantly on their guard, adopting pseudonyms and new identities, Litvinenko was open and seemingly confident. 'He never tried to hide away, never tried to disguise himself or change his looks . . . he felt very safe and he was very open. When we moved into the place where we used to live, he was very proud of this. I could see how Sasha, from being a former officer, was growing into an absolutely different person.'

In retrospect the psychology of the situation is intriguing. Here is a man who knows he is being threatened by powerful enemies. Whatever his assessment of the imminence of that threat, he knows that his own safety and that of his family would best be ensured by stepping out of the public spotlight and keeping a low profile. But he does not do so, and his response is once again revealing of his character. Litvinenko, it seems, had priorities other than safety, and those priorities involved him being very much in the public eye. He spent the next six years continuing to provoke the Kremlin and the FSB, almost daring them to come and get him.

Bukovsky tells a sobering story of how he and Litvinenko were walking in a park in Cambridge 'and the birds were singing and the flowers were in blossom, and all of a sudden there was a call on his mobile phone and it was a former colleague of his from the Lubyanka saying, "Do you think you are safe over there in England? Well, you are dreaming. Just remember what happened to Trotsky!"' Trotsky, of course, was killed in his Mexico exile by a Kremlin assassin wielding an ice-pick.

It seems madness for someone who knows he is a potential assassination target not to take cover, but remember: Litvinenko is the man who refused the chance to make peace when he and his comrades were offered a deal after the press conference of 1998.

What is common to the two situations is that Sasha would have had to back down to ensure his safety. And backing down is something he was not good at doing. As many who knew him have pointed out, Sasha was an obsessive. He hated losing face. As far as he was concerned Putin had offended him; he had challenged Putin and he was not going to make peace. Sasha was a man who insisted on total vindication. Now, in 2001, his obsessive nature was driving him to ratchet up the stakes even further. He railed at Putin from his London refuge, firmly believing him to be the guilty party in their clash of wills. For Litvinenko it was Putin who needed to be punished not him, and with the backing of Boris Berezovsky and his powerful circle Sasha set out to do just that.

His first months in London were spent doing odd jobs, including a spell as a postman, while Marina picked up her old profession, teaching ballroom dancing to middle-aged English couples who were intrigued by her exotic accent and background. But Litvinenko was biding his time, waiting for the British courts to confirm his political asylum in the UK. Once they did so, on 14 May 2001, his hands were untied and he threw himself once again into the passion that drove his life. In interviews, books and articles on anti-Kremlin websites, Sasha resumed his campaign against his former employers with a vengeance.

The list of his accusations over the next few years is quite astounding. In 2002 he suggested the FSB had engineered the horrific siege of a Moscow theatre in which 130 people died. According to Litvinenko, two of the Chechen hostage takers, whom he called alternatively Terkibayev or Abdul the Bloody, and Ruslan Elmurzaev or Abu Bakar, were working for the FSB. The attack took place at a theatre in the Dubrovka area of Moscow which was showing a musical comedy called *Nord-Ost*. Forty-two heavily armed men and women entered the theatre and took everyone present hostage, both audience and performers. The gunmen, led by the nephew of a slain Chechen military leader, threatened to kill the hostages unless Russian forces withdrew from Chechnya. With explosives set throughout the auditorium and grenades strapped to their own bodies, the Chechens released a statement declaring themselves ready to die for the cause of Chechen independence.

> The Russian occupiers have flooded our land with our children's blood. People are unaware of the innocent who are dying in Chechnya: the women, the children and the weak ones. So we have chosen this action. This action is for the freedom of the Chechen people. There is no difference where we die, so we have

decided to die here in Moscow. We will take with us the lives of hundreds of sinners. If we die, others will come and follow us – our brothers and sisters who are willing to sacrifice their lives for Allah. Russia is the true criminal.

It seems unlikely that the Kremlin would have engineered the theatre siege, but that is exactly what Litvinenko claimed, suggesting the FSB had manipulated the rebels into staging the attack. 'Terkibayev was guided by the FSB when he was in the theatre building. I know that they put the main task before him to go upstairs, get into the room where the hostages were kept, and open fire. After that it was declared that the terrorists had begun shooting and that it was necessary to begin the storm of the building.' After the assault by Russian *spetsnaz* special forces in which many hostages and all the terrorists died, Litvinenko said, 'When they tried to find Abdul the Bloody and Abu Bakar among the dead terrorists, they weren't there. The FSB got its agents out. So the FSB agents among the Chechens organized the whole thing on FSB orders, and those agents were released.'

Subsequently he claimed the two men had been given new identities and were being employed on special duties by the Russian security forces. 'Let's speak about the reality. The FSB is a terrorist organization. It is not in the interests of the FSB to search after the terrorists and detain their agent Terkibayev, a terrorist and provocateur. The FSB will continue to use him in terrorist acts and hide him in case of failure.'

Whether Abdul and Abu ever existed is far from clear. But Litvinenko's allegations – based, he said, on good intelligence sources – set the tone for much of the material he was to produce in the coming months and years.

32

BLOWING UP RUSSIA

Hard on the heels of his claims about the Moscow theatre siege, Litvinenko produced a book, together with his colleague Yuri Felshtinsky, called *The FSB Bombs Russia*, later to be translated into English as *Blowing up Russia: The Secret Plot to Bring Back KGB Terror*. It recounts the story of a series of explosions that shook Moscow and other Russian cities in September 1999. The explosions, in crowded apartment blocks, took place during the night while the occupants slept and claimed the lives of more than 300 people. Army and police experts determined without doubt that the blasts were all caused by deliberately planted bombs. The Russian government promptly blamed the outrages on Chechen terrorists and proceeded to stir up public anger against the separatist republic in the national media. On 17 September Prime Minister Vladimir Putin convened an emergency session of the Federation Council with the participation of the armed forces and the Interior Ministry. He proposed immediate action to defend Russia against the terrorist threat, including the establishment of a defensive safety cordon along the Chechen border and the commencement of aerial and artillery bombardments of Chechen territory. Shortly after, he appeared on television to announce that 'action of the most hard-line character' would be taken to deal with 'bandit bases' in Chechnya, saying, 'The bandits must be exterminated; no other action is possible here.' Quite remarkably, there had been no reported sightings of any suspects in the bombings and no clues at all to link them to any particular ethnic group, but Putin pinned the blame on the Chechens. The next few weeks proved the value of such certainty: his poll ratings, which had been languishing at around 2 per cent began to rise in step with the harshness of his

Marina and Alexander Litvinenko on their wedding day, 14 October 1994

Alexander Litvinenko (right) at the November 1998 press conference

Aftermath of the Kashirskoe Shosse apartment bombing in Moscow, September 1999

Vladimir Putin

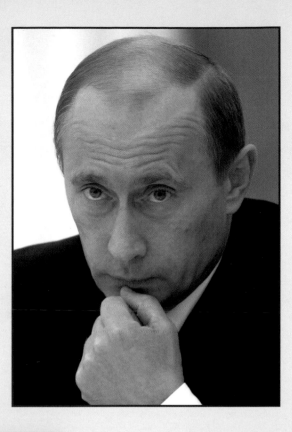

Boris Berezovsky

Above.
Marina Litvinenko at her
husband's funeral

Left.
Litvinenko's father, Walter,
accusing the Kremlin of
his son's murder

Right.
Akhmed Zakayev
arriving for Litvinenko's
funeral

Below.
Alex Goldfarb at the inquest
into the death

Below, right.
Andrei Nekrasov

Scotland Yard detectives in Moscow

Right.
Mikhail Trepashkin
at his trial in 2003

Below.
Dmitry Kovtun

Below, right.
Andrei Lugovoy

Alexander Litvinenko
in 2002 (*left*) and in
November 2006 (*below*)

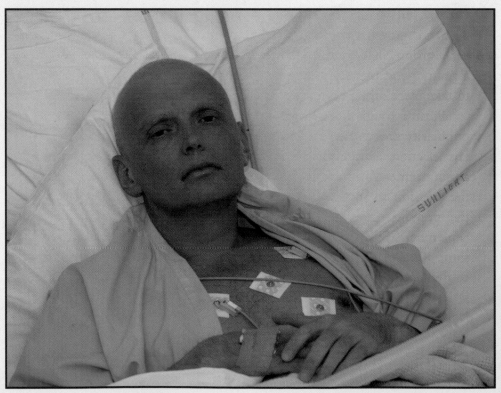

rhetoric. When he picked up the art of echoing the language of the streets, he did even better: in a carefully planned off-the-cuff remark that sounded suspiciously like a parody of Winston Churchill's 'fight them on the beaches' speech, Putin crudely pledged to 'pursue the terrorists wherever they go; if they are at the airports, we will strike them there; and if – pardon my language – we catch up with them when they are sitting on the toilet, we will wipe them out in the lavatories. That's all there is to it; the problem is over.' The prime minister who had until then been dismissed by most Russians as an ineffective nonentity suddenly seemed to strike a chord.

Citing the 'probability' that those who had bombed the Russian apartment blocks had fled to Chechnya, the Kremlin announced two weeks later that military action was necessary to strike at them 'in their own territory'. On 4 October the army launched an invasion of Chechnya. Intensive fighting followed, with some quick victories for the Russian forces.

By December the army had encircled the Chechen capital, Grozny, the separatist rebels were on the defensive and there had been no more apartment bombs in Moscow or anywhere else. By early spring 2000 Putin's poll ratings had soared to over 60 per cent, a pretty good piece of timing given presidential elections were due to take place on 26 March.

Putin's tough line over Chechnya had massively boosted his popularity and turned him from a no-hoper into a certain winner. His election as president had been virtually guaranteed by his announcement and vigorous prosecution of the Chechen War. But the decision to invade Chechnya had been made possible only by the popular anger over the apartment bombings the previous September. Even before the March ballots had been counted, some Russian journalists were beginning to smell a rat. At a press conference during a campaign event the president-elect was asked a series of questions by a journalist from the investigative newspaper *Novaya Gazeta.*

'Vladimir Vladimirovich, did you decide to launch the operations in Chechnya before the apartments were bombed or after?'

Putin replied, 'After.'

'Have you heard that, according to one version, the apartments were deliberately blown up to justify the start of military operations? That is to say, it was allegedly done by the Russian secret services.'

Putin responded angrily, 'What? We blew up our own houses? Nonsense! Total rubbish! There are no people in the Russian secret services who would commit such a crime against their own people. The very suggestion is amoral and fundamentally nothing more than part of an information war against Russia.'

But Russia is a country with a grand history of conspiracies, as well as a population of conspiracy theorists. Speculation that the apartment bombs had been planted by the FSB with the intention of boosting Putin's image as a tough, decisive leader continued. Andrei Piontkovsky was one of many influential commentators who were not convinced by the government's insistence on blaming the Chechens: 'A single, simple chain of conditioned reflexes: Chechens – terrorists – liquidate – wipe out in the toilet. It was the explosions in Moscow that put the last piece in this jigsaw. And if in the name of such absolute values as "geopolitical interests" and "the greatness of Russia" they can sacrifice hundreds of lives in Dagestan without their hands so much as shaking, then what is to stop them sacrificing human lives in Moscow?'

In 2002 Alexander Litvinenko and Yuri Felshtinsky set out to prove that the FSB was to blame. They were greatly assisted in their task by evidence from a failed bombing attempt in the city of Ryazan which had taken place at the same time as the successful Moscow bombings. After a tip-off from local residents that two men and a woman had been seen acting suspiciously in a communal courtyard, the Ryazan police discovered sacks containing quantities of a yellowish granular substance connected to detonators in the basement of an apartment block at number 14–16 Novosyelov Street. Experts arriving at the scene found that the sacks tested positive for the explosive Hexogen. The building and the surrounding neighbour-hood were evacuated and 30,000 people spent the night in the open air. Police set up roadblocks on all routes leading out of the city, and in the search for the bombers telephone exchanges were instructed to listen out for suspicious calls.

That evening, 23 September, a call from a Ryazan public telephone to a number in Moscow was intercepted by a local telephone operator, Nadezhda Yuknova. She heard a conversation in which the caller said, 'There is no way to get out of town undetected.' The voice at the other end of the line replied, 'Split up and each of you make your own way out; there are roadblocks everywhere.' The operator reported the call to the police and they traced the Moscow number. To their astonishment, it belonged to the headquarters of the FSB.

33

AN EXPLOSIVE CAMPAIGN

For Litvinenko and his partner the events in Ryazan were a godsend. The three suspects identified from the intercepted telephone call were quickly arrested and all turned out to be FSB employees. It seemed to be proof that the bombings – both the successful ones and the thwarted Ryazan attack – were part of an FSB-backed plot to kill Russian citizens in pursuit of some cynical political advantage. Litvinenko and Felshtinsky both laid the blame at Putin's door and set about excoriating the 'murderous president' with gusto.

> Before the end of September, the FSB intended to blow up residential buildings in Ryazan, Tula, Pskov and Samara ... It [was] important for the FSB to drag Russia into a war as quickly as possible, so that the presidential elections [could] be held against the background of a major armed conflict, and so that after the new president comes to power he can inherit the war together with all the political consequences it implies ... It is a simple little matter of a conspiracy with the goal of allowing the former KGB to seize power.

According to Litvinenko, the 'conspiracy' achieved its goal when Putin won the March 2000 elections: 'The FSB ... succeeded in getting its own candidate elected president ... Putin is perfectly described by the definition of a "tyrant" given by the *Soviet Encyclopaedia*: "a ruler whose power is founded on arbitrary decision and violence".'

But despite the evidence against it, the Kremlin was insistent it had nothing to do with the apartment bombs. Nikolai Patrushev, then head of the FSB, announced that the bomb in Ryazan had actually been a dummy and that the incident had been a 'test' by the security forces to check emergency procedures in case of a real attack. He congratulated the local residents on their vigilance in exposing the 'exercise'. The FSB claimed the supposed explosive material in the sacks attached to the detonator was actually sugar; the gas analyzer that detected Hexogen had simply malfunctioned.

The Kremlin's explanation was attacked by many in the Russian media and holes picked in its story. Litvinenko and Felshtinsky collated all the evidence pointing to an FSB conspiracy and inter-viewed many of those with first-hand knowledge of the events.

They completed their book in 2002 and took it excitedly to a series of Western publishers, but to their great disappointment none was interested. Some chapters from the book were printed in Moscow by *Novaya Gazeta*, but it was only two years later that Boris Berezovsky agreed to fund a private print run of 5,000 copies, in Russian, to be shipped to Russia as part of his continuing campaign against the Kremlin. Sadly for him and his two authors, the whole shipment was confiscated in transit and never reached the streets of Moscow. For the next two years they continued to seek a British or American publisher to bring out an English translation, but the prevailing climate was not in tune with the book's strident anti-Putin message. These were the years of the 'Islamic threat' following 9/11 in New York and the train bombings in Madrid; George Bush and Tony Blair were portraying Putin as a valued ally in the war on terror, and anyway the West needed Russia's oil and gas. In the end it took Sasha Litvinenko's very dramatic and public death to produce a mass-market English language edition of the book.

As for the credibility of the allegations in *Blowing up Russia*, it is clear they are based on much more rigorous evidence than Litvi-nenko's accusations of FSB involvement in the Moscow theatre siege. They cite detailed (though often anonymous) eyewitness testimonies and they have a historical precedent that adds to their plausibility.

Russia has a long history of bomb plots and assassinations, some of them politically motivated, more of them the result of business feuds and the settling of accounts. But there have been repeated incidents – never claimed by any group and never solved by the police – which have raised suspicions in the past.

★

On the evening of 11 June 1996 I was in the bar of the Radisson-Slavyanskaya Hotel in Moscow with some BBC colleagues. We had just sent our last report of the day via satellite to London and were having a quick drink before going home. Then news arrived that there had been an explosion at the Tulskaya metro station in southern Moscow. It was dark by the time the media got there, and outside the building police cordons were keeping the crowds at bay. Periodically, passengers from the platforms below emerged with blackened faces and bandaged limbs. Some of them explained that they had been sitting in the front carriage of a train on the Serpukhovskaya line when a bomb had exploded under a seat. Four people had been killed outright and dozens injured. What made the explosion suspicious to me and other journalists was its timing, just five days before Boris Yeltsin was to face a testing first round of voting in the presidential elections. With impressive alacrity, Yeltsin's key ally the mayor of Moscow had appeared at the metro station to explain to the television cameras what lesson voters should draw from the bomb: 'This savage terrorist act is part of a chain of measures to create chaos in the run-up to the elections. It is directed against the president and against me.' A few hours later Yeltsin himself made the message even more explicit, saying that the best response to the extremists was to 'vote for stability in Sunday's elections', a not very concealed plug for his own campaign. In case anyone hadn't got the message, when two trolley buses were blown up, injuring thirty-four people, Mayor Yuri Luzhkov appeared at the scene to announce he was expelling all Chechens from Moscow. There is no suggestion Luzhkov himself was behind the bombings, but there had been no investigation of the attacks, no suspects had been named and the police had no theories. Muscovites, though, were more than willing to believe they were the work of terrorists from down south.

For the next days and weeks the sight of police patrols sweeping through the city's bustling street markets was a common one, and it seemed to me that on occasion they were intent on picking up anyone with even the slightest hint of a swarthy complexion. The Kremlin and its allies were making a fairly blatant political point.

When it came to the 1999 apartment bombs, my memories of three years earlier came immediately to mind. Despite the enormity of the allegations Litvinenko and Felshtinsky were making, I did not feel able to dismiss them out of hand. The book they had written, if proved to be correct, would be immensely damaging to Putin. Litvinenko was claiming the Russian president was willing to sanction the cold-blooded murder of Russian civilians in order to make political propaganda, and he had deliberately engineered a war which was to cause untold horrors and the deaths of tens of thousands of people. It was very far removed from the image of the reforming democrat which Putin wanted to project to the world.

But would Litvinenko's allegations really provide sufficient grounds for Moscow to order his execution?

34

UNSOLVED DEATHS

On 18 March 2000 two liberal members of Russia's parliament, the Duma, demanded an inquiry into the allegations of FSB involvement in the bombings. But the application, made in the name of Yuri Shchekochikhin and Sergei Yushenkov, was turned down. Yushenkov was a veteran member of the Liberal Russia Party, which was co-chaired and financed by Boris Berezovsky; Shchekochikhin was a member of a sister party, the liberal-leaning Yabloko (Apple) group. The two men were respected politicians. When they complained about the government's refusal to investigate the apartment bombings, they received the backing of several leading public figures. They also sparked great anger in the Kremlin.

After two years of stonewalling by the Russian authorities, Yushenkov and Shchekochikhin decided to take their campaign for justice for the bomb victims into the arena of public debate. And to do so they turned to their colleagues in London.

If Alexander Litvinenko's efforts to pin the blame for the bombings on Vladimir Putin had found few backers in the West, they had by now won the keen endorsement of Boris Berezovsky. Having read Litvinenko's book, the oligarch commissioned and paid for a documentary film about the apartment bombs. Made by a French production company, its title, *Assassination of Russia; false-flag, government-sponsored terrorism*, leaves little doubt about the thrust of its conclusions. The film insists that the evidence from 1999 indicates an FSB hand behind the bombings and points out that right up to a month before the explosions the director of the FSB was Vladimir Putin. At the film's conclusion Yuri Felshtinsky sets up an either–or scenario: 'Either Putin knew exactly what was going on, and that is why he has refused to hold an inquiry, or there is another explanation – that the president doesn't really have control over the FSB.' It is an either–or proposition that will become vitally important as we consider the FSB's subsequent relations with Shchekochikhin and Yushenkov, and with other opponents of the Kremlin, including Alexander Litvinenko.

Berezovsky's film was first screened in March 2002 in London, but efforts to show it in Russia were blocked by the Kremlin. Prints of the film and consignments of video-cassette copies were seized by customs at St Petersburg's Pulkovo Airport. Sergei Yushenkov, however, did manage to bring 1,000 video copies into Russia when he flew from London to Moscow's Sheremetevo Airport.

Soon after, the parliamentary leader of Liberal Russia, Yuly Rybakov, claimed members of his party were being assaulted and some had received death threats. Rybakov said unidentified assailants had beaten up three of his employees and attacked a fellow party member; he was convinced the threats were an attempt to prevent the showing of the Berezovsky documentary. He and Yushenkov renewed their demands for an inquiry into the 1999 bombs and sent a letter to Vladimir Putin urging him to set up a special commission to investigate the events. Yushenkov, meanwhile, continued to distribute copies of the tape to members of parliament and organized a private showing of the film in Moscow.

On 17 April 2003 Sergei Yushenkov was shot dead with a single bullet to his chest. His body was left lying on the pavement outside the entrance to his apartment block. A police investigation failed to turn up any suspects, but Yuly Rybakov was convinced that the death was ordered by the Kremlin and that it was connected with Yushenkov's attempts to promote the Berezovsky film. Other Duma members claimed Yushenkov had recently quarrelled with Berezovsky and suggested *he* might have been responsible for the killing. Berezovsky himself told the *Kommersant* newspaper, 'Whatever my disagreements with Sergei may have been, he is after all my comrade. I'm lost for words.' Already, in 2003, it seemed that unexplained murders were taking place for which responsibility was being pinned variously on Vladimir Putin or on Boris Berezovsky, no matter what the evidence.

Three months later another death occurred. On 3 July 2003 Yury Shchekochikhin, the other liberal politician who had been pressing for an inquiry into the bombings, died suddenly of a mysterious allergic reaction. Many believed it was a case of deliberate poisoning, but the incident was never investigated as a murder. As well as being a deputy in the Duma, Shchekochikhin was also deputy editor of the investigative journal *Novaya Gazeta*. Under his guidance the newspaper had continued to expose corruption in post-communist Russia and had made the 1999 events one of its key causes.

After a visit to the city of Ryazan in the summer of 2003 Shchekochikhin developed a slight fever. When he returned to Moscow, his face broke out in blisters and his skin began to peel. Shchekochikhin's symptoms were identical to those experienced by the anti-Kremlin Ukrainian politician Victor Yushchenko, who fell ill just before his country's 2004 presidential elections. It was later determined that Yushchenko had been poisoned by dioxin and that he had previously had a meeting with Russian officials during which it is said he drank a bowl of soup. Yushchenko lived to tell the tale and to be elected president of Ukraine, but Shchekochikhin was not so lucky. Nine days after falling ill he died in agony. The official cause of death was given as Lyell's syndrome, or toxic epidermal necrolysis, an extremely rare allergic reaction, but his friends and colleagues believed he was poisoned. Journalists on *Novaya Gazeta* started their own investigation, but faced opposition from the authorities, who would not release samples of Shchekochikhin's hair for forensic analysis. The official file on his death was never released and is now classified as secret.

In the final weeks of his life Shchekochikhin was working on a story about the 1999 apartment bombings. His death meant that two of the four Duma deputies looking into the bombings were now dead, presumed murdered. The case was clearly of sufficient importance for someone to resort to extreme measures, and Litvinenko was absolutely convinced it was the FSB.

In fact, the fate of many who have investigated the apartment bombs has been an unhappy one. In November 2003 Mikhail Trepashkin, the former FSB man who was beaten up by Litvinenko and his cronies before eventually becoming an ally, was due to present a report on the incident to a parliamentary commission. At the same time he was acting as legal adviser to members of a family who had lost their mother in the explosions and were attempting to have all FSB files relating to the bombs made public. On 24 October, before he could complete either of his tasks, he was stopped by a police patrol, who threw a bag containing a gun into his car and charged him with illegal possession of a firearm. When he eventually came to trial, he was sentenced to four years in prison on the additional charge of 'revealing state secrets': Trepashkin had identified Vladimir Romanovich, a former FSB man, from a photofit picture as a suspect in the 1999 bombings. Romanovich was later killed in a car crash in Cyprus.

Perhaps the most high-profile person to take an interest in the 1999 apartment bombings was the investigative journalist Anna Politkovskaya. An earnest, dedicated woman, Politkovskaya had earned a reputation as a fierce critic of the Kremlin. She was born in 1958 in New York, the daughter of Russian Ukrainian diplomats, and dedicated her early life to the study of literature. Her university thesis was about the great tragic poetess Marina Tsvetaeva, whose involvement with anti-Bolshevik White forces during and after the Russian Revolution forced her into exile in Paris and a bleak suicide at the age of forty-eight. After an early career with official Soviet newspapers, Politkovskaya went to work as a columnist for *Novaya Gazeta*, the paper which published extracts from Litvinenko's *Blowing up Russia* in 2002. She spent many months on assignment in Chechnya, away from her husband and children in Moscow and living under difficult conditions, investigating atrocities carried out by Russian troops in the occupied republic. She worked closely with

Yuri Shchekochikhin on his investigation of the 1999 apartment bombings. On several occasions she received death threats as a result of her journalism and in 2001 she had briefly been forced to flee abroad following a particularly credible series of emails indicating that a contract had been placed on her life.

On 2 September 2004 Politkovskaya was sent by her editor to cover the unfolding drama in the southern Russian town of Beslan, where armed Chechen gunmen had taken more than a thousand children and teachers hostage in a local school. The building had been surrounded by Russian troops who were threatening to storm it. The stand-off was eventually to end in the death of hundreds of hostages and a fierce debate about the tactics of the Russian security forces. But Politkovskaya was not there to report it. On the plane from Moscow she was served a cup of tea and shortly afterwards fell seriously ill; she lost consciousness and awoke in hospital. Doctors said she had been poisoned and was lucky to survive.

In the months that followed, Politkovskaya was urged by her family to leave Russia and accept one of the many posts she had been offered by universities in the United States. Alexander Litvinenko gave her the same advice when she came to London, but in temperament she was very like him: once she had committed to a cause, she would not give it up. She acknowledged the danger she was in – 'People sometimes pay with their lives for saying aloud what they think,' she told a journalists' conference; 'I am not the only one in danger' – but she stayed in Russia and carried on the struggle for truth and justice. At the same time, however, she had no illusions about how hard it was to awaken public opinion to the abuses she saw happening around her.

> I will not go into the joys of the path I have chosen – the poisoning, the arrests, the threats in letters and over the Internet, the telephoned death threats, the weekly summons to the prosecutor general's office ... People don't want to know about the things I write about. It's too hard, because to accept it would

mean rethinking all their views and all their lives . . . They read it, but they don't want to think about what they've read. There's no real protest in this society any more. Society says, 'Don't worry, Mr Putin, it'll all go away.'

It was Anna Politkovskaya's determination not to let it 'go away' that almost certainly sealed her fate. On 7 October 2006, in the lift of her apartment block in the middle of Moscow, she was shot four times. It was a professional job; the last bullet was in her head to make sure the job was done. Like the tragic poetess of her youth, she was forty-eight years old.

As would happen with Sasha Litvinenko's death a few weeks later, conflicting theories immediately began to circulate about who might have ordered Politkovskaya's murder. Her colleagues at *Novaya Gazeta* suspected it was retribution for her revelations about the behaviour of Russian troops and local pro-Moscow forces in Chechnya. Other commentators suggested the murder had been done to blacken the name of Vladimir Putin. He had been the target of much of Politkovskaya's bile and, just as with Sasha Litvinenko, the president was remarkably slow to express regret over her death. Yuri Felshtinsky says the choice of date for her murder links her irrevocably with President Putin. 'You know, Politkovskaya was killed on his birthday. It was definitely someone who wanted to offer a present for Putin's birthday. I think this is the result of their understanding of his desires; there are a lot of people who like to do something nice for the boss.'

35

THE GANG FROM THE LUBYANKA

Shortly after his first abortive attempts to publish *Blowing up Russia*, Alexander Litvinenko began work on an exposé of the crimes and corruption he had witnessed in his years at the FSB. Eventually published in New York in December 2002, the book's foreword by Berezovsky's lieutenant Alex Goldfarb claims, '*The Criminal Gang from the Lubyanka* by Alexander Litvinenko . . . is a historical milestone . . . in the same category as Solzhenitsyn's *Gulag Archipelago* or *The Diary of Anne Frank*.' In reality it is a series of disjointed interviews with a Russian journalist, apparently drawing on the hundred kilos of secret files, videotapes and audio recordings Litvinenko allegedly brought with him when he left Russia. And the files appear to contain some startling revelations, including the 'fact' that Vladimir Putin was personally involved in organized crime.

While investigating the activities of Yevgeny Khokholkov, the FSB colonel with whom he clashed during his time at URPO, Litvinenko claims he discovered that he and Putin were mixed up with the mafia bosses who were Khokholkov's controllers.

> I discovered that Putin's connection with Colonel Khokholkov dated back to the time when Putin was a Deputy for Economic Affairs to the Mayor of St Petersburg . . . My informant came to see me: 'Putin will squash you,' he said, 'and no one can help you. He has no choice because he was working with the Uzbek group. There is lots of common money there' . . . He was telling me that Putin was directly linked to the mob that my investigations into Colonel Khokholkov had led me to.

Litvinenko's informant cannot, however, vouch for these allegations, because he was later conveniently (or inconveniently) killed 'by a close range direct hit from . . . a hitman on a passing bicycle'.

Before he died, though, he did, allegedly, manage to tell Litvinenko about one more 'crime': 'Remember the smuggling of precious metals in the early nineties? Putin was in charge of export licensing. You worked on organized crime? Tell me, could anyone export a kilo of metal in those days without the mob? And he was right at the centre of it all. All those he gave licences to were mob fronts.'

In his closing chapter Litvinenko explains that he really didn't want to reveal Putin's criminal past, but thought he had better do so because the man just happened to become president.

> As a security agent, I have every reason to suspect Mr P. of criminal complicity. There is nothing unusual in that – in my time I have seen hundreds of similar situations. Sure, Mr P. happens to be the President of Russia. But the crimes were committed when he was a humble Deputy to the Mayor of St Petersburg. Admittedly, the evidence is indirect and cannot be used in a court. And, of course, if Mr P. were not the President, I would not have publicized it . . . But he is the President, and there is no possibility of questioning him. He is accountable by a different standard. So he must respond to my questions before the public.

When even Litvinenko says that evidence against Putin is 'indirect and cannot be used in court', the allegation has to be treated with extreme caution. After the book was published, Litvinenko's intelligence sources apparently provided him with yet more interesting 'facts', namely that Vladimir Putin was an international drugs dealer.

> I would like to add some information which you won't find in the book, concerning the connections of Russian President Putin with the international Colombian drug cartels . . . It became known to me that Putin, together with members of the Tambov organized crime group, closely collaborated with one of the Colombian drug clans. The drugs produced in Colombia were illegally distributed in European countries, and the money from their sale was laundered through a German company, in which Putin functioned as a consultant until 2000, i.e. until he was elected President of Russia.

Litvinenko's accusations were growing more and more fantastic.

He went on to allege that the FSB was responsible for the murder of Anatoly Sobchak, the St Petersburg mayor Putin had been working with in the early 1990s, and for the death of Galina Starovoitova, a leading figure in Russia's democracy movement. Then came the claims that the FSB had trained al-Qaeda leader Ayman al-Zawahiri, that Carlos the Jackal, Yassir Arafat, Saddam Hussein, Abdullah Ocalan and 'all the bloodiest terrorists in the world' were connected to the KGB and the FSB. 'The terrorism infection seeps out from the offices of the Lubyanka Square and the Kremlin,' he said, 'and it contaminates the whole world.'

In April 2006 a British member of the European Parliament claimed Litvinenko had told him that Romano Prodi, the Italian prime minister, was 'the KGB's man in Italy'. In July 2006 Litvinenko compared Putin to the Russian rapist and serial killer Andrei Chikatilo, and made wild allegations about Putin being a paedophile, 'a fact that was known to many people' including – Litivinenko claimed – the editor of a Russian newspaper who died in an aeroplane crash under suspicious circumstances just a week after trying to publish an article on the subject.

By 2006 the patience of his friends and colleagues was wearing thin. Boris Berezovsky was getting increasingly exasperated with his former protégé, whose flights of fantasy he felt were undermining his own credibility. Vladimir Bukovsky says he and Berezovsky had both tried and failed to curb this loose cannon, who was in danger of making the anti-Kremlin opposition a laughing stock: 'I tried to persuade him not to make those sexual allegations against Putin. I nearly had a quarrel with him. Marina tried. Akhmed tried. I told him he should never do it unless he has clear proof. Otherwise you undermine your credibility with the public. But he was very stubborn, you know. Sometimes, you could persuade him; sometimes you could not.' Vladimir Putin must have been incandescent.

36

BEREZOVSKY ASCENDANT

By the summer of 2006 Boris Berezovsky's patience with Sasha Litvinenko was close to exhausted. Litvinenko was no longer the man who had arrived in London six years earlier. Back then he had been the archetypal FSB graduate – rational, calculating and coldly efficient in everything he did, a man of action used to wielding power and getting results. But six years out of Russia, six years out of the vortex of daily operations, had changed him. Sitting on the sidelines in London had left Litvinenko disoriented and more than a little manic; his friends saw a touch of desperation in him that had not been there before.

For Berezovsky in particular Sasha was no longer the valuable asset he once had been. In 2000 his information – the fabled one hundred kilos of documents – had been current and highly valuable, but with every year that went by Sasha's knowledge and his contacts in Russia had become less and less relevant. In the intelligence game old material, no matter how spectacular, loses its worth very quickly; from being a trump card in the propaganda war with the Kremlin, Litvinenko had become an irrelevance. Whatever his personal feelings about Sasha – and he says he always felt gratitude for the help he gave him in 1994 and 1998 – Berezovsky was a businessman. In March 2006 he told Sasha that he was cutting the monthly allowance he had paid him since he arrived in England. From now on Litvinenko would have to be more enterprising in finding his own sources of income.

For Sasha this was a hard blow. He responded by looking for consultancy work with British companies hoping to operate in Russia – the business which eventually brought him into contact with Lugovoy and Kovtun. But he also flung himself into frenzied efforts to persuade his patron that he was not as dispensable as Berezovsky seemed to believe. Sasha's way of proving his value was to redouble his search for material – any stories, any rumours that could be used as ammunition against Vladimir Putin. This was the period when he came up with his allegations about Romano Prodi, and about Putin and paedophilia. It reflected the desperation he was feeling and it increased the reluctance of his friends and allies to take him seriously.

In his last weeks Sasha seems to have been frustrated and unhappy; he was spending more and more time besieging Berezovsky with new 'intelligence' he had gathered, new schemes he had thought up to discredit the Kremlin. He was pushing his boss to back his allegations, trying to impress him with his enthusiasm, trying to win back his waning approbation. An acquaintance recalls that Sasha would spend hours, sometimes the whole day, sitting in Berezovsky's waiting room. Even when he was told Berezovsky was out and not coming back, he would still wait. Litvinenko was 'terrorizing him', says the acquaintance, 'bombarding him with all sorts of ideas, imaginings, plans and information . . . most of which turned out to be worthless. In the final months Boris became very irritated every time Litvinenko brought him "something interesting". He tried to hide his irritation, but he couldn't always do so.' When Sasha came to Berezovsky with the Scaramella papers on 1 November, Berezovsky told him to get lost. All in all, Litvinenko was becoming an embarrassment.

The cooling relations between the two men have been cited in some quarters as evidence for Moscow's claims that Berezovsky may have been responsible for Litvinenko's murder. The Kremlin's interpretation is simple: Sasha was becoming a nuisance, so Berezovsky spotted a way to get rid of him, with the added bonus of framing Putin and the FSB for the crime. Had Litvinenko's behaviour reached the point where Berezovsky viewed him as more valuable dead than alive?

It seems an outlandish suggestion and Berezovsky strenuously denies it. His enemies in Russia suggest that certain episodes in his past indicate a willingness to be ruthless in getting what he wants. They point to the violent deaths of Sergei Yushenkov and Vladimir Listyev at times when they had fallen foul of Berezovsky, but no proof was ever offered to implicate him in those murders either. Could Boris Berezovsky really have ordered the death of a friend and ally in order to gain a political advantage? The answer may lie in an examination of his past.

*

I first remember Berezovsky from the mid-1990s in Moscow, just as he was making his name as one of the richest and most powerful men in Russia. When I had left Moscow three years earlier he had only recently given up his job as a mathematician research fellow at the Academy of Sciences to go into the used car business. By the time I came back, in 1995, he was a multimillionaire and controlled the distribution network for all Russian-made cars throughout the former Soviet Union.

Organized crime was rife, and as with all big firms his company, Logovaz, paid one of the crime groups to protect it from the others – in Russian this was known as buying your *krysha*, or roof, and everybody did it. Berezovsky's security men happened to be Chechens, among the fiercest in the business. In 1993 a Slavic group known as the Solntsevo Brotherhood tried to muscle in on Berezovsky's territory, but a showdown with the Chechens on the busy Leninsky Prospekt left three of them dead and many others wounded. In 1994 Berezovsky himself narrowly escaped death, first when his apartment door was booby-trapped with a grenade, and then in the 7 June car bombing that killed his driver. So threatened did he feel that he briefly left Russia at one stage for the sanctuary of Israel, where he acquired joint Israeli citizenship.

The Russian police could offer businessmen little protection in those days of Wild West capitalism; like many in the FSB they were deeply involved in criminal rackets themselves and were more likely to be committing crimes than solving them. The United Nations commission on crime recorded 5,700 organized crime groups in Russia, with an estimated three million members. Murder was little more than a business tool. It was often easier to wipe out a rival than compete with him, and few of the contract killings were ever solved. It is a way of thinking that has endured in some quarters to the present day, and in considering possible motives for the killing of Alexander Litvinenko it would clearly be wrong to rule out possible business considerations among the other theories.

Back in 1994 Berezovsky's car distribution network was selling 45,000 vehicles a year, bringing in revenues in the hundreds of millions of dollars. At the same time he was embarking on a massive fund-raising exercise to build a new 'people's car', which he claimed would be Russia's answer to the Volkswagen. He did so by selling bonds to the public and raised fifty million dollars from people who put their meagre wages into the scheme. But Berezovsky never built the car factory and thousands of small investors were left out of pocket. It was the first of many acts that would make him deeply unpopular with large sections of the Russian population.

He was, however, increasingly close to the new clan of Western-leaning, market-oriented politicians gaining power in Russia. One of Berezovsky's many talents is to identify the right people to be friendly with and to keep courting them until they succumb; persistence is definitely his strong suit. In the early 90s he knew the person he really needed to get close to was the president, Boris Yeltsin, and he knew exactly how to do it. Yeltsin's closest confidant at that time was his bodyguard and the head of Kremlin security, General Alexander Korzhakov. Korzhakov was the president's old friend and drinking partner and wherever Yeltsin went, he was sure to be. I find it hard to picture one of them without the other. At all Yeltsin's public appearances, including the day he emerged victorious from the besieged Russian White House following the attempted August coup, Korzhakov was there with him.

So Berezovsky knew the way to the president was to court his bodyguard. First he bought himself membership of the sports club where Korzhakov hung out; Berezovsky is anything but sporty, but that didn't deter him. Then he trailed his prey everywhere he went. Korzhakov has said that he would be taking a shower after a tennis game and suddenly Berezovsky would be in there passing him the soap. Eventually, it worked. Korzhakov introduced Berezovsky to his boss and the relationship blossomed. Within weeks Berezovsky had made himself indispensable by doing a string of favours for Yeltsin and his family, including printing and publishing the president's memoirs in Russia and abroad.

In return, Berezovsky enjoyed favourable treatment from both Yeltsin and Korzhakov in his increasingly complex dealings. When Berezovsky complained of business rivals, Korzhakov is said to have sent people to lean on them. Korzhakov has since claimed that Berezovsky insistently and repeatedly asked him to kill Vladimir Gusinsky, his competitor at that time, although it should be said that in his memoirs Korzhakov's accounts of events are often highly colourful and exaggerated.

In November 1994 Yeltsin agreed to privatize the main state television station and did so in an auction with only one bidder. Berezovsky became the owner of a 49 per cent stake in ORT, a channel with 180 million viewers and the reputation of being the official source of information that all Russians should trust. The trade-off was that Berezovsky would ensure ORT always supported Yeltsin.

Within weeks of becoming the channel's major shareholder, however, Berezovsky was in deep conflict with its general manager, Vlad Listyev. On 20 February 1995 Listyev announced that he would not allow Berezovsky a monopoly of the station's advertising revenues and that he was going to introduce a new system of 'ethical standards' for ORT's advertising money. On 1 March Listyev was shot dead.

Acting on an alleged tip-off, the Moscow police raided Berezovsky's offices in a massive show of strength. Evidently fearing that he would be fingered for ordering the murder, Berezovsky went straight to Korzhakov's office in the Kremlin, where he and another ORT director recorded a video appealing to the president not to believe he was to blame.

They warn the president that 'a theory is being prepared and witnesses are already on hand to the effect that Vlad was killed by Berezovsky'. 'Yesterday,' says Berezovsky on the video recording, 'NTV [a rival channel] aired a programme where essentially, or in thinly veiled fashion, I was identified as the person who arranged and carried out the murder of Vlad Listyev ... According to other sources, there is a mafia thief sitting in jail who has made a declaration that my deputy gave him a contract for Vlad's murder.' Berezovsky and his colleague appeal to Yeltsin for the investigation to be 'handled personally by Korzhakov and the FSB, above all not by the police'. Finally they claim that they know who really killed Listyev: it was not Berezovsky but his rival Vladimir Gusinsky. The appeal seems to have worked because the Moscow prosecutor in charge of the case was fired shortly afterwards. No suspects were arrested for the murder, and no evidence presented against Berezovsky or Gusinsky.

Confirmed as the undisputed arbiter of ORT, Berezovsky moved quickly to expand his empire. A controlling interest in the cash flow of the national airline Aeroflot brought a lucrative new revenue stream and he installed his old partner Nikolai Glushkov as the company's general director. Together with a young tycoon named Roman Abramovich he bought the oil giant Sibneft, which would eventually earn them both billions. But Berezovsky coveted power and influence just as much as wealth. He was now pursuing media interests with a passion, soon adding Channel Six TV, the magazine *Ogonyok* and the newspaper *Nezavisimaya Gazeta* (literally, the *Independent*) to his stable.

It was his media clout which gave Berezovsky the trump card in 1996, when he and his fellow oligarchs united to provide a monopoly of media support and an estimated two billion dollars of financial backing for Boris Yeltsin's successful re-election campaign. In return the businessmen were offered sweetheart deals to purchase much of Russia's national wealth, in the form of fabulously valuable state industries 'privatized' to them for a song. Berezovsky talks with pride of the deal he did with Yeltsin, and of the benefits it brought him: 'It is no secret that Russian businessmen played the decisive role in President Yeltsin's victory. It was a battle for our blood interests.'

The months following the 1996 elections were the apogee of Berezovsky's business and political career. This is the period in which he was appointed deputy secretary of the National Security Council and became the key figure in Moscow's negotiations with Chechnya. There is no conclusive evidence, but cynics have attributed his influence over the separatist rebels to the long-standing Chechen 'gangster' connections he made during his time in the car distribution business; and critics say he was in cahoots with the rebels and made money from their cause, including the kidnapping and ransoming of hostages. FSB Director Nikolai Patrushev claimed to have evidence that Berezovsky had extensive economic dealings in Chechnya, including financing the separatists' military operations. But it is undeniable that his influence helped build a fragile peace that lasted from 1996 until the Second Chechen War of 1999.

For Berezovsky, though, triumph was only a small step away from disaster. At the height of his powers, with his struggle for wealth and recognition finally paying off, the controversies over his alleged criminal past seemingly behind him and with his name now recognized throughout Russia, Berezovsky's fatal miscalculation was to underestimate one man: Vladimir Putin.

37

PUTIN, THE MAN FROM NOWHERE

When Boris Yeltsin appointed the little-known former FSB man prime minister in August 1999 few people expected him to last long. He was the archetypal unknown technocrat; his poll ratings were infinitesimal. But it was precisely this nonentity status that made him so attractive to Berezovsky. Boris Yeltsin claims he first identified Putin as his successor in late 1998. Berezovsky's star was still high at that time and it is beyond doubt that he would have played a role in shaping Yeltsin's decision. We have already seen that Berezovsky regarded Putin as an ally and that he was largely instrumental in getting him appointed director of the FSB. But when he pushed Yeltsin to choose Putin as the next president, Berezovsky was a turkey unwittingly voting for Christmas. At the time Berezovsky felt sure of his own power and ability to influence events. It was only a couple of years since he had, in his own words, 'played the decisive role' in getting Yeltsin elected and he was pretty sure he could do the same for the next president. So a candidate without his own power base, a nonentity, would be perfect for his purposes; if he got Putin elected in the same way he had Yeltsin, the new man would be saddled with a debt of gratitude to him that he would work long and hard to repay.

Even before becoming prime minister Putin had seemed to give Berezovsky the right sort of respect, and Berezovsky took this as a sign that the new man was assenting to his protégé status. In a key episode, during the period when Yevgeny Primakov was prime minister, Berezovsky reports that he was impressed by Putin's behaviour. Primakov's campaign to indict him on criminal charges was causing Berezovsky difficulties, but Putin nonetheless took the daring step of attending a birthday party for Berezovsky's wife, making him one of only a few high-ranking officials to show up. He even brought flowers. When Berezovsky said to him, 'Volodya, don't you think you might get in trouble for this?' Putin replied, 'But I'm your friend.' This, Berezovsky declared in a later interview, demonstrated to him that Putin put loyalty and respect before public opinion.

In fact, Putin's knack of being in the right place at the right time had served him well for most of his career. A graduate of the law school of Leningrad University, he had joined the KGB in 1975 and been assigned to overseas spying duties. Unlike Litvinenko, whose KGB career always involved the physical implementation of decisions made by others, Putin was part of the organization's intelligence-gathering elite. In 1984 he was posted to East Germany and spent six years working closely with the GDR's feared secret police, the Stasi. The fall of the Berlin Wall saw the young lieutenant colonel called back to his native city and a fallow period in his career. Moved into the KGB reserve, he found a post as a foreign affairs adviser at Leningrad University. It did not pay well and Putin struggled to feed his wife and two daughters. But fortune smiled again when Anatoly Sobchak, his old law-school professor, was elected mayor of Leningrad. Sobchak was a leading light in Russia's pro-democracy movement; I remember him as a tall, inspiring, intellectual figure, committed to reform and eloquent in his support for human rights. He evidently saw similar qualities in his old pupil because he offered him a post on the city's Foreign Relations Committee with responsibility for attracting Western trade and investment.

By 1994, with Leningrad now renamed St Petersburg, Putin became Sobchak's first deputy, but disastrous elections in 1996 saw the mayor voted out of office and his colleague decided to go with him. Once again, however, he turned a setback into a step forward. Another old friend, Anatoly Chubais, was now Boris Yeltsin's chief of staff and he invited Putin to join him in the Kremlin. He was appointed first deputy manager of the Russian state's overseas property portfolio, including embassies and trade missions. It was a job with endless opportunities for personal enrichment and several of his colleagues seem to have taken advantage of them. By all accounts Putin did not, a fact which casts even more doubt on the accusations of corruption that Alexander Litvinenko was later to level against him. In March 1997 Putin's silent rise through the apparatus of power saw him appointed first deputy chief of staff to the president, where he made a name for himself as an unbending enforcer of the Kremlin's authority over the country's regional governments and a stickler for rules and regulations. A year later Boris Berezovsky had adopted the dour young technocrat as his protégé and manoeuvred him into the top job at the FSB.

At first Putin seemed to be keeping his side of the unwritten bargain with his mentor. Berezovsky was being dogged by criminal cases against him which Prosecutor General Yuri Skuratov appeared determined to pursue. Government subsidies to Berezovsky's ORT channel had been investigated and bankruptcy proceedings were opened against the station. Aeroflot had been audited and irregularities discovered that led to the freezing of Berezovsky's bank accounts and those of his partner Nikolai Glushkov. Despite several heavy hints from Berezovsky and his patron Boris Yeltsin, Skuratov was clearly not getting the message that he should lay off. So, in February 1999, Putin ordered the FSB to investigate Skuratov himself. A few weeks later a videotape of a naked man enjoying the favours of two attractive call girls was sent to the country's media outlets and immediately shown on national television. The man was identified as the prosecutor general; Skuratov's credibility was destroyed and his resignation followed. Putin had done Berezovsky a favour and paid off at least part of his debt; it was widely assumed he would carry on doing so.

38

BEREZOVSKY CAST ASIDE

In August 1999 it was Berezovsky who persuaded Boris Yeltsin to appoint Vladimir Putin prime minister, an appointment that carried with it the president's imprimatur as heir apparent. In December's parliamentary elections he rallied his media outlets and financial resources behind Putin's Yedinstvo (Unity) party and promised to give him the same support in the presidential elections of 2000. Some newspapers, largely of the more scandalous type, speculated that Berezovsky may even have had a hand in the September 1999 apartment bombings which helped his protégé into power, although no evidence was ever produced to support this.

Berezovsky told me a story to illustrate how much Putin seemed to value his help, and how close he seemed to be to his mentor at that time.

> I don't hide that I helped him and supported him. As far as making him prime minister, I participated in that; for the parliamentary elections of 1999 I created all the ideology of his new party, Yedinstvo. The whole idea was created by me; the ideology was created by me and we won the parliamentary elections in December 1999. [After the election] I was on my way to my country house and he called me on the mobile phone. It was already late and he asked, 'Where are you?' I said, 'I am on the way to my country place,' and he said, 'I would ask you very much to turn back and come to the White House.' And I came back and he was alone and he said, 'Boris, I just want to tell you: I can never overstate what you have done for me – your ideas and your energy and how you created this party. And I just want to tell you: I don't have a brother; you don't have a brother. Now you are my brother forever.' And I felt he was saying that sincerely

and for sure I was happy, because I really believed he would continue the path of democracy; he had told me that many times.

Putin may have been sincere in his gratitude, but behind the apparent affection we have already seen that Putin was finding Berezovsky's yoke increasingly irksome. The November 1998 press conference had left him exasperated and secretly plotting his revenge; his agreement to stitch up Skuratov had gone against his notions of propriety and he felt he was increasingly being drawn into a pact with a ruthless, unpopular figure. It was not just Berezovsky's failed automobile bond scheme that had aroused public resentment; he was widely disliked for the flaunting of his ill-gotten wealth, his rumoured connections with Chechen 'bandits' and – very importantly in a deeply anti-Semitic society – the simple fact that he was Jewish.

For the moment, however, Putin needed Berezovsky's help. Presidential elections were looming in March 2000, and as long as Berezovsky's ORT TV backed his candidacy – and shamelessly slandered his main opponent, Yuri Luzhkov – Putin was content to string Berezovsky along. But all the time he was secretly gathering evidence of his patron's misdeeds with the firm intention of using it against him once he was elected president. Berezovsky seems to have sensed this, because he decided to run for a seat in parliament and the legal immunity from prosecution it confers. Elections to the Duma were a novelty at that time and it did not take too much effort for a rich man to schmooze his way into a seat. Berezovsky was duly elected as deputy for Karachaevo-Cherkessk, a distant region of the north Caucasus, and once in the Duma, he set up his own political party, Liberal Russia. Meanwhile, Roman Abramovich became the new member for Chukotka, a frozen waste in Siberia. Both men probably breathed a sigh of relief.

Then in the presidential elections Berezovsky kept his word and helped to get Vladimir Putin elected, evidently hoping to continue the same symbiotic relationship he had had with Boris Yeltsin. But the new president did not seem impressed. Like Prince Hal in Shakespeare's *Henry V*, Putin seemed bent on throwing off his old cronies to take on the mantle of his destiny. To Putin, Berezovsky had been like Falstaff, a pleasant and useful companion in the past, but not fit to be seen with a king.

On 8 July 2000, three months after his elevation to the presidency, Putin declared war. In a nationally televised address he announced that Russia would 'no longer tolerate shady groups that divert money abroad, that establish their own dubious security services and block the development of a liberal market economy'. Whatever the truth, it was quite clear to everyone that he was setting his sights on one group. For Boris Berezovsky – and for the other oligarchs like Mikhail Khodorkovsky, Vladimir Gusinsky, Mikhail Fridman, Vladimir Potanin and Roman Abramovich – the writing was on the wall: they needed to make a choice between what Putin would view as going straight, getting out or going under. For Berezovsky, who had supported Putin all the way to the presidency and expected his gratitude, it was a cruel blow. At the beginning of August he went to see his former protégé for what would turn out to be the last time. As he told me about the clash of titans that took place that day, it was clear that every detail remains fresh in Berezovsky's mind.

> I remember well my last meeting with Vladimir Putin. It was in August 2000, after the tragedy of the *Kursk* submarine ... ORT Television was very critical of him and so on. And I went to see the head of administration, Voloshin, who was my friend and ... he said I was playing against Putin and if I did not return my shares in ORT I would follow Gusinsky to jail. I was very surprised and I don't even understand how I controlled myself. There was an ashtray and I was tempted to put that ashtray on his head. So I said, 'OK I don't want to talk to you any more; I just want to speak to Vladimir.' Next day I came and Putin said the same thing – ORT is very corrupt ... Putin said ORT is very corrupt. I said it is strange you didn't know that before, when ORT supported you

– and only now is it become corrupt . . . And we both spoke in a very arrogant way – both me and Putin. Putin said, 'You should return your shares under my personal control . . . I will manage ORT on my own.' I said, 'I will never return you my shares!' And after that he started to call me Boris Abramovich – before he used to call me Boris – and I continued to call him Vladimir. And a bit later he said, 'OK, goodbye,' and he stood up and started to move away and I said, 'Goodbye forever!' And that's it: it was the last meeting I ever had with him.

The next day Berezovsky sent Putin a note saying that he was taking Russia in the wrong direction and adding, 'If any time you need my real help in solving Russia's problems you may call me.' But the rift between Russia's two most powerful men was final. Putin never rang Berezovsky, and Berezovsky embarked on his years of bitter opposition. In retrospect, he told me, it was the moment that everything changed.

The most terrible thing during that meeting was that he accused me of deliberately trying to destroy him, that I was using false information against him . . . After that meeting, I realized he was really – it was new for me – that he is really . . . not a good man. This story helped me see he was a wrong sort of person . . . on the personal level. Before it was a political battle, but now for the first time I recognized he was also not my friend. There was something wrong about him as a man. And it was soon confirmed because after a few weeks they reopened the Aeroflot case against me and it was definitely done on the orders of Putin. And several months later they took my house off me, where I lived with my family. It's all the result of that meeting in August 2000. It was all the result of that.

Shortly afterwards, criminal cases were revived against Berezovsky declaring him the main suspect in the embezzlement of funds from Aeroflot and in large-scale fraud at his Logovaz car company. In the coming months his stake in ORT was sold, and his Channel

Six TV was closed by a ruling of the Russian Arbitration Court. The man who did more than any other to bring Putin to power responded to the president's declaration of war by accusing him of establishing 'an authoritarian regime'. Having pulled the strings of the Russian state for so many years, Berezovsky was furious that he was now being manipulated himself. 'This campaign against the oligarchs is well orchestrated,' he said at the time. 'It is aimed at destroying independent big business in Russia. I don't want to be a puppet. I won't go every day to a show which someone has been directing, especially when I don't like the director. If the president decides it is in his interests to lock me up, he will lock me up. If he decides it is not in his interests, he won't.'

In fact, the president did not get the chance to lock him up. When a criminal case was brought against Berezovsky for defrauding a regional administration out of thirteen million dollars by the illegal sale of cars from the giant AvtoVaz car maker, he fled to the West, living first in Paris and then moving permanently to London in late 2000. When he looks back now, it is clear he finds it hard to hide his resentment at the way Putin turned against him.

> I met him for the first time at the very beginning of the 90s. He was very helpful. He became a friend, and at that time I started doing business in Switzerland, and he travelled with me to ski and so on. We were not very close friends, but we were friends. Putin went into the presidential election promising to continue the policies of President Yeltsin. He declared democracy necessary, freedom of the mass media, freedom of political life and the market economy. But when he became president, in a very short time he completely changed his mind. I was completely against all that and not without arguments. I had a lot of arguments why it was a mistake . . . Three months later they put my friend Nikolai Glushkov in jail. I recognized there was no way for me to stay any more, and I left Russia.

Even at that late stage Berezovsky says he believed he had a deal with Putin, namely that his relinquishment of ORT would be reciprocated with the release of Glushkov from jail. Glushkov, the man Berezovsky had installed to run Aeroflot, was not released, and this clearly rankles. Berezovsky says it is evidence of Putin's ultimate treachery. (So deeply did this bother Berezovsky that he eventually employed an undercover agent to try to engineer Glushkov's escape. In a twist that will have intriguing ramifications for our investigation of the Litvinenko case, that agent was none other than Andrei Lugovoy.) In exile in London since the end of 2000, Berezovsky's anger has festered and grown. He feels the loss of his business empire in Russia, but even harder to bear is the disappearance of his power and prestige. When I ask him if he regrets having supported Putin, having made him president only to be cast aside, there is a momentary glimpse of the sense of betrayal which fuels his quest for revenge.

> Well, no one likes to admit they made a mistake, OK? I definitely made a mistake in my understanding of his character, of his vision of Russia. But I can tell you – I knew him ten years before he was elected president. I definitely had very positive experiences with him together, and he was very brave at several very complicated episodes of my life and so . . . I really thought all the time that he was a good person and that his understanding of the future of Russia was correct. I knew there were better candidates than him, but they had no chance of being elected. I do not support losers.

When I ask Berezovsky if he can forgive Putin, he invokes the tenets of the new religion he has embraced since arriving in the West.

> You know that for a Christian to forgive is much better than to seek revenge. It is clear. And it is clear Putin is a weak person . . . I am a Christian and I forgive everything . . . even Putin, but to forgive does not mean losing your true direction and I never want to lose my direction . . . In 2000 I knew what Putin was like, but the West kept thinking he was moving Russia to democracy and he was just fighting against 'robber barons' like me – as Mr Soros

described us – and it was hard for me to explain: I don't fight Putin; I fight the regime he created. Many people say, 'Oh, there is Putin and he fired Berezovsky because Berezovsky just went stealing property off Russia and Putin is just fighting the rich oligarchs.' But it is wrong. I was the closest of anyone to Putin at that time, and when he started to go bad I had a very complicated choice. I had the chance to stay with Putin and to be number one, there is no doubt, but I knew that at the end ... There is a big difference between me and my former friend Roman Abramovich: we were friends and partners, and he had the choice just like me and we made two completely different choices – two different paths. He made his choice and I don't have the power to change him, but inside I feel he is wrong. And I told him, 'Roman, if I stay with Putin, finally he will lose and everyone would realize what he was and would see his true face ... deep inside he is just *Homo sovieticus*. He will lose and I will lose and I will be killed and he will be killed ... I will be the first and he will be the second. But if I leave him now, I know it will be a big battle. I know he will use his power against me, but I have a chance of surviving ... I will continue on my own path of understanding life. I will not be a loser in my own eyes.' It was a hard choice.

Berezovsky's 'hard choice' left him exiled in London and plotting to regain power in Russia. In 2005 he told the BBC, 'If I am presented with any political project that could realistically bring down Putin, then I will support it. The day Putin goes, I am back in Russia ... My strategy of attacking is the same: to change the Putin regime, which is very dangerous for Russia and for the world. And I think we have done a lot towards that because Putin's image is damaged now, damaged a lot ... And I participate personally in doing that and I am happy about that.'

It is the loss of power that haunts Berezovsky. His response has been to thunder and rail from his London exile, his jibes and threats growing ever more intense as the months go by. With the muzzling of the press and the limitations on political activity in Russia, he and his London-based allies have become the centre of the real opposition to the Kremlin. At first Putin tried to make light of Berezovsky's hostility; when he was asked about him at a news conference in July 2001, he replied, 'Boris Berezovsky – who's he?' But Putin knows Berezovsky is a real and credible threat that is not going to go away: he is a billionaire with the resources, the connections and the motives to make life difficult for him. He is not someone the Kremlin can safely ignore.

In the years after 2000 Moscow issued a series of arrest warrants for Boris Berezovsky on fraud and embezzlement charges. An outstanding Interpol arrest warrant meant the only country he could travel to outside the UK was Israel, where he was protected by his dual nationality. His application for political asylum in Britain dragged through the courts – Litvinenko's had been granted much earlier – and in March 2003 a renewed Russian demand for his extradition resulted in him being briefly arrested and released on bail. The following September, when Berezovsky attended a hearing at Bow Street Magistrates Court to contest the extradition, Judge Timothy Workman declared he was rejecting the Russian demands as the British government had decided to grant Berezovsky political asylum – there was a legitimate fear that returning to Russia could expose him to persecution. For Berezovsky the news that he was now beyond the legal reach of the Kremlin was a victory. For President Putin it was an intensely infuriating setback. The Russian Prosecutor General's Office announced immediately that it would challenge the decision. On 13 November Judge Workman rejected another Russian government extradition request, this time for Akhmed Zakayev, the Chechen leader and Berezovsky's exiled colleague, because of a 'substantial risk' of torture or death. An exasperated Kremlin publicly accused Workman of playing 'cold war politics'.

Two months later, in the quiet Hertfordshire village of Furneux Pelham to the north of London, eighty-three-year-old Robert Workman was killed in an apparently motiveless murder when he opened his front door to what police described as a professional hit man.

Robert Workman was a retired colonel in the British army with no connection whatsoever to the world of hit men and assassinations, except that he shared a surname with the judge who granted Moscow's exiled enemies protection from the FSB.

39

A COUP FROM LONDON?

Boris Berezovsky is a charming man and easy to like. He can be witty, amusing and very good company. But he has a past. And in that past there are things he would rather forget. He and Alex Goldfarb once asked me if I would like to make a movie of Berezovsky's life. 'It will be like Al Pacino in *Godfather II*,' Goldfarb said. 'Only you will make it back to front . . . Pacino starts out as the incorruptible young man determined to stay straight; then he gets drawn into the shady dealings of Marlon Brando and the Cosa Nostra. But you will show Berezovsky going in the opposite direction. Maybe in his young days he was a little bit shady, but now you will show he has become honest and incorruptible.' Looking back, I think they were joking.

After five years in England Boris Berezovsky was living a life of great material comfort. He had settled his family into an attractive Georgian country house with beautiful rolling grounds in the upmarket town of Egham in Surrey, fifteen miles west of London. Every day he was whisked to and from his office near Piccadilly in central London in a black chauffeur-driven limousine; his children were at the best schools and he and Yelena could afford to enjoy the finest things in life without stinting. It was not bad for a former mathematician from a poor Jewish family in Moscow.

Berezovsky's sixtieth-birthday party on 23 January 2006 was a sight to behold. In the splendour of a great English country estate marquees were pitched on every lawn; tuxedoed waiters carried gleaming trays of food; champagne and vodka flowed and an orchestra played late into the night. Boris and Yelena had invited hundreds of guests from England, Russia, Israel and beyond. The night was a triumph. Alexander Litvinenko was there, so was Yuri

Felshtinsky, and so was a man who continues to crop up in this account, Andrei Lugovoy. Felshtinsky sat next to him that night and says Lugovoy appeared relaxed and charming.

For Berezovsky it was a pleasure to treat his friends so generously, but he has never struck me as a man who can switch off and savour life. He is knowledgeable about fine wines and seems at ease swirling a vintage Bordeaux in his glass. For the rest of the time he is on the move, constantly thinking, pacing, rattling out ideas in his quick-fire Moscow Russian, a taut bundle of electricity looking for a lightning rod. Since I met him in London in 2003 Berezovsky has struck me as unhappy. His public persona is the same, self-confidently polite, considerate, seemingly lit by an unfailing bonhomie, but now there is the darkness of exile in his life, the long shadow of Moscow that keeps him from the sunlight. It is tempting to describe Berezovsky in his London splendour as a bird in a gilded cage, but that is not quite right. I never felt he lived for luxury or wealth. He enjoys it, that is for sure. And he clearly enjoyed making it. Alexander Lebed, the fierce Russian general turned political power broker, said of him in his robber baron period of the mid-90s, 'Berezovsky is not satisfied with stealing – he wants everybody to see him stealing, and stealing with impunity.' Berezovsky would dispute it was stealing, but it was as if the acquisition of fabulous wealth was a game for him, or rather a challenge. He was challenging a Russia where power belongs to the elite and where the elite is not Jewish, where you can succeed if you are born in the right circles, if you are a party member, if you have the right connections. His life's purpose was to succeed without any of that, and he did so. In his heyday he delighted in flaunting his success and thumbing his nose at the establishment. But it did not last long.

When Berezovsky finally got to the pinnacle of power, the pinnacle of influence, of standing, prestige and *acceptance*, one man took it all away from him. The cage Berezovsky has occupied in his London exile since 2000 is the cage of a troubled mind which will never be happy till it has righted the wrongs Vladimir Putin has done it.

On the morning after his sixtieth-birthday celebrations Boris Berezovsky was in a buoyant mood. There had been a good deal of fighting talk the previous evening and the leaders of the anti-Putin opposition were all in good heart. Berezovsky has maintained friendly relations with one Moscow radio station since he left Russia and that morning he picked up the phone to dial the number of Radio Ekho Moskvy (the Moscow Echo). In a wide-ranging interview he spoke at length about his political views and his plans for the future. But at one point the euphoria of the occasion seems to have got the better of him and he uttered the following words: 'President Putin violates the constitution and any violent action on the opposition's part is justified today ... That includes taking power by force, which is exactly what I am working on.' Berezovsky said he was deliberately making his plans public and had been working on them for eighteen months. 'The regime has lost its legitimacy. Neither Putin nor the parliament are legitimate. They are anti-constitutional, because they have made a number of anti-constitutional decisions ... This is absolutely against the spirit and the language of the constitution.'

And since there was no chance of a fair election, Berezovsky added, the only way to get the regime out was a coup: 'There is only one way out – a coup, a forced seizure of power ... Every day I talk to lots of people who are certain the existing regime should be changed, and see there is no chance of this happening legally, by an election. This regime is leading Russia into an abyss. Besides, it is deprived of ideology. The regime is doomed, and I want to see it collapse before Russia collapses.'

Berezovsky said he was planning to fund the coup with his own money, 'earned by honest labour'. He was doing so because 'it is vital that the Russian people realize just talking is not enough, that it is time for action.'

Asked whether he felt his remarks might endanger his own

security, Berezovsky gave the same confident response that Alexander Litvinenko always gave: 'My security is guaranteed by the state I live in. The UK takes care of all its residents, including the immigrants.'

It seems Vladimir Putin was tuned in to Radio Ekho Moskvy that morning because a few days later a letter arrived at the British interior ministry, the Home Office. It was from the Russian Prosecutor General's Office and was a renewed extradition request for the 'self-styled political émigré' Boris Berezovsky. This time the charges were not trifling accusations of fraud and embezzlement; the warrant accused him of attempting a coup against the legitimate government of Russia and plotting acts aimed at the armed seizure of power. Berezovsky had gone too far and the British foreign secretary, Jack Straw, was not amused. 'I am aware of the comments made by Mr Boris Berezovsky in an interview on January 24,' Straw fulminated. 'Advocating the violent overthrow of a sovereign state is unacceptable, and I condemn these comments unreservedly.' Somewhat ominously, he reminded Mr Berezovsky that the British government could review his status as a political refugee at any time. A hasty message was dispatched from Berezovsky headquarters to the Home Office claiming that the remarks in the interview had been misconstrued and it was not clear if the extradition request contained any further evidence. Lawyers' opinions were that Berezovsky's statements were political in nature, and if there were no evidence other than these remarks the extradition request would likely fail as being politically motivated. But the oligarch had been put on a final warning. Even the outspoken Sasha Litvinenko was horrified by Berezovsky's rhetoric, commenting to a British academic, 'I warned him that he cannot talk about changing the political regime in Russia by force but he ignores me. They will get him. He is not careful enough.'

40

THE LONG ARM OF MOSCOW

In the end, of course, the person they got was not Boris Berezovsky but Litvinenko himself. It seems moreover that the poison which killed Sasha in 2006 was not the first time an attempt had been made on his life. In the six years since he arrived in London in November 2000 Sasha Litvinenko had ratcheted up his rhetoric against Moscow, and Moscow had responded with increasingly serious threats against him.

In the early days the noises from the Kremlin were little more than rumblings. Andrei Ponkin, for instance, one of the FSB men who took part in the 1998 press conference, was used to blacken his former comrade's name in the Russian media, alleging among other things that Berezovsky had hired Litvinenko to do his political dirty work and had paid him one and a half million dollars for doing it. The two other stool pigeons, Gusak and Shebalin, were also back in harness at the FSB and they too were working on revenge.

In 2002 Litvinenko received a telephone call from his friend Mikhail Trepashkin in Moscow. After Litvinenko had beaten him up and forced him out of the FSB, Trepashkin had become a prominent liberal lawyer, taking on cases that others were too scared to contemplate, including the suit brought by the victims of the 1999 apartment bombs. Unlike Litvinenko and his URPO bully-boy cronies, Trepashkin is a contemplative, quietly spoken man, an intellectual well versed in the complexities of Russian law and with enough courage to use that knowledge to embarrass the Kremlin. After 2000 Trepashkin had served as Sasha's eyes and ears in Russia, passing on to him information about developments in political circles and in the security forces. The information he was ringing him about now he considered of vital importance: Trepashkin had heard that Shebalin and some other FSB men were planning to assassinate the 'traitor' Litvinenko. Sasha's friend Vladimir Bukovsky was aware of the plot as it unfolded, the panic it caused and the efforts to thwart it.

> The intention to murder Sasha is not a new one. The first attempt against him was made in 2002. It was thwarted because Sasha was tipped off from Moscow by Trepashkin that a certain colleague of theirs had been given the task of carrying out his murder. So Sasha knew it in advance. There were two guys, former KGB officers, who arrived in London. Sasha tipped off the police and the police sent them back. The guy's name who came here was Shebalin, one of the guys at Sasha's 1998 press conference. So again they used someone who was known and trusted and had access to the intended victim. That's the usual technique of KGB assassination.

Trepashkin confirmed Bukovsky's account in letters smuggled out of the prison where he has been held since he was arrested in 2003.

> I warned Alexander Litvinenko about the creation back in 2002 of a group for his destruction . . . In August 2002 I reported about a meeting I had near the Kitay-Gorod metro station [in Moscow] with former URPO officer Mr V.V. Shebalin, at his request. At that meeting he declared that he was once again working for the FSB and that 'a very serious group' had been created to 'fuck everybody connected with Berezovsky and Litvinenko'. He told me that if I agreed to drop my interest in the 1999 apartment bombings and started cooperating with the group, I would be 'left in peace' . . . I replied that I can't stomach violence, especially murder.

Trepashkin says Shebalin threatened him with violence or arrest if he did not help in the plot to kill Litvinenko by providing intelligence about the exiled agent and his family.

He asked me to check out Litvinenko: find out where he works, his pattern of movements, his regular meeting places. He asked me to get details of the book he was writing. It was obvious to me that they wanted to send one person in advance to check out his whereabouts, and then the group would follow. Getting access to radioactive material would have been no problem for FSB officers.

Trepashkin's contemptuous refusal may well have paved the way for his own arrest the following year.

I told Shebalin, 'Forget about Litvinenko! He's in London. And enough with all these dirty settlings of personal accounts!' That spineless coward Shebalin ... had thrown himself at the feet of the sleazy FSB bosses and offered to work as an agent provocateur and false witness against Litvinenko and his circle. They took the bastard! He saved his skin. And he got into the group that was scheming to destroy both Litvinenko and his supporters.

Yuri Felshtinsky, Litvinenko's friend and co-author, told me he too was warned he was in danger in 2002, although he says he does not think practical measures for assassinations had yet been taken. 'There was talk that a group of people were preparing to organize Litvinenko's assassination. Since they talk to each other, those FSB officers, the idea to kill Litvinenko would be discussed many, many times starting from November 1999 because that's how those people think. That's how they think: OK, Litvinenko went public with that press conference – we should kill him. It's very simple.'

It is the chilling logic of a security organization where mortal hatred of traitors has long been a watchword. In the days of the Soviet Union it was an unwritten rule of the Cheka, the NKVD and the KGB that it was the automatic duty of any serving agent who encountered a defector from the security services, whether in Russia or abroad, to kill him. Felshtinsky believes the same thinking may have been behind the prolonged scheming and plotting to eliminate Alexander Litvinenko, but he says it is unlikely Shebalin himself would have been nominated as the assassin.

Serious people – whom Shebalin considered to be serious – were saying, 'We must kill your Litvinenko, *your* Litvinenko, because you went together to that press conference.' Shebalin considered this to be a credible threat. I don't think Shebalin himself was preparing to kill Litvinenko. For two reasons: first of all Shebalin never worked abroad – he was always an internal Russia person. To kill someone in Russia, OK, he would organize it, but to kill Litvinenko in London, that is not his territory. And second, if he was planning to kill Litvinenko personally, he would keep it quiet. At the same time I have to say that I received an email from Trepashkin myself. It said a team was being sent to Boston to assassinate me, and Trepashkin said this was a credible threat. I heard from Sasha saying he had received two emails from Trepashkin: one was about Shebalin trying to organize his assassination and the other was about a group which was being sent to Boston to assassinate me. I had doubts about the seriousness of these threats, though. They didn't trust Trepashkin, so maybe the information they were feeding him was not completely reliable.

I asked Felshtinsky whether an FSB assassination would need the explicit sanction of the very top echelons in the organization and he said it would not. 'The discussions were at the level of colonel – Shebalin and Co. – rather than at the level of the generals ... although maybe it was being discussed at the generals' level too.'

The supposition that FSB killings may be sanctioned at the level of colonel is an important one. Andrei Nekrasov says Litvinenko was keenly aware of it – aware that an assassination can happen without an explicit order from the top. As in the case of Anna Politkovskaya, it could be as simple as 'someone wanting to do something nice for the boss'. 'Sasha said to me, "You couldn't imagine the lifestyle, the atmosphere, the code of those people. There is a code of honour; it's about cliques and friendships and allegiances ... 'He's my friend; I'll do anything for my friend.' It's not even 'for my country'; my country's just a pretext. The subtext is the allegiance between members of the organization itself. It's either money or this loyalty to a group."'

41

CLARKE OF THE YARD

Deputy Assistant Commissioner Peter Clarke of Scotland Yard's Anti-Terrorist Command had read the files. He had seen all the speculation in the British media and spoken to many of the people who have informed the account of events laid out in the preceding chapters of this book. When I spoke to his informants, they told me his questioning – or that of the detectives he had sent on his behalf – had been thorough, detailed and extremely knowledgeable. One of his interviewees, the senior KGB officer Oleg Gordievsky, who defected to Britain in 1985, told me that he sensed Clarke and his officers may have become emotionally involved in the case and were deeply committed to solving it, that they felt an almost personal sense of responsibility and regret for not having been able to protect Sasha from his enemies.

> The police know very well what happened. They spoke to Sasha every day before he died. So there is nothing unexplored. They spoke for several hours to Marina, his wife. And they talked to all the people that Sasha spoke to when he was dying. They spoke to me twice. The police are working very well. They know everything. I can tell you, just between us, that people from the Metropolitan Police came down to me five days after he died to apologize that they could not have protected him.

Those who know Peter Clarke speak of him as a meticulous, thorough and dedicated officer 'married to his job'. An intelligent man with years of experience of policing in London, Clarke rose rapidly through the ranks of the Metropolitan Police but, in the words of one former colleague, he never lost the feel for hands-on police work and has remained very much a 'copper's copper'. A long spell in charge of Scotland Yard's Royalty Protection Group gave him responsibility for the security of the Queen and the royal family, as well as the thousands of foreign diplomats working in the British capital. He dealt with sensitive international cases on many occasions, including alleged terror plots with Israeli and Middle Eastern connections. In June 2002 he was appointed head of the Met's anti-terrorist branch in the wake of the 9/11 attacks in New York. Given the task of preparing Britain for the perceived threat of increased bombings and suicide operations, he initiated new counter-terrorism strategies implemented by police forces across the country. After a successful operation to identify and capture those responsible for two waves of bombs on London Underground trains in 2005 Clarke was awarded the MBE, a decoration conferred by the Queen on those who have performed an outstanding public service.

At the time of Sasha Litvinenko's poisoning Clarke's unit was already carrying out more counter-terrorism investigations than ever before. With police capacity challenged by the rise of Middle East terrorism, the last thing Clarke needed to hear was that his men would now have to deal with Russian-related plots as well. However, after negotiations with the Metropolitan Police commissioner, Sir Ian Blair, Clarke secured a promise that he could have – within reason – the extra resources he needed; it was a high-profile case with international implications and Scotland Yard's efforts would be very much in the public eye.

Clarke's first move was to call together the detectives and researchers who would be working on the investigation and lay down some strict ground rules. There would need to be great sensitivity in the police work, he said, especially if evidence were to be uncovered supporting the widespread speculations about Kremlin involvement in the murder – the prime minister himself had already made clear that Britain's relations with Moscow were at stake. With a nod in the direction of the press officers in the room Clarke said there would be tight control over information about the case. He was happy to make periodic statements through the Met's website or in person if necessary, but he was counting on all present to make sure there were no unauthorized leaks about the course of the investigation.

Then he set about creating individual teams of detectives with specific responsibilities: one to research the recent history of Litvinenko's life in London, to question friends and acquaintances; another to look into his past in Russia and liaise with Moscow about the possibility of information exchange; and a third, priority team, to collate information from the beat police officers and forensic specialists who were trying to establish who went where and did what on the days around the presumed date of the presumed poisoning.

The first hours of Clarke's investigation were inevitably chaotic. For the weeks while Litvinenko had been lying sick in his hospital bed the case had been in the hands of local police and a detective superintendent from the Met's Specialist Crimes Directorate. The new team needed to assimilate everything they had accumulated, including the interviews recorded with the victim, his wife and friends. In addition there were new witness statements to be taken, new locations to be swept by the forensic teams and hours of CCTV footage to be examined. London is the most monitored city in the world, with cameras constantly surveying most public locations, and Clarke's men knew they would be helped by what these revealed. Meanwhile, British officials were being sent to talk to the Russian ambassador in London, Yuri Fedotov, and the inquiry team needed to provide a representative for that meeting too. To add to his troubles, the press office was pushing for a statement to feed the ravenous hunger of the media; Clarke asked for it to be as bland as possible and signed off the following:

> We continue to carry out a thorough investigation into the circumstances surrounding Mr Litvinenko's death. Detectives are carrying out an intensive investigation. We will trace possible witnesses, examine Mr Litvinenko's movements at relevant times, including when he first became ill and identify people he may

have met. There will also be an extensive examination of CCTV footage. As part of the investigation police are liaising closely with experts to search for any residual radioactive material at a number of locations where Mr Litvinenko may have visited. No arrests have been made in connection with the inquiry.

The following day, one of the detectives uncovered the allegation of the 2002 assassination plot against Litvinenko by his former FSB colleagues. To his astonishment, further research revealed that another attempt to kill him had apparently been made in 2003. Shortly before Litvinenko was due to appear at a British parliamentary hearing into state-sponsored terrorism, Molotov cocktails were allegedly thrown at the front door of his house. He had reported the incident to the local police station, but no action had been taken and no suspects identified. After the attack Litvinenko began to take more interest in his personal security, regularly changing his mobile phone number and telling journalists not to reveal where he lived.

A female police liaison officer was assigned on a continuing basis to Litvinenko's wife and son. Her reports to DAC Clarke contained heartbreaking accounts of Marina and young Anatoly's sadness at Sasha's death, as well as their fears that they too might be targeted by his killers. But there was a moment of levity in the inquiry room when photographs were produced of Litvinenko celebrating the acquisition of his British citizenship by wearing a kilt and wielding a claymore. One detective sergeant pointed out that, despite his apparent Scottish leanings, Sasha had actually hung an England flag on the front of his house during the soccer World Cup and, according to an interview on Britain's Sky Television, his wife seemed to have him down as a committed England fan:

'He really like England. Really. When he put flag on the balcony before World Championships he said, "I'd like everybody will see I support England in football," and when it's finish, I ask him, "Would you like to take it off?" But he say, "No. Everybody, I'd like everybody will see I support England."'

There was less amusement among the detectives studying the transcript of Litvinenko's evidence to the 2003 British parliamentary committee. 'The Russian secret services are getting more aggressive,' Sasha claimed. 'They are threatening my relatives. There are thirty-two [Russian] secret service agents working in England. They follow us and prepare our liquidation . . . Since then my persecution has become more intense – a bomb was thrown through my window. I am being persecuted . . . When a secret service goes after an individual . . . they have no chance.'

42

FOLLOW THE POLONIUM

Peter Clarke's detectives were starting to make progress. The priority team of investigators dealing with the who, what and where of the murder had got a break. The diagnosis of polonium poisoning had given them an important lead they were now figuring out how to follow. The detectives knew of course that polonium 210 is a deadly poison – Sasha Litvinenko's agonizing death was proof enough of that. But at a special briefing from the Metropolitan Police's scientific investigations department they had discovered quite a lot more about it, including one fact which was going to help them enormously. According to the police scientists, polonium 210 is rare, and – importantly – the radioactive signature it leaves behind is very distinctive. When it comes into contact with people and objects, the isotope spreads a trail of contamination with specific radioactive alpha particles – such a trail if followed successfully could lead Peter Clarke's investigators directly to the person or persons who killed Litvinenko.

To pin down the science behind the detective work, the Metropolitan Police took advice from Britain's top experts. Dr Nick Priest, professor of environmental toxicology at Middlesex University in the north of London, is the UK's leading authority on radioactive contamination; he has worked on the clean-up of Chernobyl and the decontamination of former nuclear weapons sites in Russia and eastern Europe. Most importantly for the Litvinenko case, in his early research career he carried out practical experiments with polonium aimed at establishing toxicology norms for detecting and identifying its presence in humans.

When I spoke to him in his laboratory at the Centre for Risk Management he told me how as a young scientist at the forerunner of Britain's Health Protection Agency he had methodically injected polonium into rats to determine its effect on a living organism. The results of his observations allow doctors to diagnose the poison if ingested by a human. Professor Priest wears his erudition lightly – he is a genial, relaxed man – but listening to him describe the processes that polonium triggers in a living being brought home the devastation that Sasha Litvinenko's body would have been subjected to.

> If polonium is ingested, it goes into the gut and the stomach. It will very quickly cause vomiting and that will remove some of the radioactivity. But a large amount will remain behind and will travel through the gut. In the top of the small intestine about 20 or 30 per cent will be absorbed into the bloodstream, depending on the form of the P210. In this case it was likely to have been in a simple chloride solution. It will then travel around the blood and will penetrate the fluids around the cells in the body. It will irradiate the cells and will penetrate deep into those cells that have a high division rate, for example in the follicles, the skin, the gut wall and the bone marrow. This produces acute radiation syndrome, which means the depletion of bone marrow, the loss of the immune system, the depletion of lymphocytes in the blood, a drop in white blood-cell count, and the loss of hair. Much of the P210 goes into the liver and will cause liver damage, jaundice and yellowing in skin colour. The destruction of the inner gut wall will lead to peritonitis, toxic shock syndrome and possible heart attack.

Polonium had subjected Sasha Litvinenko to a terrible death but it could also, said Dr Priest, lead the police to his killers.

> They probably didn't realize how easy it is to follow a radiation trail. It's easy because there is a massive difference between the amount that was administered to Litvinenko and the amount you need to determine contamination. It's billions of times more . . . a becquerel is one count per second, emitting one alpha particle per second, and there were around four billion becquerels in the source material. When you've got differences of that order, it

means that everywhere they went, wherever they handled the material, it was contaminated and they left a trace.

I suggested to Dr Priest that the killer or killers must have been very naive if they thought their trail would not be discovered, but he disagreed. In many ways, he said, the choice of alpha-emitting polonium had been a sophisticated one. 'The choice of polonium was clever because, unlike the majority of isotopes, it does not emit any gamma energy. Gamma energy is what airport radiation scanners are programmed to test for, so polonium won't show up on them. It's easy to transport because it looks just like water and it can be carried in neutral solutions. There's no need to carry it in an acid solution; it's colourless, odourless and transparent.'

In addition, said Dr Priest, the neutral nature of the polonium solution means it could easily have been split into two or more smaller vials, making detection even less likely, and transported into Britain by two or more people before being poured into the vial used to administer it. This is an important hypothesis because it would later help the police understand why so many seemingly disparate radiation trails were showing up and why the killer or killers seem to have been so contaminated themselves.

Dr Priest said that whoever planned the murder would have known that cases of polonium irradiation are so rare – there had been none in Britain – that doctors do not even test a patient for it. Test procedures did exist forty years ago when polonium was used in the weapons industry as the trigger for nuclear devices, but they are not routinely administered today. So there was every likelihood that the source of Litvinenko's death might have gone undetected forever.

Polonium looks like water, tastes like water and there is no way it could be detected in a cup of tea. You would just pour a small vial of it into a cup and the person would not even know he had been attacked. Unlike most other poisons, there is no antidote for polonium. In hospital they tested him with a Geiger counter and found no gamma radiation, but that's because it was all alpha radiation with the absence of a gamma signature ... Polonium is not a current analysis technique – the analysis has not been used for years now. And if the doctors hadn't figured out that it was polonium, they would never have traced the trail across London.

As we have seen, polonium was identified only on the day of Litvinenko's death; had he died a day earlier the killers might have got away undetected. In fact they could probably consider themselves unlucky because the dose of radiation they administered – estimated at over twice the lethal dose – would have killed most people much more quickly; it was only Sasha's strong constitution that enabled him to survive for twenty-three days.

As for where the polonium came from and who could have had access to it, Dr Priest says Britain and most Western countries stopped producing it years ago. Nowadays, it is used as an anti-static agent in the photographic industry, and the vast bulk of production takes place in Russia.

The polonium could have been ordered, or stolen, from a reactor ... I know from personal experience that security in Russia is very low at these reactors ... polonium is pure – it has only one isotope – so it is virtually impossible to identify which specific reactor it comes from. It could have come from the Russian authorities ordering it or it could have been purloined: they could have paid a reactor supervisor to 'dip a source'. A few micrograms would not be missed since they are producing gram-size quantities. It would never have been detected.

What surprises Nick Priest is the contrast between the sophistication of the organization behind the murder – 'This type of attack takes a lot of planning and there's a lot of thought gone into it. It's not something that anyone could just do just because they had some polonium. I'd be surprised if they hadn't tried it out before' – and the apparent amateurishness of those who actually carried it out. 'The assassins seem to have got a big dose [of contamination] ... It amazed me that these trails were left. Either they thought they would never be detected, or the people who carried it out had received no training and had not been told the dangers of what they were dealing with. That's the most likely – they were just told, "Pour this into his tea." With proper training, you wouldn't leave this contamination trail.'

As for how the killers contaminated themselves and the people and places they came into contact with, Professor Priest says there seems to have been a remarkable lack of precautions taken.

> They must have opened the vial. If it came from an 'official' source, the external surfaces of the vial would have been cleaned by the organization providing it and any radiation removed. Although, if it came from an illicit source, the outside of the vial might have been contaminated from the start. They either opened it in Moscow or in London, possibly to pour two or more small doses into one vial. As soon as they did so, their hands and clothes would have become contaminated and anything they touched would have been contaminated . . . cups, chairs, tables, aeroplane seats. It is very easy to spread and very easy to detect. It is quite credible that they could have contaminated a briefcase which then would contaminate an aeroplane. Then, if you drank an irradiated drink, the contamination would spread from the cup to your lip; if you wiped your mouth, it would spread to your hand; if you shook someone's hand, it would spread from hand to hand. At the same time an irradiated cup would spread contamination to a hotel kitchen, to the cleaning staff, to the dishwasher, to a dishcloth . . . and to all customers who later used that cup. It's just logical. And Litvinenko could have transmitted it by shaking someone's hand or by kissing his wife.

The radiation trail was fatal for Sasha Litvinenko, it was highly dangerous for his assassins who became contaminated, but it was a godsend for the Metropolitan Police. Briefings from Nick Priest and other experts explained why the polonium trail would be so valuable to their inquiries.

A radiation trail is like a paper trail. But a paper trail can go in either direction. A contamination trail can only go in one: it always goes from higher levels to lower levels. Therefore you can look at the comparative levels of radiation at different locations; you can work out the chronology of the events and the vector of the trail. It's like footprints: it always points in one direction. It allows you to follow the trail back and see who contaminated whom. In this case, the vector of the trail was not from London to Moscow; it was from Moscow to London.

43

RADIATION PANIC

It is standard practice for the Metropolitan Police to reconstruct the movements of a murder victim in the day or days before his death. They had interviewed Sasha Litvinenko on his deathbed and had a good idea where he been on 1 November. Now as they went round the central London locations he had visited that day, they were finding one alarming common factor – radiation.

There was radiation at the Itsu sushi bar on Piccadilly, where Litvinenko had met the Italian Mario Scaramella; there was radiation in the Pine Bar of the Millennium Hotel, where he had met Lugovoy, Kovtun and Sokolenko; there was radiation in the offices of Boris Berezovsky, where he had gone to photocopy the Scaramella documents; there was radiation in the car of Akhmed Zakayev, who had taken him home; and there was radiation in Litvinenko's own house. There was also radiation at several locations Litvinenko had not visited, although the police were keeping these secret for the moment as potential material evidence in a future prosecution.

What they could not keep secret was the potential risk to public health. Just as Nick Priest had predicted, radiation at the Millennium Hotel had been found not only in the Pine Bar, but in the hotel kitchens too. A teacup was found to be highly contaminated; the dishwasher in which it had been cleaned was contaminated and so was a dishcloth. For the police it was all useful evidence, but for the Health Protection Agency it was a red alert. Officials from the HPA discreetly asked the hotel management for access to their staffing rosters. Armed with the details these provided, the police set out to contact every member of staff who might have been on duty on 1 November and the following days – not just waiters and staff from the Pine Bar, not just kitchen staff, but room service staff as well;

there was clearly doubt in the mind of Peter Clarke's men over just where the contaminated cup had come from.

At least seven of the staff had been affected by radiation. All were referred for medical examination and the doctors who dealt with them were instructed to wear protective clothing. The results of tests showed varying levels of contamination and the authorities issued a statement saying, alarmingly, that the effects on their future state of health could not at this time be accurately predicted.

The HPA was painfully aware that in addition to the staff, hundreds of guests had passed through the Millennium Hotel and many more customers had eaten at the Itsu sushi bar. Some Itsu staff were also contaminated, but the levels there did not seem as high as at the hotel. Nevertheless, the HPA decided to issue an appeal for everyone who might have been in either of the two affected locations to contact their local health authority immediately. The result was a tidal wave of phone calls and queries that Britain's National Health Service found hard to cope with.

Then on 29 November came the news that radiation had been found on two British Airways planes operating on the Moscow–London run. BA told the media that up to 33,000 passengers and 3,000 staff had potentially travelled on the 221 flights made by the short-haul 767s after the 'low levels of radioactive traces' were thought to have been left on board. Experts were preparing to examine a third aircraft in Moscow. What followed next was not panic but was not far from it. Emergency lines to the health service's call centre, NHS Direct, were swamped; medical staff manning the phones moaned that they had not been warned the announcement was going to be made and had received no briefing on how to identify those at risk or what advice to offer them. In retrospect Professor Nick Priest believes the authorities may have overreacted, but he says the scale of the operation they implemented suggests they were seriously alarmed that they might be facing a major terrorist attack. 'The public health procedures were those for a dirty bomb or a radiological attack. The police at the hospital and at

Litvinenko's house were military police. In the view of the authorities this was the first person ever to be killed by polonium that we knew about. It was all new and unprecedented.'

It was, for all intents and purposes, the world's first experience of international nuclear terror.

PART FIVE

44

ON THE POLONIUM TRAIL

If Nick Priest was right and the trail of radiation really was like following a burglar's footprints in the snow, the Metropolitan Police simply had to establish where the footprints were and which way they pointed. But to Peter Clarke things were not looking quite so simple. The 'footprints' he had found looked suspiciously like they went round in circles, as if there might be more than one radiation trail, and sometimes seemed to lead backwards instead of forwards.

The first important discovery Clarke's men had made was that radiation traces were not confined to the locations visited by Sasha Litvinenko: another, independent polonium trail followed the footsteps of Andrei Lugovoy and Dmitry Kovtun. The police knew there was contamination at the site of their meeting in the Pine Bar; they knew there was contamination at locations they visited after that meeting; and – crucially – they had now discovered there was radiation at several locations they had visited *before* the Pine Bar meeting. The reason this discovery caused so much excitement was that radiation at or after the meeting with Litvinenko could have come from Sasha himself: it could have rubbed off on the two Russians in the way Nick Priest and others had outlined. But radiation on Lugovoy and Kovtun before the Pine Bar meeting could only have come from them.

Scotland Yard now had a lead to follow and two potential suspects to investigate. Clarke's priority team was charged with reconstructing Lugovoy and Kovtun's movements and quickly established that they had been coming in and out of Britain for many weeks, if not months. Yuri Felshtinsky reported that he had seen Lugovoy on the evening of 12 October outside Henry's Café Bar at number 80 Piccadilly. Worryingly, the British police could find no passport or immigration records for him at that time and initially suspected Felshtinsky had mixed up the dates, but Felshtinsky had kept the receipt for a cash machine transaction he made that night and it located him exactly where he said he was.

Lugovoy and Kovtun's next appearance seems to have been on 16 October, and this time there were official records of their movements. From passport and immigration lists detectives were able to establish that the two men flew from Moscow to London on a flight operated by the Russian airline Transaero. Scotland Yard knew the plane was a Boeing 737 with the registration EI-DDK, but when they approached Transaero with a request to examine the plane, the company refused. That night Lugovoy and Kovtun stayed at the exclusive Parkes Hotel, with rooms starting at £199 ($380), in swanky Knightsbridge just round the corner from Harrods. When police arrived with a forensic team, they were shown to the two rooms the men had occupied and quickly discovered that both were contaminated with radiation. A table in one room and a door handle in the other were showing traces of alpha energy, the distinctive signature of polonium. Two days later the men returned to Moscow. Again Transaero would not allow the plane they had used to be examined. But the discovery of radiation at the Parkes Hotel was of vital significance to the police: it proved that the polonium was in the UK as early as 16 October.

On 25 October Lugovoy again flew from Moscow to London, this time on a British Airways flight, number BA875. The plane, GBN-WX, was tested by detectives and Health Protection Agency staff and found to show traces of radiation on one seat and an overhead luggage locker. Scotland Yard will not give any further details, but unnamed sources quoted by the BBC said that the locker may have been contaminated by Lugovoy's briefcase and that a second consignment of polonium may have been brought to London that day. Certainly, there was no doubt about the hotel where Lugovoy stayed. The Sheraton on Park Lane, another upmarket hotel in another upmarket area, was tested and found to show high levels of contamination. In particular, room 848 on the eighth floor had radiation levels as high or higher than those found in the Pine Bar. The Metropolitan Police moved quickly to contact all guests who had used the room after 16 October and urged them to undergo a medical examination. The corridor on which room 848 is located was sealed off and remained so over two months later. On 28 October Lugovoy returned to Moscow on the same BA plane on which he had arrived.

That same day Dmitry Kovtun flew from Moscow to Hamburg, where his German ex-wife and their young child live. He flew on an Aeroflot plane, which the Russian authorities would not release for radiation testing, but German police were able to examine the Hamburg flat he and his wife stayed in that evening. It was contaminated, and so was Kovtun's BMW in the parking lot outside. The German authorities concluded that Kovtun had brought polonium with him from Moscow and said they wished to question him on suspicion of importing radioactive material. Hamburg's Chief Prosecutor, Martin Koehnke, announced that he considered there was reason to suspect Kovtun may have been among those responsible for Litvinenko's death.

On 31 October Kovtun and Lugovoy both flew to London for their final visit. The British Airways plane taken by Lugovoy, GBN-WB, was again found to be contaminated; the polonium trail now strongly suggested that the isotope had been brought into London repeatedly. That evening Lugovoy went to the Down Street offices of Boris Berezovsky and the two men shared a bottle of wine. Berezovsky had employed Lugovoy since the mid-1990s, first as a bodyguard and later as a security consultant. Their relationship had continued after Berezovsky fled to London; they were long-term acquaintances and evidently close enough for the always busy Berezovsky to spare time for a drink and a chat with him. It was a relationship that would be closely examined when police investigations began to point towards Lugovoy as a suspect in the Litvinenko murder.

When Peter Clarke's men examined Berezovsky's office, the chair on which Lugovoy had sat that evening was found to have very high levels of contamination. After the meeting Lugovoy went back to the Millennium Hotel on Grosvenor Square, where he was staying along with Dmitry Kovtun and Vyacheslav Sokolenko. Police later found two bedrooms, numbers 101 and 441, to be heavily contaminated; they will not say who slept in which room but there was a strong suggestion that Sokolenko's room was not one of those affected.

Having followed the radioactive footprints in the days leading up to 1 November, the police were now concentrating on the day itself. They knew Litvinenko had had two scheduled meetings, and from a detailed examination of CCTV footage and cash-register receipts had been able to establish their order and timings. The Itsu meeting with Scaramella had taken place shortly before 3.30 p.m. and the Pine Bar encounter with Lugovoy and Kovtun began an hour later at 4.30. Would the radiation trail point to Sasha's murderer?

The first measurement for 1 November was taken from the Oyster card Litvinenko had used to pay for the bus journey from his home into central London. An Oyster card is a season ticket in the form of a top-up credit card; the passenger touches it against an electronic reader every time he takes a bus or an Underground train, and the card creates an electronic record of the times and routes of all journeys taken. In the case of Litvinenko's ride on the number 134 bus the card allowed detectives to trace which vehicle he had travelled on and who was driving it. They tested both Litvinenko's card and the bus itself, and found no radioactivity on either. This was a strong indication that Sasha had not been poisoned before the time his bus journey ended, at 11.30 a.m. on 1 November. Then Litvinenko went into a newsagent's shop and browsed the shelves. He bought a bottle of water and picked up a newspaper. Again, the shop was tested and no trace of polonium was found on either the premises or the objects Sasha had touched.

But next came the Itsu sushi bar, and this time there was plenty of evidence of radiation: detectives found a table and two chairs unmistakably contaminated with alpha energy. For the police it was an important discovery and raised immediate suspicions: this was Litvinenko's first recorded meeting after the negative tests of the bus journey and the shop, and it was the first location to link him to the presence of radiation. He was clean before the Itsu meeting but apparently contaminated afterwards.

This was circumstantial evidence that the sushi bar was the most likely scene of the poisoning. In addition, Litvinenko himself had initially fingered Scaramella as the man he suspected of attacking him. The day after they got the results from the sushi bar, the British police took Mario Scaramella into 'protective custody'. A test on a urine sample he provided was sent to the Atomic Weapons Research Establishment at Aldermaston and swiftly returned with sensational news: it had tested positive for massive polonium poisoning. The evidence was building . . .

45

SUSPECTS GALORE

Now things started to get complicated. Scaramella vocally protested his innocence: 'Not only did I not kill him, I think my role in this affair was very marginal. I simply happened to meet him on the same day that something horrible happened to him.' And forensic results from the site of Litvinenko's second meeting, with Lugovoy and Kovtun in the bar of the Millennium Hotel, were about to throw the whole case into confusion.

Working behind protective screens, police scientists had trawled the bar area and nearby kitchens for polonium and discovered the place was teeming with alpha radioactivity. It was on a table and several chairs; it was strongly present in a teapot and in one teacup; it was in a dishwasher and on a dishcloth. These were the highest and most specific levels of contamination found anywhere on the polonium trail and pointed strongly to this being the location where Alexander Litvinenko had been fatally poisoned. The evidence gathered from witness statements and from the radiation measurements led the police to believe that during his meeting in the Pine Bar Litvinenko had drunk a cup of (probably green) tea and that this was the most likely source of the deadly poison which ultimately caused his death. Indeed, quite powerful circumstantial evidence, including Litvinenko's own deathbed testimony, suggested the tea had been prepared while Litvinenko was waiting for Lugovoy to fetch him from the lobby and it was sitting on the table ready for him when he arrived. Tests at the places Sasha visited after the Pine Bar – the photocopier he used in Berezovsky's office, Zakayev's car in which he went home, his house in Muswell Hill – revealed that he was now leaving a trail of alpha particles everywhere he went. The finger was pointing at the Pine Bar, and at Lugovoy and Kovtun.

But the Scotland Yard detectives were puzzled. If they were right that the polonium was administered at Litvinenko's second meeting, then how come the sushi bar he had visited an hour earlier, when he was presumably still clean, was also contaminated? And how come the man he had met there was showing alarming signs of radiation?

A second forensic team was dispatched to the sushi bar to make sure there had been no mistake, and they returned with exactly the same results: a table and two chairs contaminated but at lower levels than those found in the Pine Bar. It was a conundrum. The police had learned from experts like Nick Priest that the vector of a radiation trail is always from high to lower levels – the contamination reduces as the carrier moves from place to place. But in this case the timings made a nonsense of the science: the contamination in the Pine Bar made it almost certain Litvinenko was poisoned there, so how could he have spread radiation to a place he visited an hour earlier?

Peter Clarke ordered his men to revisit the timetable of Litvinenko's movements they had drawn up for 1 November. Could he have had another meeting, a third meeting, before either of the two they already knew about? Could he have been poisoned even before Itsu and the Pine Bar? Detectives spoke to everyone who knew Sasha and who might have further information, among them the small group of former KGB men who live in London. Two of them, Oleg Gordievsky and Boris Volodarsky, advanced a startling theory: that after he got off the number 134 bus that morning Sasha had gone directly to another meeting. This was in the Millennium Hotel but not in the Pine Bar, and was with Lugovoy and another, unnamed Russian, most likely in the bedroom of one of the men, and it was at this meeting that Litvinenko's tea had been poisoned.

Because of the interest the police took in this theory, I questioned Volodarsky about it. He is a cultured, intelligent man who came to Britain in 1987 after years training as a KGB special operations officer. In perfect, almost unaccented English he explained to me what he believes happened that day.

> The whole Pine Bar meeting in the afternoon lasted twenty-five minutes and it was all filmed [on CCTV]. If something suspicious happened at that meeting we would already know about it. At that meeting the guys were relaxed and celebrating. It is clear that he was not poisoned at that moment ... he was poisoned between 11.30 a.m. and 1 p.m. It happened in the Millennium Hotel but not in the Pine Bar. There were two meetings. The first location was not entirely confirmed; it could have been in a hotel room, with two people, Lugovoy and one other person. A second operation had been planned [for the afternoon meeting]. This is normal practice to plan two operations. If something fails with the first, you have the second one. The second operation was planned with Lugovoy, Kovtun and Sokolenko as the three-man team to take part. But that never happened. It was not necessary because Litvinenko was already poisoned on the morning of 1 November. When they met on the evening of 1 November, it was no longer necessary to carry out any operation.

Oleg Gordievsky says the alleged morning meeting took place in a fourth-floor room in the Millennium Hotel and was attended by Lugovoy, Kovtun and a mysterious third man introduced as Vladislav. Vladislav allegedly made the tea that Litvinenko drank, using water from a kettle in the room. According to Gordievsky, Sasha spoke about the incident in hospital before he died. His recollection was that 'the water from the kettle was only lukewarm and the polonium 210 was added, which heated the drink through radiation so he had a hot cup of tea. The poison would have showed up in a cold drink.'

The theory sounds plausible. Sasha's friend Andrei Nekrasov reports a conversation with him on 8 November, seven days after his poisoning, which at the very least leaves open the possibility of an earlier meeting. 'There's confusion about it. My impression from a conversation with Sasha on 8 November was that Lugovoy was first. But then the media reported it was the other way. Maybe he met Lugovoy twice.'

The KGB/FSB modus operandi with its two-pronged approach to special operations was confirmed to me by other intelligence sources. If Sasha really was poisoned in the late morning or early afternoon, it might explain why radiation was found at all the later places he visited, including the sushi bar. And the radioactive teapot and teacup at the Millennium Hotel might have come from room service in the morning rather than from the Pine Bar in the afternoon.

But the scenario has serious flaws. Scaramella was seemingly so heavily contaminated that the radioactivity could almost certainly not have rubbed off from Sasha's handshake or even the kisses the two men exchanged that day. And what about the evidence of Marina Litvinenko, who has no knowledge of an earlier meeting? Marina seems convinced the poisoning happened in the Pine Bar. 'In the Millennium Hotel Sasha told me he met Lugovoy and during this meeting he drank tea. And he said the tea was already served on the table. And he just took this cup of tea and he didn't finish it all. And he later said the tea was not very tasty.'

But if there was no morning meeting, where did the radiation at the sushi bar come from? Scotland Yard's finest were starting to discover some interesting facts. From talking to Marina and to friends of Sasha they already knew that he was a big fan of sushi and that Itsu was his favourite place to eat it. Quite separately, Yuri Felshtinsky, his old friend and colleague, had mentioned that whenever he came to London Litvinenko would say 'Let's meet as usual' and that meant Piccadilly. It seemed the landmark statue of Eros in the middle of Piccadilly Circus was the place Sasha always met anyone who came to London to see him. And the nearest branch of Itsu to Piccadilly Circus is the now infamous one, just five minutes walk away. Piecing all the information together, the detectives realized that Sasha Litvinenko had been in the Itsu sushi bar on many occasions, not just for the 1 November Scaramella meeting. In fact – crucially – they discovered he had been there two weeks earlier, on 16 October. And his companions at lunch that Monday were Andrei Lugovoy and Dmitry Kovtun.

46

NARROWING THE FIELD

The police now had a record of Litvinenko's previous meetings with the two men from Moscow, and it was a surprisingly long one. For the Itsu lunch on 16 October they were able to pinpoint the exact table where Sasha had sat with Lugovoy and Kovtun. Next they asked Scaramella to point out the table where he had met Litvinenko on 1 November. And then they compared the findings of the forensic teams that had combed the premises. All the evidence was that the radiation traces were not at the Scaramella table, but at the one where Sasha had met the two Russians. It was a major break-through, and the first suggestion that Litvinenko may have been attacked not just once but at least twice.

The police already knew that Lugovoy and Kovtun were contam-inated when they flew into London for the 16 October meeting – their rooms at the Parkes Hotel were evidence of that – indicating that they brought the first consignment of polonium with them on that trip. If they had brought the poison into London, was it not likely they were intending to use it? Could they have tried to poison Litvinenko at that meeting? Or could they have merely been making a dummy run, a rehearsal for the real thing?

Oleg Gordievsky believes it was the latter. 'This was a general rehearsal. Everyone involved in operations – secret services, military officers – performs general repetitions of their operations. This day was a rehearsal. They had poison with them because all warfare substances are meant to be at hand. They arrived, they made up nonsense, but they didn't decide themselves to use the ampoule.'

But when I asked Boris Berezovsky what he knew about the events of 16 October, his reply was startling. 'As I understand it, they had a meeting with Alexander on 16 October in this sushi bar.

And what I know is that Alexander felt bad for the first time after this meeting. I think that the dose of polonium that they used on that occasion was not enough to kill him . . . and that's the reason why they made the second attempt on 1 November.'

Berezovsky seems in little doubt that 16 October was a genuine assassination attempt. If a polonium vial was opened that day, it would explain why traces of radiation were still clearly evident on the table and chairs when forensic investigators swept them at the end of November, six weeks later. But it still would not explain the troublingly high level of Scaramella's own contamination. The police were perplexed; it was the one anomaly stymying the whole investigation. Then, on 30 November, the jigsaw gained its final piece: further medical examinations had revealed that Scaramella was not contaminated at all! The boffins at the Atomic Weapons Establishment in Aldermaston had got it wrong. Nick Priest thinks he knows why and it is not surprising: 'It is clear that mistakes were made early on. Polonium is not a current analysis technique and there was cross-contamination of samples in the lab. Litvinenko had millions of becquerels in his urine [his urine was there too].'

With the riddle of Scaramella and the sushi bar seemingly solved, it was looking ever more likely that the poisoning had taken place exactly where the radiation trail suggested: in the Pine Bar on the afternoon of 1 November. Scaramella was little more than an innocent bystander who had been in the wrong place at the wrong time, as he himself had claimed all along. But if not Scaramella, what of Lugovoy and Kovtun?

By the time the police completed their investigations, they were long gone. Back in Moscow they were protesting their innocence, with Lugovoy saying, 'I have the feeling someone is trying to set me up as the fall guy in all this.' To bolster their case they were both admitted very publicly to hospital, apparently suffering from radiation poisoning. Kovtun was photographed with no hair and his lawyer announced he was critically ill or even in a coma. The Russian authorities let it be known that they believed the two men were also victims of an assassination attempt and that the Prosecutor General's Office would be opening an investigation into 'the murder of Alexander Litvinenko and the attempted murder of Dmitry Kovtun'.

In London Peter Clarke's team was uncovering yet more evidence linking Kovtun and Lugovoy to the polonium trail. Radiation was found at the offices of Erinys and Titon International, the two security firms the men had visited with Sasha before he was poisoned. A spokesman for Titon confirmed that it had employed Litvinenko as a paid consultant and that he in turn had brought two Russian security consultants to visit them. Traces of polonium 210 had been found in their offices and the premises had been closed by the police pending further investigations. Finally, radiation was identified at the Pescatori restaurant north of Piccadilly, where Lugovoy is said to have dined on 1 November before meeting Litvinenko.

By early December Scotland Yard were certain that to solve the Litvinenko case they would need to speak to Andrei Lugovoy and Dmitry Kovtun. A flurry of correspondence with the Russian Prosecutor General's Office resulted in permission being received for nine detectives to fly to Moscow and they duly arrived on 4 December.

47

TO MOSCOW

When the Scotland Yard detectives touched down at Moscow's Domodedovo Airport that Monday afternoon, they had little idea what to expect. The team was led by a detective chief superintendent and included three Russian-speaking specialists from the Metropolitan Police's Counter Terrorist Command SO15, but even they had no experience of such operations, let alone one with such implications for international relations that it was being played out in the spotlight of the world's media.

Acutely aware of the potential for negative publicity, the Russian authorities had decided to keep the Scotland Yard men as far away from the press as possible. After a few handshakes and strained smiles at the airport, the Brits were ushered into a people carrier and whisked into Moscow to the headquarters of the Russian prosecutor general on Bolshaya Dmitrovka Street. Yuri Chaika sent his deputy to greet them and wish them a productive stay in Moscow, but then the Russians produced a written set of instructions for the British to follow with a long list of dos and don'ts that made clear the limitations being placed on them. All interviews, said the instructions, would be carried out by Russian officers, with the British being allowed to attend only as witnesses; no suspects would be extradited to Britain; if any prosecutions were to prove necessary, they would be carried out on the territory of the Russian Federation. The Prosecutor General's Office, said Chaika, would detail a representative to assist them at all times, a not too subtle euphemism for twenty-four-hour surveillance. That evening the detectives were guests of the British ambassador, Tony Brenton, at the UK embassy overlooking the Moscow River. For the next two weeks they would work out of a suite of offices in the embassy which had been swept for bugs and was deemed secure.

The following day Yuri Chaika made clear his irritation with the British presence when he faced lengthy and searching questions at a boisterous press conference. Asked if he expected imminent arrests in the Litvinenko case, he snapped, 'Scotland Yard can't arrest Russian citizens. If they have to be investigated, we can do that in Russia. We can instigate an inquiry and put them on trial here.' He pointedly added that Russia had no extradition treaty with the UK and that the British were in Moscow very much thanks to the goodwill of the Kremlin. 'If they want to arrest citizens of the Russian Federation, it would be impossible because of the Russian constitution. They will not be questioning any suspects. Any questioning we will do on their behalf . . . They can request permission to attend the interviews, but . . . that does not mean permission will necessarily be granted.'

At the same time the Russian foreign minister, Sergei Lavrov, was attacking the West for 'politicizing' the Litvinenko case and said British insinuations of high-level Russian involvement were 'unacceptable'; the affair was, he said, 'damaging UK–Russian relations'.

Over the next few days the British media was full of stories of how the Russians were impeding the detectives' investigations. In fact the Scotland Yard team was making remarkably good progress. Within twenty-four hours of arriving, they had had their first meeting with Dmitry Kovtun. For a man who had recently been said to be at death's door, the detectives thought Kovtun was looking remarkably well. So too was Andrei Lugovoy, whom they met two days later.

No official information on the interviews was released by either side, and unofficial sources were remarkably tight-lipped too, but Andrei Lugovoy has spoken about his meetings with the British, which he says he actively welcomed as a chance to prove his innocence in the eyes of the world.

> As soon as my name started to be mentioned in connection with this affair . . . I consulted my lawyers. The next morning I got

straight in touch with the British embassy. I told them on the telephone that we should meet so we can clear up everything that has been going on. They called me back and said OK, great. I agreed to meet them at a time they proposed ... It was a very constructive meeting and I am absolutely satisfied with how it went. I have met the British police. Dmitry has too. We both had a lawyer with us. The meeting was informal, because there is no legal basis for holding it. We have both signed statements ... And they said they were very grateful to us that we had come forward.

Lugovoy and Kovtun were concerned to put their side of the story to the British police and keen to tell the world that they had nothing to hide. Apart from protesting their innocence, Lugovoy says they gave the detectives a detailed explanation of what happened after Litvinenko fell ill.

[Litvinenko] rang me at 7.30 on the morning of 2 November and he said, 'Andrei, you know, I'm not feeling too good. My stomach's turning inside out.' Then he rang me again that same evening and said he wasn't feeling any better ... I had been planning on going to Madrid and he said, 'I've got a good business contact in Madrid; I'll have to put you in touch with him' ... Then I rang him on 7 November. He was already in hospital. His wife picked up the phone and handed it to him. We chatted and I asked him about his health. He said he had been unconscious for two days and thought he had probably been poisoned ... But he said he was feeling a bit better and hoped he might get out of hospital soon. We agreed to talk again in a week and I rang him on 13 November. By then he had already named that Italian as being ... Well, all the press were writing about it. We spoke just for a couple of minutes; his voice was heavy. He was sure he had been poisoned. I said, let's be in touch ... Then my name suddenly cropped up [in the media]. But I can categorically affirm and I am ready to prove – and Alexander and his family and his friends and everyone who met him knew this perfectly well – that I met him on 1 November, and they know perfectly well that I met him *after* Scaramella. And they know where I met him.

At this stage Scotland Yard had not yet announced that they knew about the crucial meeting with the Russians in the sushi bar on 16 October. By insisting so strongly – and his language at this stage changed from a rather casual conversational style to a much more formal 'I categorically affirm . . .' – Lugovoy was making what he clearly believed to be a telling point: if he had met Litvinenko *after* Scaramella and there was already radiation at the Scaramella meeting, then Scaramella must be the culprit.

> After all when I spoke to Alexander on the phone we had a completely ordinary, normal conversation. Nobody was accusing anyone of anything. He didn't even mention such a thing . . . I think maybe Scotland Yard should be looking at more than just the two names that are being mentioned at the moment; they should be looking at all the contacts he had not just over the last month, but over the last year. That's what they should be starting from – looking at all his movements, all his statements in the press, all his mobile phone calls and all his landline calls, including those with Russia and other countries, Spain, London, Moscow.

48

THE KREMLIN BITES BACK

While Lugovoy and Kovtun were protesting their innocence, the Russian authorities were mounting a concerted campaign to counter Western suggestions that they had had a hand in the Litvinenko murder. The problem for Moscow was that the British were moving ever closer to naming their suspects, and the men whose names were in the frame were former FSB operatives whose involvement would be hard for the Kremlin to explain away. Indeed, they were not just ordinary FSB men; both Lugovoy and Kovtun had served in the Kremlin Regiment of the KGB's Ninth Directorate, carrying out security duties for top Kremlin officials. In the early 90s, Lugovoy had been charged with protecting the foreign minister, then the prime minister and – intriguingly – the head of the presidential administration. But it was not these posts the Kremlin was keen to highlight now. Much more useful for their purposes was the fact that Lugovoy's last position in the FSB had been to work with the then head of the National Security Council, Boris Berezovsky, and that when Lugovoy left the FSB, he was taken on full time in Berezovsky's staff. Indeed, Kremlin sources were quietly reminding journalists that at the time of Litvinenko's death Lugovoy had been working for Berezovsky and perhaps they should draw their own conclusions.

In public, the Russian authorities were using powerful members of the national parliament to direct accusations towards Berezovsky. Head of the Duma's Committee on Security Mikhail Grishankov did not mince his words: 'This is yet another scheme by Berezovsky. Berezovsky has been out of the news for a while, so he has masterminded this scheme.' Former FSB Director Nikolai Kovalyov, whom Berezovsky ousted in 1998 to make way for the appointment of Vladimir Putin, is now chairman of the Duma Committee on Veterans' Affairs. In the chorus of anti-Berezovsky rhetoric, his voice was particularly strident.

> Litvinenko is a figure of the distant past in Russia's political life. In Britain he has been Berezovsky's right arm. Therefore it cannot be ruled out that Berezovsky was precisely the one who would benefit most from organizing this poisoning. Berezovsky has long been forgotten in our country. He has disappeared from TV screens and pages of the mass media, and he needed to show his presence before the forthcoming parliamentary and presidential elections. Berezovsky has close links to Chechen terrorists. It means we should not rule out the possibility that for a payment they organized the murders of both Politkovskaya and Litvinenko.

Duma member and retired FSB Colonel Gennady Gudkov had previously mocked Litvinenko's illness as the result of too much moonshine vodka. Now he was dead Gudkov was quick to name the culprit: 'This looks like a brilliant performance, and Berezovsky is a master of staging them. The authors should be sought among his closest entourage.'

Regarding the polonium trail leading to Lugovoy and Kovtun, the Kremlin had a quite breathtaking explanation, suggesting Litvinenko and Berezovsky had been working in London on a dirty bomb, and that it was they who had contaminated the two Russian visitors. The state-owned news agency Novosti ran a long explanation of how it all had happened. A nuclear physicist and professor at the prestigious Kurchatov Institute, Alexander Borovoy, was quoted as saying:

> The worst part of the story is that it was like a rehearsal for a dirty bomb. The incident shows that something dangerous is cooking in the terrorist kitchen, with menacing ideas and plans that can generally be described as a crime. Litvinenko or one of his close friends have somehow got hold of polonium. From them we can trace a connection to those whose dream is to get hold of a dirty

bomb – terrorists. It is a fact that terrorist number one, Osama bin Laden once bought from shady arms dealers three containers with weapons-grade fissionable materials. The world was saved then only because the dealers cheated bin Laden by selling him medical waste, which also set off the Geiger counter. We were probably lucky this autumn too, because something apparently went amiss in London. Polonium doesn't forgive lax attitudes. In my view this is a warning to us. Terrorists could have acquired a horrible weapon. We must wake up to reality and take emergency measures to stop radioactive terrorism!

Rhetoric about nuclear terrorism and comparing Litvinenko and Berezovsky to Osama bin Laden might make Moscow's accusations sound somewhat over the top, but the kernel of the argument – that Lugovoy was a long-time Berezovsky friend and employee, and that he was working for him at the time of Litvinenko's poisoning – cannot be so easily dismissed. So did Berezovsky have a case to answer? I would have to put it to him directly.

49

THE CASE AGAINST BEREZOVSKY

It was a warm summer evening in Moscow and Paul Klebnikov had been working late. Just before 10 p.m. he left the offices of the American *Forbes Magazine*, where he was a senior editor, and set off to walk home. He never got there. An unknown assailant lowered the window of a car and shot him nine times. Paul was still alive when the ambulance arrived at Moscow's City Clinic Number 20, but he died in a corridor on his way to the emergency room. It was 9 July 2004 and Klebnikov was forty-one. The American-born son of Russian émigrés, with degrees from UC Berkeley and the London School of Economics, he had been covering Russia for fifteen years. A few years earlier he had published a book entitled *Godfather of the Kremlin; Boris Berezovsky and the Looting of Russia*. It was not complimentary. Among other things Klebnikov accused Berezovsky of having 'a history replete with bankrupt companies and violent deaths. The scale of destruction was extraordinary ... Many of his business ventures ... were marred by the assassination or accidental death of key players.' Klebnikov says he was warned by a Russian government minister not to publish the book: 'With a guy like that, you have to be very careful ... Over here we don't talk, we shoot ... They can do anything ... With a foreign journalist, they aren't going to think twice about it.'

In 2003 Berezovsky won a libel suit against Klebnikov in a London court. When Klebnikov was shot dead the following year, he told the news agency Novosti, 'I cannot say who is behind all this. I am aware of his careless handling with facts, which was cleared up in the British court. Unfortunately, he used to invent many facts and someone must have disliked this very much.'

The Russian media speculated extensively about who had killed

Paul Klebnikov. Now they were doing the same about Alexander Litvinenko, and in both cases they were touting the name of Boris Berezovsky. There was no evidence that he was responsible for the Klebnikov killing, but when I sat down with him in his London offices to discuss the Litvinenko murder the Russian accusations were fresh in my mind. Berezovsky was his usual charming self. He was drinking mineral water but insisted on serving me a cup of hot tea. We chatted for a few moments about various matters and then I asked him to explain his relationship with Andrei Lugovoy. How was it that the man Scotland Yard seemed to be fingering as a key suspect in the murder of Alexander Litvinenko was actually his friend and paid employee? Berezovsky thought for a moment and replied that he had been surprised to hear the evidence against Lugovoy.

> You know, I went to see Alexander. I went to Barnet Hospital. Scaramella's name was in the press at that time. At hospital he told me, 'I have very serious information for you, Boris: on that day I met Lugovoy and some other people; I think they poisoned me.' I was very surprised because I knew Lugovoy and I didn't think he could do such a thing. I started to think that maybe it is a special operation by the KGB against me – that they wanted to implicate me through Lugovoy, that I knew Lugovoy and that they were building up a story that I gave the order to Lugovoy. When Alexander told me the first time about Lugovoy, I was very surprised.

Berezovsky says the fact that polonium was used in the murder is proof the Kremlin's accusations against him are groundless.

> If it had not been polonium, I am sure they would have created that story, the Russians. No doubts! Maybe you remember how step by step they changed their story. Initially they said, 'Oh it's just stomach problems;' then when it was thought it was thallium, the Russians said, 'Oh no it's not thallium, it's just bacteria;' then when polonium was discovered, they said, 'OK, maybe it was

thallium . . . but not polonium!' Putin played this sick game at the EU summit in Finland. He said, 'We don't have any evidence that he was poisoned.' It is typical KGB!

In fact the Kremlin was insisting that the discovery of radioactivity at Berezovsky's offices – in the room next to where we were now sitting – was conclusive proof that Berezovsky *was* involved in the murder. Nikolai Kovalyov again led the attack.

Boris Berezovsky's involvement has been further proved . . . The container [of polonium] was handed over to Litvinenko, but the curious young man got into it or did something wrong, contrary to Berezovsky's scenario. Another possibility I do not rule out is that there was some plan aimed against Litvinenko. Perhaps Boris Abramovich [Berezovsky's patronymic] wanted to kill several birds with one stone . . . Berezovsky has already taken care of his alibi . . . He will say he had expected polonium traces to be found in his office, and will start saying on all corners that the special services tried to kill him.

The accusations were based on the contention that Berezovsky benefited most from Litvinenko's death: he could use it to blacken the name of Vladimir Putin; he could use it to revive the idea that his own life was at risk and that he still needed asylum from a British government which was beginning to tire of his presence. Berezovsky denies all such accusations and insists the Kremlin is trying to deflect the blame away from itself. 'Russia is trying to point at someone else to change the direction of the investigation. But they are not lucky this time, because the polonium [trail] is clear evidence of how it happened . . . Russia is in very serious trouble now . . . in particular Putin himself; because polonium looks like it left a fingerprint all over the world.'

But even if it were true that he had not ordered the murder, why had Berezovsky continued to trust a man who seems to have been involved in it? Was it not clear to him that Lugovoy was acting as a double agent for the Kremlin?

'For you it was clear; for me it was not,' he told me. 'I spent a very complicated time in Russia and I know that Lugovoy nevertheless created a bodyguard team that protected me. At least I am still alive; many others were murdered. It is the only criterion of success of a bodyguard ... When I got control of ORT TV station, Lugovoy organized the security ... Right up to the last moment I had relations with him, and about seven or eight months ago I was calling him and asked him to protect my daughter who had moved to St Petersburg ... And also I knew Lugovoy had been in jail with my partner Nikolai Glushkov, and OK only for a very short time—'

I interrupted Berezovsky at this point. Lugovoy had been convicted in 2001 of allegedly trying to help Berezovsky's Aeroflot partner Nikolai Glushkov escape from prison. The operation was widely rumoured to have been mounted on Berezovsky's instructions. When Lugovoy was found guilty, he was sent to jail but quietly released soon afterwards. The episode had aroused suspicions that the FSB was trying to give Lugovoy a cover story that he had 'gone bad' – that he had cut his ties with the agency and proved his loyalty to Berezovsky. For some observers it was a classic example of a security force trying to infiltrate a double agent into the confidence of an opponent. I asked Berezovsky again: Didn't he sense that Lugovoy had been deliberately sent by the FSB to spy on him and ultimately to help in the operation against Litvinenko?

He admitted he had thought about it: 'OK, you can always have doubts about someone who has been in the KGB. You are correct. I do not dispute this. Alexander always said, "Boris, in the KGB there is a way in, but no way out." And I want to tell you that only Alexander demonstrated the way out. He was really exceptional ... It was his very strong choice to fight against this organization [the FSB].'

I recalled something Berezovsky had said in the past: 'I am very bad at understanding people. I don't know who is traitor, who is good, who is bad.' I asked him if he felt he had been negligent in allowing Lugovoy such access to his circle in London and to the lives of those around him. He had invited Lugovoy to his birthday parties, he had kept him informed of his business dealings and he had not warned Sasha Litvinenko to steer clear of him. Berezovsky acknowledged it was a thought he had grappled with.

> OK, I tell you. Many people ask me, do I feel guilty that Alexander is killed? But honestly my answer is no, I don't feel guilty. I don't feel guilty because of two reasons: first, it was Alexander's firm choice to do what he did, the same choice that I made; and second he was no less protected than I was . . . And I told you that just the evening before I had a meeting with Lugovoy in my office and drank wine with him and he could have the same chance to poison me like he did with Alexander . . . He came here on 31 October and I invited him into my room. I asked my secretary to bring us some wine. We shared a bottle between the two of us. And I mean between the two of us literally, because there was no one else there. And afterwards the police found that the most radioactive place here was the chair Lugovoy had been sitting.

I asked Berezovsky if he had remained in touch with Lugovoy after Litvinenko's murder and was astounded to hear that they had continued to speak on the telephone.

> I can even tell you that he, Lugovoy, called me just five days ago [6 February 2007] – the first time after Alexander died – and he told me, 'Boris . . . I want just to clarify: did you say that I am guilty, or did you say that Alexander told you I am guilty?' And I say him, 'The second. As far as I am concerned, I don't know. If you ask me, do I think that you are guilty, I tell you I don't know. But I have a lot of facts that make me think you are guilty . . .' And he said me, 'Which one?' And I said, 'Very simple, the trace of polonium! Even in my office. The chair where you were sitting now is destroyed. They took this chair, and only this chair, because the radiation was 800 times more where you were sitting than even where Alexander printed the photocopies. And this is the first fact. And this trail follows you all over Europe . . . It is a fact. But the most important fact is that you are not here. If you are

not guilty, then you know you are not guilty, then come here, go to Scotland Yard.' And I tell him, 'I have my personal experience – it's not Russia here! I had nine cases in British courts, including against the government, and all of them I won. I know that if you are right, you win.' And I told him, 'Come here. I give you the best lawyers; I pay for them. I give you the . . . I help organize the best coverage of your story for public attention. That's it – it's the only way to clean things up!' And he said, 'Oh I will think about that,' and so on. Will he come? I don't know. I have impression that he is not independent to take this decision; that there is another alternative, that there is someone behind him that doesn't allow him to do this step.

50

HOME FOR CHRISTMAS

On 20 December the nine British detectives in Moscow were told it was time to leave. Prosecutor General Yuri Chaika handed them transcripts of the Russian police interviews they had attended and informed them that their 'joint inquiry' was over. Some of the policemen were relieved – they'd had sixteen days in Russia and didn't fancy the prospect of Christmas away from home – but there was dissatisfaction too. The mission had achieved some of its goals: the interviews with Lugovoy and Kovtun had helped firm up some suppositions the investigators had already arrived at, but there had been obstruction from the Russian authorities when it came to other interviews they wanted to carry out. In particular, they had been refused permission to speak to Mikhail Trepashkin, the former FSB man who had provided details of the alleged 2002 plot to kill Litvinenko. The Russian prosecutor had contended that Trepashkin was a criminal serving time in a penal institution; his evidence was by definition untrustworthy and the British should give it no credence. Trepashkin had let it be known that he had new information about the Litvinenko murder but the detectives had argued in vain to be allowed to talk to him.

It was perhaps the irritation felt by some at Scotland Yard over the Russians' intransigence that led to the first spate of leaks from the inquiry. Shortly after the investigators got back to London several newspapers reported that the police had decided to indict Lugovoy and Kovtun. The *Daily Mirror* reported a police source as saying, 'We are 100 per cent sure who administered the poison, where and how,' and adding that they would officially declare Lugovoy and Kovtun the guilty parties in a forthcoming file to be submitted to the Crown Prosecution Service. The *Independent on*

Sunday cited a senior Scotland Yard official as confirming that charges would be laid but speculating that the suspects would never be brought to justice because of Russia's refusal to extradite them: 'The odds of getting someone to face trial at the Old Bailey [London's criminal court] are somewhere between slim and none.'

Behind the scenes the police were continuing to build evidence for their case. Despite their failure to interview Trepashkin, they had obtained several letters from him smuggled out of prison, containing some of the new information he had spoken about. The letters, which were certified authentic by Trepashkin's friends and relatives, gave details of an alleged plot by officers within the FSB to take revenge on Litvinenko and other 'traitors'.

> Back in 2002, when I refused the offer to work against Litvinenko, I believe they were preparing me for the role that Lugovoy, Kovtun and Sokolenko carried out in 2006. I do not, therefore, believe that the murder was done on their own initiative. As I understood it, the initiative was coming from another group within the FSB, whose creation had been sanctioned at the very highest level. The group includes both active and former members of the FSB.

Trepashkin's letters spoke of a unit in the VKR (Russia's foreign counter-intelligence agency, the Vneshnyaya Kontr-Razvedka) which has been developing poisons to use against targets abroad.

> Earlier, I described a concrete situation about the use in the FSB of special poisons for the physical destruction of people. Already in 1994 certain of the officers of the VKR were sneaking these poisons out from development sites and were attempting to sell them to businessmen they knew for the elimination of competitors. These poisons do not leave traces in the organism. Most often, autopsy results list cardiac failure as the cause of death. The poison is usually applied by aerosol or with a brush to the steering wheel and door handles of an automobile, in a place where an air conditioner is working, on telephone receivers, and so forth. In the instance described by me, there were ten kinds of poisons of

various effect (through the respiratory passages, through the skin of the hands, through the conjunctiva of the eyes and so forth). Traces of such poisons are present in the murders of Kivelidi, Shchekochikhin and others. It cannot be ruled out that such poisons have been used for the murder of A.V. Litvinenko ... I will add the following information. As far back as 2001, I was asked by the FSB to phone Litvinenko in London, and find out if he was writing a book [about the FSB]. I learned that he was currently working as a postman. A little while later I was told it was being considered to send him a letter with poison [anthrax] powder. Such things were being widely talked about at that time in the USA.

As for the motive behind Litvinenko's killing, Trepashkin was convinced it stemmed from the FSB's desire for revenge for his whistle-blowing press conference of November 1998.

I greatly regret that human rights advocates did not give due attention to what A.V. Litvinenko was talking about way back in 1998, when he ... told about contract murders and abductions of people committed on the orders of the leadership of the FSB. Maybe the death of A.V. Litvinenko, who fell a victim of vengeance with impunity, will finally force those who are engaged in protecting human rights to pay attention to what is going on. Litvinenko was asked at that time: what can you expect for yourself after such high-profile revelations? He replied, 'If there isn't good support, then the criminal murderer-generals will fire us and strangle us like puppies' ... And they did: they started to strangle everyone involved with the 17 November 1998 press conference, to get rid of them like so much unneeded waste. Litvinenko and I are not the last in the chain of those being pursued. You remain silent? Tomorrow any one of you may find yourself in this chain.

And Trepashkin sent the British police a warning not to trust the assistance of the Russian authorities, suggesting that one of the FSB officers involved in helping them may have actually taken part in the plot against Litvinenko.

They need to be speaking to this serving FSB officer. I believe he is of key importance to their inquiries ... I know that the prosecutor's office is helping Scotland Yard in investigating Litvinenko's murder. But I don't trust the state prosecutor's office. Their help is like the help of a murderer who promises to find his victim's killer. They decided to destroy me slowly, placing me in conditions which are dangerous for my health and my life. But Alexander, because he was abroad, they decided to destroy quickly.

On 31 January Scotland Yard decided they had enough evidence to send a file on the case to Britain's Crown Prosecution Service. A spokeswoman for the CPS said there was nothing to prevent Britain seeking the extradition of someone from a country with which it has no extradition treaty, 'but if there is no extradition treaty and we think that the people won't be extradited, there's not much point doing it'.

When a reporter from the Reuters news agency rang Andrei Lugovoy for his comments on the Scotland Yard decision, he said, 'You can say on Reuters that when Lugovoy was read the report about my extradition, Lugovoy gave full-hearted, healthy laughter.'

51

TRADE OR JUSTICE?

If Andrei Lugovoy was laughing, Tony Blair must have been struggling to see the funny side. The decision on whether or not to seek the extradition of the Russians was the sole prerogative of the British judiciary, and politicians were not supposed to play any part in it. Blair had recently earned opprobrium for intervening to halt a corruption probe into a case involving a British defence firm and the Saudi government, so he did not want to run a similar risk over this one. On the other hand, Moscow was already hinting that trade with the UK could be adversely affected if London insisted on making a fuss over the Litvinenko affair. Fearing damage to Anglo-Russian relations, Downing Street reportedly sent firm instructions to Scotland Yard that it should keep quiet about the case.

In early February Trade Minister Alistair Darling was dispatched to Moscow to try to smooth things over. With British firms investing $5.5 billion in Russia in 2006 and Russian companies raising $15 billion with share offerings on the London Stock Exchange, Darling announced that the UK is – and intends to remain – Moscow's number one trading partner. 'Our relationship is robust. Where there have been difficulties, we need to talk frankly as partners.' He added, 'We did discuss the [Litvinenko] case and, in parallel, the Russian requests for their own extraditions,' an indication, seemingly, that Moscow was now linking its cooperation over Lugovoy and Kovtun to British collaboration over extraditing Berezovsky and Co.

The priority for Darling's trip was to shore up Britain's access to Russian oil and gas, a market in which Moscow had been increasingly flexing its muscles. With 30 per cent of the world's gas exports and oil production far outstripping all its rivals, Russia knew it could afford to twist Darling's arm, and he could hardly afford to offend them. So it must have been particularly unhelpful and irritating to the minister that anonymous Scotland Yard sources were quoted the same day insisting they had enough evidence to try, and to convict, Lugovoy and Kovtun. The minister held to a firm line of smiles and 'No comment.'

When Darling got back to London, it was not long before the outline of a deal seemed to be emerging to placate the Russians: the British Home Office was reported to have signed an agreement for Russian police to come to the UK to visit dozens of sites and interview up to a hundred designated people. All were allegedly witnesses or suspects in the Litvinenko affair but most were in fact exiled opponents of the Putin government which Moscow had long been wanting to get its hands on. Top of the list was Boris Berezovsky, the man the Kremlin would most like to extradite back to Russia. And he was not happy about it.

> Russia is blackmailing Scotland Yard. Russian officials say they will allow questioning in Russia if Britain allows Russia to question people in Britain. I said, fine, they can question me if it helps Scotland Yard find those who killed my friend. I have the impression that Scotland Yard knows who committed this crime and they know very well who is behind it – that is, the Russian state machine. The Russian prosecutor's office is well aware of it too, so their actions are a diversion tactic. They know who actually contracted and carried out this crime. They know not only as much as the investigators of Scotland Yard, but a lot more, because they have had access to information first hand.

Berezovsky told me he was angry the British government seemed to be putting its relations with Moscow ahead of the search for the truth about Litvinenko's murder.

> I'm sure the government would like very much to hide, to stop this story. They want to be nice with Mr Putin and so on, because they are weak . . . but if that is so, it means they are no longer the

guarantor of the protection, of the safety of their people. It means they should leave, step down. The problem for the British government is that if they don't discover every single link in the chain from the cup of tea that Alexander Litvinenko drank right back to the place where the polonium was produced, then no one in this country can feel safe any more – not you, not me … We will not allow this country or Russia to stop this story. It should be absolutely clear for the government that there is no chance to stop this story.

Berezovsky did, however, agree to meet the Russian investigators on certain conditions: 'First, it cannot take place in the Russian embassy as I do not trust the Russian authorities. They are capable of any kind of provocation. And second, before the meeting the representatives of the Prosecutor General's Office must be checked for all kinds of poisonous substances and for weapons. If these conditions are met, then I don't see any reason why we shouldn't meet.'

Alex Goldfarb said he would agree to speak with the Russians too, but only 'if British security experts can rule out the possibility of them putting polonium in my tea'.

52

THE THIRD MAN?

As Scotland Yard awaited a decision from the Crown Prosecution Service, suspicions were emerging that the hit squad sent to kill Litvinenko may have contained a third man. With the media speculating that only Lugovoy and Kovtun were named in the indictment, several sources who had given evidence to the police were keen to let it be known that they had told detectives about another, third suspect. The sources of the evidence were former KGB and FSB men themselves, now living in the UK. One of them, Oleg Gordievsky, told me that Moscow would never send just a two-man team: 'This was a very well organized KGB operation ... in all the details. A rehearsal in the middle of October, and then repeated on 1 November. It was a classic three-man KGB operation, with the classic agent group. That means a group of three agents, a troika.'

Former FSB special operations officer Boris Volodarsky agrees. He told me that the mission involved one operative carrying out surveillance on the target, and that Lugovoy had been tracking Litvinenko for a full year; a second agent would bring in the weapon, in this case the polonium; and a third man would carry out the actual killing.

> Lugovoy, Kovtun and Sokolenko are not professional murderers, despite serving in the Federal Protection Service. They are not the actual killers. Lugovoy and Kovtun scouted out the ground and the professional killer came in at the last moment to do the murder and then disappeared without trace. That is his job; that is how we have been trained – you enter the country and you leave the country unnoticed, in a quite short space of time. Planning a special operation takes a long time but he appears and disappears, that is normal operational practice.

246

Russians refer to a professional assassin as a *keelyer*, a rather sinister adaptation of the English word. I asked Gordievsky if he knew the identity of this third man.

> He was a KGB killer; he was trained to kill. He joined them just for a moment solely to put the poison down. And that man who put the poison, he disappeared. He came to the country certainly under an EU passport because he had to come into Heathrow without any checks, which he did, and then he disappeared from the country in an unknown way. They've been checking the airports and there is no record of him. So he most probably changed his passport twice. For me as a former member of the department, it is absolutely clear. He changed his passport when he arrived; wherever he stayed in some hotel under some different passport; and in the evening of the same day – or maybe in the morning of the next day – he left Britain under another passport. So now when the British will demand extradition of the main killer, it will be very difficult.

I asked both Gordievsky and Volodarsky if they thought the mysterious Vyacheslav Sokolenko could have been the third man, but they said that he was at most backup for the logistics men, Lugovoy and Kovtun. Gordievsky says the *keelyer* would have been a specialist, whereas the others were double agents trained in infiltration. '[In 1996] Lugovoy and Kovtun were told to officially leave the FSB because that made it easier for them to distance themselves from the security forces. The FSB can say, "We don't know them; they left our service long ago." Lugovoy even spent time in prison, so he's "a criminal" and "not one of us" and so on. They officially left the FSB. That makes it easier for them to carry out such a dangerous mission; to get close to their target.'

Lugovoy himself vehemently denies that any third person was with him and Kovtun at the meeting in the Pine Bar of the Millennium Hotel: 'There was no third man. I want to make that perfectly clear. Dmitry and I met Litvinenko on our own ... As for the man supposedly sitting next to Dmitry Kovtun on the plane coming to London from Hamburg, there was none. Kovtun was on his own . . . We didn't bring anyone to meet Litvinenko.'

According to my former KGB contacts, the anonymity of the *keelyer* in an FSB-style troika is always carefully preserved. He is not known by the victim and his true identity is kept secret even from the other members of his team. As with the spy rings of cold war times, the agents operate in cells; no cell can implicate another because it does not know names or identities. In a troika the key feature is deniability: the third man comes and goes with no trace and no connection to the logistics men who have paved the way for him.

Such a structure does of course presuppose an overarching command, a person or group of people with overall control of the agents in the field. Oleg Gordievsky says the organizers of the assassination were efficient to the point of ruthlessness; they put operational priorities first and were prepared to sacrifice the safety of their own agents. Crucially, he believes, the operatives were not told about the danger they were running by handling polonium. Lugovoy and Kovtun both reported radiation poisoning when they returned to Moscow and Gordievsky says the *keelyer* in particular would have been exposed to a potentially lethal dose.

> They didn't realize that they were being exposed to such toxic poison. The KGB [*sic*] didn't tell them; the KGB framed them, set them up. They even framed their own illegal, the man who put the poison ampoule in the tea. He didn't realize what the ampoule was all about – that you touch the ampoule and three years later you are dead. The KGB needed to conceal the truth from them in order to use them, to exploit them. Now he will die probably in three years of cancer. Those three people didn't realize what kind of poison it was – they knew it was a poison, but they didn't know they will also die because of leukaemia. It is the greatest shock in their lives. Now they will die – they are people in their fifties, strong, fit men. All three of them will die in a few years.

In fact, the medical evidence is not as conclusive as Gordievsky claims. There is no certainty the men will contract leukaemia, although there are instances where polonium has had that effect. The daughter of Marie Curie-Sklodowska, who discovered the isotope and named it after her native Poland, was accidentally exposed to a very small dose of it when a vial was broken and she died of leukaemia ten years later. Yuri Felshtinsky agrees that those arranging the kill would probably have kept the nature of the poison secret from those who were handling it: 'It's of course understandable that Lugovoy knows Litvinenko is going to be poisoned, but I'm sure that Lugovoy would not ask, "By the way, how are you going to poison him? What kind of poison am I going to use?" He is a military man. He was working for the FSB for many years. I'm sure he would not ask extra questions because the general rule is that the less you know, the better it is for you.'

With such a level of secrecy within the operation and the identity of the putative *keelyer* deliberately cloaked in anonymity, the chances of ever finding the alleged third man seemed remote. The British police believed they may have identified a suspect from CCTV airport footage from 31 October. He was described as tall and powerfully built, in his early thirties with short black hair and distinctive central Asian features. But no pictures of the man were published and no arrests made.

A picture of Alexander Litvinenko was hitting the headlines, though. A video recording of a government shooting range in Moscow showed a blown-up photograph of his face peppered with bullets from FSB agents. As a 'traitor' Sasha was obviously considered fair game.

53

THE BUSINESS CONNECTION

Somewhere in my files there is a photograph. It is a snapshot of a smiling group of people at the BBC office in Moscow on some formal occasion in late 1996. I recognize all of those present – they were friends and colleagues. On the right of the photo, also smiling but a little apart from the main group, is a sharply dressed American – double-breasted grey suit, brightly coloured tie – in his early forties. Paul Tatum was the co-owner of the building that housed the BBC offices and those of other broadcasters from Europe and North America. I say co-owner because he was in partnership with some Russian businessmen of Chechen extraction whom we often noticed in the foyer. That occasion was the last time I saw Paul. A few weeks previously his partners had told him they wanted to buy out his share of the building. Paul refused. On the evening of 3 November 1996 a man with a Kalashnikov walked up to him as he left the building and shot him eleven times. I saw the ambulance take his body away. His mistake had been to underestimate the ruthlessness of some Russian businessmen and the nonchalance with which they use murder as a solution to commercial disagreements.

By the end of December 2006 the theories advanced about Litvinenko's death in the main attributed his poisoning to political reasons. But a new explanation was now emerging, and this time the theory suggested that, like Paul Tatum, Sasha was killed as a result of a business dispute. Having lived in Russia at the time of the gangster wars that swept Moscow, I knew the idea should not be ruled out.

A fifty-three-year-old former FSB major living in Washington DC by the name of Yuri Shvets had been collaborating with Litvinenko in the consulting business he had started after Berezovsky cut his monthly allowance. Shvets, who defected in 1993, revealed that Litvinenko had been hired on behalf of a 'major British corporation' to investigate several Russian firms it was thinking of investing in. Sasha had asked him to help in the process known as due diligence and Shvets had agreed. Due diligence means checking that a firm is financially robust and worth investing in, but also that it is not tainted by corruption. When I spoke to Shvets's partner Robert Levinson he made clear how crucial such work can be for deals worth millions, and sometimes billions of dollars: 'Russia is a big priority. It needs lots of careful due diligence. Few countries need it more than Russia. Large companies want to know should they do business with Russian firms. Are they connected with organized crime? Do they have any kind of record of criminal activities? Is the firm's registration in order? Are they connected with money laundering?'

Levinson is a former FBI man who has been investigating Russian companies for many years. When I spoke to him in a crowded bar he was careful to check our conversation was not overheard. He has himself suffered intimidation by Russian firms who don't like what he has found out about them. 'I was asked to investigate [a major Russian business group] and their alleged links to two organized crime gangs in Moscow. [The business group] found out that I was investigating them and spread the word that I was taking money [to come up with false information]. The aim was to undermine me, destroy my reputation and discredit whatever I came up with.'

The suggestion now being made by Yuri Shvets was that Litvinenko was also being intimidated by a Russian firm he had been investigating, and that the intimidation in his case had included the ultimate sanction. According to Shvets, he and Litvinenko had been given a one-year contract at a fee of $100,000 to investigate five Russian individuals on behalf of a reputable British company. Their research had revealed serious doubts about the probity of one of the men, a tycoon who was also a 'close confidant of Vladimir Putin' and a 'senior Kremlin official'. The eight-page dossier they produced labels him a 'powerful and vindictive man'. In rather shaky English, it concludes, 'Many people view him as a remnant of former times and fits more to the Josef Stalin times than to the modern Russian environment.' As a result, the British firm had pulled out of a multi-million-dollar deal which had been close to completion.

What happened next, says Shvets, was a chain of events that led directly to Sasha's death. The dossier was completed on 20 September 2006 and Litvinenko took it directly to the headquarters of the company which had commissioned it. Two weeks later he showed it to his supposed friend Andrei Lugovoy. He was hoping to develop a business relationship with Lugovoy carrying out investigations inside Russia, and he gave him a copy of the dossier to explain what a due diligence report should look like. But Shvets says Lugovoy was a long-standing double agent and FSB informer who 'rushed' back to Moscow to show the dossier to his bosses. They passed it on to the Kremlin official discredited in the report who thus discovered why the British firm had pulled out of the deal with his company. Shvets says Litvinenko's dossier cost the as yet unnamed man 'millions of dollars'; it also raised the possibility that Litvinenko was privy to further 'difficult' information exposing high-level corruption and might be passing this on to the British secret services. Shvets believes the Kremlin official could have ordered Sasha's execution as a punishment and a warning to others. Neither the British company which ordered the due diligence dossier nor the security firm which acted as its intermediary in hiring Litvinenko – possibly Erinys or Titon International, which confirmed Sasha was indeed working for them – has commented on the matter, although both have been interviewed by British investigators.

For his part, Yuri Shvets passed a copy of the due diligence file to Scotland Yard. He did not publicly name the Kremlin official and businessman he alleges it concerns, but from the extracts I have seen it is clear that the man in question is Viktor Ivanov, a career FSB man and now President Putin's deputy chief of staff.

Putin and Ivanov have known each other for many years, working together first in the Leningrad KGB and later in the mayor's department after the city was renamed St Petersburg. As with so many top officials in Russia today, Ivanov has also carved out an impressively lucrative business career: he is currently chairman of Russia's leading missile defence company, Almaz-Antei, and – since November 2004 – chairman of Aeroflot.

In the murky world of Russian high finance Shvets's theory is far from implausible. Ivanov certainly has the business connections that could make him of interest to a big British investor . . . and the target of an investigator like Sasha Litvinenko. As a senior Kremlin official and long-time KGB man, he would also have had little problem gaining access to polonium or any other poison.

But there are serious flaws in the scenario. For a start, the timings seem implausible. Shvets says Litvinenko gave the dossier to Lugovoy some time around 4 October. Lugovoy then had to take it to his FSB boss, who had to pass it on to Ivanov, who then had to make all the arrangements for an assassination that seems to have begun just a few days later with the 16 October meeting in the sushi bar. It seems a remarkably tight timetable for such a complex plot to be hatched and executed. Neither does the theory explain why surveillance on Litvinenko appears to have been going on for almost a year before the dossier was produced; according to all accounts, Lugovoy had been courting him since the end of 2005. Even if we accept that the Shvets–Litvinenko dossier was the last straw, the final impetus to trigger a plot which was already under way for other motives, it is hard to lay the blame at Ivanov's door. Journalists who saw him at the EU–Russia summit in Helsinki the day after Litvinenko's death report that he was 'in a panic' and anxiously going round the press asking who they thought was behind the killing . . . but that of course is no evidence of anything. In fact the fingering of Ivanov is almost too convenient: from the point of view of the anti-Kremlin camp it has all the right ingredients, including a dossier of dirt and allegations of murder against a man who incarnates the values of the FSB and, to top it all, is close to the hated Vladimir Putin.

Even some of the Kremlin's harshest critics find the scenario hard to swallow. Litvinenko's friend and neighbour Akhmed Zakayev says he was not aware of any dossier or investigation that could have led to Sasha's murder. 'I'm doubtful of Shvets's version. [Litvinenko] was conducting a general case against the FSB and the Kremlin regime . . . not a special commission for, or from, someone.' But Boris Berezovsky is less categorical: he says there might have been business considerations behind, at the very least, the timing of the poisoning.

> I think there were reasons why it was Sasha . . . and why it was now. Sasha had been telling me what operations he was engaged in at the time – not actual operations, but the people on whom he was gathering very serious evidence of participation in criminal dealings. Knowing Sasha, I understood that this was in fact very serious, because he was truly a very good operative . . . Certainly he was investigating in favour of – I don't know who – in favour of some people who pay interest to that . . . His interest was to discover the crimes created by the FSB and personally by people in the top level of the government.

This sounds like it might fit the bill for the Shvets dossier theory; Viktor Ivanov is undeniably a 'person in the top level of the government'.

But the biggest drawback to the dossier theory is the dossier itself. The extracts I have seen contain material which is already widely known, which is taken from anti-Kremlin websites or which comes directly from Litvinenko's own book *The Criminal Gang from the Lubyanka*. After a factual biography of Ivanov, the tone of the dossier's allegations is very similar to the attacks Litvinenko made on Vladimir Putin, accusing him and several other Kremlin figures of links to organized crime, specifically to the Tambov mafia group. Litvinenko advances the same allegations of drug trafficking and consorting with Colombian mafia groups, the same story of money laundering through a named German company and the same accusations of smuggling precious metals out of Russia. All the allegations relate to the early 1990s when Ivanov was working with Vladimir Putin in the St Petersburg city administration and all have been in the public domain for several years. None of them is substantiated with any new evidence, nor seems especially damaging to Ivanov. The Kremlin will not comment on the dossier or the allegations it contains, but it seems very unlikely on its own to have served as the trigger for a murder.

What it does do, however, is raise the possibility that Litvinenko's assassination is linked to internal Kremlin politics. Under the current Russian constitution Vladimir Putin must step down as president when his second term of office expires in March 2008. Jockeying for position by his potential successors was already beginning in the latter part of 2006 just as Sasha was killed, and the emerging favourite seemed to be the liberal-minded first deputy prime minister, Dmitry Medvedev. But Medvedev's hard-line enemies within the Kremlin were said to be horrified by the thought of a pro-Western, pro-market figure becoming president.

The theory runs that the hard-liners, led by the Chief of Staff Igor Sechin, his deputy Viktor Ivanov and Defence Minister Sergei Ivanov (no relation to Viktor), may have organized the Litvinenko affair to destabilize the political scene in the run-up to 2008. Their aim would be to persuade Putin that he needs to anoint a successor tough enough to keep a dangerous international situation under control and to stand up to the threat from the exiles and the West, or to declare a state of emergency, cancel the elections and suspend the constitution so that he could himself stay on as president. The hard-liners – the aptly named *siloviki* or power group – are considered anti-Western and anti-democratic with speculation that they would be willing to tear up the constitution in order to preserve their own power. Nothing can be proved, but they were the group that had the most to gain from killing Litvinenko and, as the faction to which the FSB is most loyal, they were the people with the means to do it.

Three months after Alexander Litvinenko lay dying in a London hospital bed, on Valentine's Day 2007, the *siloviki* seem to have got their reward: President Putin announced he was promoting Sergei Ivanov to the post of first deputy prime minister. The liberal Medvedev was no longer the favourite in the presidential race.

54

LITVINENKO THE BLACKMAILER?

At roughly the same time as Yuri Shvets was revealing the dangerous commercial investigations Litvinenko had been working on, another source was emerging with allegations that Sasha had been involved in some shady business of his own. Just as the Western media was uniting to blame the Kremlin for poisoning a British citizen on the streets of a British city, an unexpected counterblast appeared in the columns of a Sunday newspaper.

Julia Svetlichnaya, a thirty-three-year-old Russian who describes herself as a politics student at London's University of Westminster, had gone to the London *Observer* with information which if true would blacken Litvinenko's name. Svetlichnaya said she had contacted Sasha in the course of researching her thesis on the war in Chechnya, and in a series of meetings between April and June 2006 he allegedly gave her details of a blackmail plot he was planning to carry out. 'He told me he was going to blackmail or sell sensitive information about all kinds of powerful people, including oligarchs, corrupt officials and sources in the Kremlin,' she said. 'He mentioned a figure of £10,000 that they would pay each time to stop him broadcasting these FSB documents. Litvinenko was short of money and was adamant that he could obtain any files he wanted.' The implication was that Sasha had gone ahead with his blackmail plans, and that one of his targets had reacted by silencing him for good. This was a godsend for the Russian authorities, who had been taking a battering at the hands of the British press and badly needed something to tarnish the saintly image of Litvinenko which was beginning to dominate the international debate.

Svetlichnaya claimed she had over a hundred emails from Litvinenko and had recorded hours of conversation with him. She certainly had lots of colourful detail about their encounters: 'We met in summer. We ended up walking round Hyde Park for hours. He told me shamelessly of his blackmailing plans aimed at Russian oligarchs. "They have got enough, why not share? I will do it officially," he said. After two hours of traipsing around the park, I suggested we sit down somewhere. "Professionals never sit and talk, they walk round so nobody can overhear their conversation," he muttered darkly.'

The picture of Litvinenko painted by Svetlichnaya is very different from the innocent family man the media had been portraying. She describes him as 'ranting' against the Kremlin and motivated by self-aggrandizement. '"Every time I publish something on the ... website," he said, "I piss them off. One day they will understand who I am!"' She says he would boast about his power to blackmail the rich and famous and even asked her if she would like to become his partner in the enterprise. 'He did not seem worried. Quite the opposite; he sensed he could finally make some money of his own after years of being supported by his friend Boris Berezovsky.' And she suggests Litvinenko had already started implementing his blackmail plans during the period before his death, including claims that some of his files documented the business practices of certain British firms.

The timing of Svetlichnaya's revelations was so convenient for the Kremlin that some commentators cast doubt on both their accuracy and her motives. It was alleged that the main focus of her studies at Westminster University was not Chechen politics, as she had claimed, but art. Since her theses were on 'Art and absence' and 'Art and empire', her motives for interviewing Litvinenko appeared to be not as obvious as she had suggested. A Norwegian publication discovered she was also working for a mysterious Russian company called Russian Investors, which other newspapers suggested had links to the Kremlin or to pro-Kremlin oligarchs. The local newspaper in her hometown of Cherepovets, 400 miles north of Moscow, proudly reprinted Svetlichnaya's comments and reminded readers that her father was the well-known Communist Party official and former first secretary of the First of May Regional Committee of the CPSU. Svetlichnaya's co-researcher was found to have been the Manchester branch organizer of the Revolutionary Communist Party and a contributor to the magazine *Living Marxism*. None of this would mean that the version of her dealings with Sasha was wrong, but the historian and author Vadim Birstein wondered pointedly whether their stories about Litvinenko might have been 'disinformation disseminated by the FSB'.

In person, Svetlichnaya is a slim, attractive woman but unsmiling, guarded and wary in the way she responds to questions. Her speech is hesitant and peppered, in both Russian and English, with 'you know'. She is eager to talk about her views on Russia today and at pains to point out that she is an 'academic'. She obviously resents accusations that she is working for the Kremlin and says she has financed her own life in England. Her mother helped with the down payment to buy a flat, she says, but otherwise she has paid for herself and for her university fees by part-time work as a journalist.

Svetlichnaya met Litvinenko through Boris Berezovsky and says she noticed immediately that relations between them were not good. 'Talking about Litvinenko, Berezovsky told me, "He's a *GeBeshnik* [a derogatory term for a KGB man]. You have to filter what he says. The man rambles about lots of things; you'll have to sort it out for yourself."' And she says Litvinenko seemed to resent the way Berezovsky had begun to treat him. 'Litvinenko told me himself that Berezovsky had slashed the money he paid him right down. He said that he used to have money: "They used to pay me, but now it's finished; I've got make my own money." Why do you think he started chasing after Lugovoy and all the others? He was broke. His house didn't even belong to him. He had big financial problems.'

According to Svetlichnaya Litvinenko's mental state was fragile.

> He would send me two or three emails every day with all sorts of information. Right at our first meeting he told me how he'd been

the deputy head of an FSB department whose job was to eliminate inconvenient people. I wouldn't say he was desperate, but there was something not right about him. I thought maybe he was suffering from post-traumatic stress disorder. His psyche seemed disturbed and he didn't quite realize it himself. In his conversation he used to jump around all over the place; everything just got lumped together. I tried to keep him on one thing at a time, but I can't even remember half of the stuff he talked about.

She paints a picture of an unstable, narrow-minded and very bitter man, driven not by principles but by an obsessive determination to avenge himself on a world that has done him wrong.

He was very emotional and very negative. There was a negative tone to everything he said. He said he was against the Russians and respected only the Chechens; he said he was an opponent of Putin and a supporter of democracy and all the rest ... But he was mercenary-minded. He was a trader in negative information; that was his speciality. Right from his KGB days, he was always collecting negative information about people. He asked me to join him in selling negative information. He said, 'I can find stuff out about anyone, absolutely anyone. Tony Blair ... BP ... I've got information about BP ... I can find it on anyone ... Let's find a journalist and slip them something about Tony Blair ... then next time they'll have to pay us.'

In view of Yuri Shvets's suggestion that Litvinenko's due diligence work was taking him into the territory of big business deals, the mention of BP is an intriguing one. What information had Litvinenko discovered? Svetlichnaya will reveal nothing further. As for the target of Litvinenko's alleged blackmail plot, she is more forthcoming, casually slipping in details which hint very strongly at the unnamed oligarch's identity.

I said to him, 'You say you are protecting people like Abramovich and Khodorkovsky from the FSB, but now you're saying they ripped off their money.' And he said, 'I've got a file on ...' And he told me the name of the oligarch. 'I've got concrete plans. I'm going to blackmail him because that vermin has ripped off so much money . . . He's a Kremlin stooge and he's got such an easy life. He should be made to share it . . . I need to feed my family, too.'

That description, together with Svetlichnaya's subsequent confirmation that the target of Litvinenko's alleged blackmail lives in the UK, strongly points to Roman Abramovich, but Svetlichnaya will confirm only that Litvinenko 'had a lot of hatred towards this man' and called him a Judas. In fact, there is no proof that Litvinenko had the evidence he boasted about to Svetlichnaya.

Asked if Litvinenko had used the word 'blackmail' unprompted by her, Svetlichnaya says he used it repeatedly, but asked if she has this on tape, she admits she has not. In the end, her testimony about Litvinenko's alleged blackmail plans may or may not be true; she may or may not have had ulterior motives in making it public at a time when British opinion was becoming overwhelmingly unfavourable to the Kremlin. But the portrait she paints of Sasha in his last few months does ring true. It is clear he was a desperate man and was being driven towards increasingly desperate acts.

55

THE YUKOS CONNECTION

Shortly after the death of Alexander Litvinenko the British press reported that yet another central London location was being examined for the possible presence of polonium radiation. Litvinenko and Andrei Lugovoy had during one of their meetings reportedly visited an office building at number 1 Cavendish Place, between the shopping districts of Oxford Street and Regent Street. The offices belong to a risk assessment, corporate intelligence and security firm called RISC Solutions Plc. Before adopting its current name the company was known as ISC Global and was headed by a British lawyer called Stephen Curtis.

On 3 March 2004 Curtis was in a private helicopter flying from London to Bournemouth in the south of England. One mile from its destination the helicopter spun out of control and crashed. Curtis, aged forty-five, and his pilot Max Radford died instantly. An inquest jury returned a verdict of accidental death on both men, but it emerged that shortly before the crash Curtis had received death threats and reported that he felt he was under surveillance. He had told a relative, 'If anything happens to me in the next two weeks, it won't be an accident.'

The source of the death threats was never established, but it was subsequently revealed that ISC was part-funded by two Russian oligarchs, Mikhail Khodorkovsky and Leonid Nevzlin, billionaire owners of the massive Yukos oil company and involved in a long-running battle with the Putin government. They had allegedly paid six million pounds to ISC over three years and had been using it to run a covert propaganda campaign against Putin and his close allies. It was claimed the company had been tasked with gathering intelligence to 'discredit Putin and those around him'. Most of the named targets were career KGB and FSB men now in positions of power in Moscow. The anti-Kremlin smear campaign was stepped up after Khodorkovsky was arrested in Russia and thrown in jail. Even the coroner at Curtis's inquest conceded that his death had 'all the ingredients of an espionage thriller'. Two former Scotland Yard detectives ran the security and information side of the business and in February 2006 an ISC insider made allegations to the authorities that the company had been paying serving British police officers to hand over sensitive information regarding Russian oligarchs in London and Moscow. All the charges were denied.

As to why Litvinenko and Lugovoy might have been visiting the firm's headquarters in November 2006, a clue emerged when it was revealed that Litvinenko had held a meeting with Leonid Nevzlin just weeks before. Since the Kremlin had arrested Mikhail Khodorkovsky in 2003 and begun the legal proceedings which eventually bankrupted his £21 billion empire, Nevzlin had been the top man in the Yukos management, living in exile in Israel and part of the diaspora of Russian oligarchs railing against the Putin regime. Litvinenko had reportedly flown to Tel Aviv to hand over another dossier of negative information, this time allegedly revealing damaging details about how the Kremlin had gone about discrediting and taking over Yukos. Litvinenko is understood to have warned Nevzlin that he had uncovered a plan by the Kremlin to claw back millions of pounds from exiled Yukos executives by what one source described as 'a covert campaign of intimidation and murder'. Three months later, at the beginning of January, sixty-four-year-old Yuri Golubev died in London. He was a senior Yukos executive and longstanding partner of Khodorkovsky and Nevzlin. His body was flown back to Russia; the cause of his death has not been revealed.

Following Litvinenko's murder, Nevzlin was questioned by police. He confirmed that Litvinenko had indeed flown to see him in Israel and that he did receive a file from him, which he had since handed over to the British authorities for examination. As for the contents of the dossier, Nevzlin said, 'Alexander had information on

crimes committed with the Russian government's direct participation. He had only recently given me and my attorneys documents
that shed light on the most significant aspects of the Yukos affair.'

If the content of the dossier was indeed damaging for the
Kremlin and if it had become known to the Russian security services
in October 2006, this could have provided yet another motive for
Litvinenko's poisoning.

The Kremlin, however, had a different interpretation. Russian
Prosecutor General Yuri Chaika announced that Moscow believed
Nevzlin was himself a suspect in the murder. No possible motives
were suggested for why he might have wanted Litvinenko dead, but
the Prosecutor General's Office said it would be seeking to question
him. It would also be asking the Russian investigators due to visit
Britain to interrogate eleven senior former Yukos executives who
currently live in London. Sources in Moscow were now suggesting
that the only way Britain would ever get Lugovoy and Kovtun
extradited would be to hand over the émigrés and political
opponents the Kremlin had long been pursuing in the UK. Chief
among these was of course Boris Berezovsky. For Vladimir Putin the
Litvinenko affair had at first looked like a dark cloud; now perhaps
a silver lining was starting to emerge.

PART SIX

56

TAKING STOCK

After many weeks working on *The Litvinenko File* and having spoken to so many different people with conflicting theories, stories and points of view – all propounded to me with the unblinking vehemence that Russians reserve for politics, both pro- and anti-Kremlin – I was beginning to wonder if I would ever get to the bottom of the case. I had started by posing two key questions: who had killed Alexander Litvinenko and what was the motivation of the person or people who ordered his death?

On the first question, a broad consensus seemed to have emerged around two names – Andrei Lugovoy and Dmitry Kovtun – to the point where Scotland Yard apparently felt sure enough of its ground to send a file to the Crown Prosecution Service, and the media and public opinion were proclaiming them guilty. The evidence against the men was circumstantial but seemingly weighty. The name of Vyacheslav Sokolenko had receded a little from the frame, but the spectre of a mysterious and as yet unnamed third man had been raised by sources with close links to the Russian security forces.

As to whether the killing really had been the work of the Federal Security Service, the question remained tantalizingly unresolved. Moreover, even if it was the FSB, it was still completely unclear at what level the operation might have been planned and authorized. Had it been at the top, in the corridors of Vladimir Putin's Kremlin? Or by individual officers (or groups of officers) with their own agenda to pursue? If it had not been an FSB operation at all, could it have been motivated by commercial conflicts Litvinenko had either stumbled into or deliberately stirred up? Had it been the result of blackmail he was carrying out? Was it revenge by criminals he had targeted way back in his anti-mafia years in Russia? Chechen blood vengeance for his actions during the war? Or was it – as strident voices in Moscow were claiming – a 'provocation', a double operation staged by enemies of the Kremlin deliberately to blacken the name of the Russian president? Could Boris Berezovsky have cynically sacrificed his own friend and ally in a demented bid to frame Vladimir Putin? Or was it the result of infighting between clans within the Kremlin itself, trying to destabilize the political situation and influence the selection of Putin's heir apparent before the elections in March 2008?

As I mulled over all these questions I began to empathize with Deputy Assistant Commissioner Peter Clarke's reaction when he first opened the Litvinenko file back in November 2006. He had reportedly been 'flabbergasted' by the range of activities which could have given rise to a motive for murder, and now I understood exactly what he meant. I knew I was getting close to the point where I would have to follow in the footsteps of Clarke's investigators. I would have to trace the polonium trail back to its source in the capital of the Russian Federation, and I would personally have to interrogate the men and women who knew the truth.

57

TRAVELLING EAST

Aeroflot was a delight. Friendly, smiling crew, a modern Airbus and edible onboard food . . . it was hard to reconcile this experience with the hundreds of Aeroflot journeys I had taken in the past, many of them internal flights on rickety old Tupolevs and Ilyushins with broken seat backs and missing safety belts, with peasant traders transporting live chickens and, once, a goat. My abiding memory of those days was of a panic-stricken stewardess rushing to stop a brightly clad Uzbek lighting a portable gas stove in the aisle moments before he would have blown the pressurized cabin to pieces.

But it was not just the air travel that had changed. The welcome at Sheremetevo Airport was now courteous and efficient with none of the ritual humiliation foreigners were previously subjected to; there were gleaming glass and steel high-rises along the road into town and a proliferation of neon signs advertising Western commodities as well as coffee shops and designer stores . . . something seemed to have changed in the way the city was thinking and acting, something intangible but readily perceptible to anyone who had known the place in the old days. Gorbachev used to talk about 'new thinking' – about rejecting the authoritarianism and arbitrary injustice of Soviet times and adopting democratic principles where the authorities can be held accountable for their actions – but these ideals seemed to get forgotten in the chaos of the Yeltsin years. Was Putin's Russia now escaping from the old Soviet stereotypes and the repressive mentality of the cold war? Was it really emerging into the sunny uplands of democracy, tolerance and a law-governed state? As I re-immersed myself in the city I had known so well, I sensed that finding the answers to these questions would be crucial in my quest to uncover how and why Alexander Litvinenko had met his cruel death.

The first hint came from my unofficial taxi driver, who drove an old Volga and took payment in euros. He was a grizzled fifty-year-old with a broken nose and a baseball cap. Early in our acquaintance we drove past the building on the Garden Ring where I once lived as the BBC Moscow correspondent. When I told him that I had lived there 'a long time ago' he misunderstood, and jumped to the conclusion that I was a Muscovite who had been taken abroad at an early age by my Russian parents. I didn't disabuse him because the thought seemed to make him immensely well disposed towards me – he called me by the familiar *ty* instead of the formal *vy* and lamented the influx of outsiders that had left 'us Muscovites' in the minority in 'our own city'. As he was obviously in a chatty mood, I asked him what he thought about 'that Litvinenko' – as all the Russians I met seemed to refer to him – and he shrugged. 'Akh, it's all politics. I guess it was the *spets-sluzhby* [special forces] that got him, don't you? He was a traitor. Before this job I was in the Alfa Group' – my ears pricked up; Alfa Group soldiers were the toughest of the very tough *spetsnaz* troops – 'and I think we would have done the same in my day. We would have done it all a bit simpler, though. We used bullets, not polonium.' It wasn't a great start in my search for the new, caring, sensitive Russia.

Further inquiries produced more encouraging results: talking to a group of younger people on Pushkin Square I heard some sympathy for Litvinenko but widespread scepticism that the Kremlin ordered his death. 'I think twenty years ago maybe it could have been the FSB,' said Igor, a tall, well-spoken physics student. 'That was the old way of doing things. But now I think we are more civilized. Putin is an FSB man, but he is a democrat too. He will not stoop to such things.' The others in the group were equally impressed by the Russian president, saying he had brought order and stability after the stormy seas of the Yeltsin era. But when I pressed them there was a grudging acceptance that some areas of society, including the security forces themselves, may not have moved on from the old ways of behaving. There was agreement that the FSB was a multi-headed Hydra, with cliques and competing interests, so that it was hard to say if its activities were all under the control of the Kremlin or of Putin himself. 'I don't rule out the possibility that FSB were involved,' said Nina, a student of art and design, 'because they have many goals that they pursue, including commercial goals and goals of self-protection. Maybe some FSB were protecting themselves from Litvinenko. But it does not mean that Russia killed him.'

Drawing a distinction between the activities of the FSB and the will of the state was a common reaction among those I spoke to, as was an almost universal admiration for Vladimir Putin. Could a man like Putin really have sent his killers to assassinate a renegade like Alexander Litvinenko? It was a question that could only be answered in the Kremlin.

58

TO THE KREMLIN

It was six o'clock on Monday evening and the snowstorm had set in for the day. Cutting down the side of GUM, the massive iron and brick Victorian department store that stares across Red Square to the Kremlin, I could see barely ten feet in front of me. Compacted ice had left the cobbles treacherous underfoot while a fleet of snowploughs was weaving a moto perpetuo on the Square, trying vainly to keep the snow at bay. I was heading for the Spassky Gate, with its iconic clocktower and illuminated red star looming through the swirling flakes.

The red brick of the Kremlin wall emerged from the gloom and I was unexpectedly transported back to the first time I had come here, twenty years earlier. Then I was a nervous young reporter setting foot in the long-forbidden seat of Soviet power, issued with a coveted pass to attend Gorbachev's groundbreaking Congress of People's Deputies where real debate was happening in Russia for the first time, where democrats like Andrei Sakharov, Anatoly Sobchak and Alexander Yakovlev were slugging it out with the communist dinosaurs.

Now, in 2007, I couldn't help wondering if much had changed. The welcome at the Spassky Gate was pretty much the same: three uniformed guards with rifles and a metal detector. But there was, I thought, a subtle difference: instead of the old silent stare and deliberately sceptical examination of my documents, the guards allowed themselves a welcoming smile and wry comment about the snowstorm. Then from the shadows a figure stepped forward and called my name.

Aleksei was in his late twenties or early thirties, slim, nondescript in dress and appearance, and cheerily informal. We chatted easily as we walked through the courtyard between the Kremlin wall and the State Armoury and then turned into a less than imposing door in the wall of the long yellow-stucco building which houses the presidential administration. This was, clearly, the back entrance to the seat of power. Once inside, the security began again with another metal detector and the surrender of my mobile phone to the guard. In the elevator taking us to the third floor I asked Aleksei how long he had worked in the Kremlin and who he worked for. The answer was a smiling seven years and a somewhat embarrassed, 'Actually I work for the FSB, but don't worry, I'm not a spy.' He was, he said, providing security to the president and other top officials and the thought crossed my mind that he was doing the same job that Lugovoy and Kovtun had once done.

We were strolling down a series of long wide corridors, the same corridors that Kremlin leaders had trodden for the last ninety years. With their brown wood panelling, rows of doors, parquet floors and worn strips of carpet, they would have been as familiar to Lenin and Stalin, to Khrushchev and Brezhnev as they now were to Putin. At the end of one corridor I was ushered first into an anteroom where a couple of officials sat typing and then into a very large corner office, four-square with a conference table and twelve chairs. At the head of the table a wide desk was covered in papers, and behind it a full-size Russian flag and a map of the world covered most of the wall. Dmitry Peskov enjoys the confidence of the president and the perks of the responsible position he occupies. He is a sprightly man in his early forties, a career diplomat who became close to Putin from the moment the president was first elected, impressing him with his energy, intelligence and knowledge of the world. Putin appointed Peskov head of information for his administration and takes him with him wherever he goes. On the day I came the two were between trips to Sochi and Volgograd. Over a cup of hot Georgian tea I tried to gauge if his boss really could have been involved in the Litvinenko poisoning, or if the accusations against Putin were merely the fabrications or wishful thinking of enemies at home and abroad. Peskov is indignant about the allegations and their timing. He and Putin were together at the Russia–EU summit in Helsinki the day Litvinenko died, and he feels the Berezovsky camp deliberately stage-managed events to embarrass Putin in the spotlight of the world's media.

> When we heard that it was serious and that his life was in danger, we were already in Helsinki. And then it was announced that he had died just one or two hours before the [president's] press conference. So from that point of view the timing was indicating that it was a frame-up, that it was an attempt to frame Putin. The attention of all the media, especially the European media, was focused on that event and there was some suspense over whether the new negotiation agreement [with Russia] would be accepted or not, so the timing for framing Putin was actually excellent.

Peskov is an earnest, sophisticated man, far removed from the bullying, stonewalling Kremlin officials I was used to in the 1980s and 90s. He comes across as reasonable, and sincere in his love for his country and his faith in his president. He knows Putin intimately – he works with him every day – and feels personal resentment on behalf of his boss.

> The whole story when Mr Litvinenko was in hospital was well orchestrated; it was spread into the media in a very talented way. What pushed the trigger for the entire anti-Russian, anti-Putin hysteria was that mysterious note [Litvinenko's alleged dying statement]. I say mysterious because the note was announced about thirty or forty minutes before the Helsinki press conference. We had heard that for the last couple of days Litvinenko was not conscious, but suddenly a note appeared that was said to be written personally by him. Before the note we were not commenting on the story. He was very sick, and when he was about to die I doubt he would want to write something. And I'll be frank with you, we know that some PR companies were involved in that case and they were communicating that story to the media. And given the style of the text of that note, I can presume that it is the joint

effort of someone who hates Russia – who hates Putin personally – and that degree of hatred is a characteristic of a very few people living in London, of Russian origin and also very talented communicators who know how to use wordings in order to burn the flame of hatred. In my opinion, that was the aim and from the point of view of starting that hysteria they lit the torch.

When I asked Peskov if he was accusing Berezovsky, his answer was reasonably clear: 'I'm not naming him personally, but from the description of course it gives you the possibility to guess.'

I knew that Dmitry Peskov had discussed the Litvinenko case with Putin at great length and given him advice on how to respond to the accusations against the Kremlin, on how to remain calm and measured in the face of what the president believed to be an unjustified personal affront against himself.

You know, I would never discuss that [advice] in public. But nevertheless, what is obvious is that the president felt himself necessary to express his condolences to the family of Litvinenko. He accepted that that it was a human tragedy – a man died – but he never tried to camouflage, to hide the fact that he was not fond of Mr Litvinenko. And you will find very few people in my country – including his first wife, by the way, and his two children – who are fond of him or who are proud of him. This is not the case in my country.

It was a strange sensation, sitting in the heart of the Kremlin, discussing the personal feelings of the most powerful man in Russia. Through two large windows I looked out over the distinctive crenellations of the Kremlin wall at the snow blowing through Red Square beyond. Would the previous occupants of these quarters have been so open with a foreigner?

I recalled the words of Akhmed Zakayev who was convinced that Vladimir Putin had personally ordered the killing of Litvinenko: 'His former teacher once described Putin as small-minded, malevolent and unforgiving,' said Zakayev. 'I believe that Putin personally hated Litvinenko and couldn't forgive him that he had betrayed the homeland and the system.' I pressed Dmitry Peskov for his views; I asked him to tell me how President Putin felt about the allegations levelled at him personally, how it felt to be accused of murder. Peskov said he would not discuss such things in public, but I later spoke to another source close to Putin who knew about his feelings.

'The president is very upset by this,' he told me. 'He is upset by these accusations made personally about him. He simply can't believe that people are saying these things about him *as a person*. He's very angry about the way the British press has named him as a murderer – that's why he won't speak about it any more.' I asked my source why, if this was the case, Putin had refrained from expressing his anger and hurt. He told me, 'The president doesn't like his feelings being discussed in public.' It was, I thought, quite a revealing moment.

St Basil's Cathedral and GUM loomed out of the snow and the gloom. The clock on the Spassky Tower chimed its distinctive peal for seven o'clock. I put it to Dmitry Peskov that even if President Putin had not personally ordered the Litvinenko killing, it could still have been the unauthorized work of the Russian security services. Had the president ordered an inquiry to make sure the FSB was not involved? 'Look, I don't know. I am being very frank with you now. It's not a question of Putin not being sure if such an involvement was possible or impossible. It is hard for us to imagine that there is the slightest idea that such a possibility could exist. For us the tiniest possibility is out of the question. There is not even the tiniest possibility, not even a hypothetical possibility of our special services being involved.'

Up to now I had been convinced by what I had heard. On the balance of evidence I was coming to the conclusion that Putin himself had had no hand in the murder. But this was something different: despite Peskov's assertion that the FSB had not been involved, he could offer no evidence that ruled out the possibility of a freelance operation, or that suggested Moscow had even tried to rule it out. When I pressed him he told me, 'For that purpose [checking the possibility of an FSB involvement] our prosecutor's office has opened its own investigation.' It was clear where I would have to go next.

59

THE PROSECUTOR

The Office of the Prosecutor General of the Russian Federation is at number 15A Bolshaya Dmitrovka, a sharply ascending street that runs from the back of the Bolshoi Theatre. On the morning I was due there, temperatures had plummeted to $-20°C$ and walking up the sloping ice-covered pavement I found it a struggle to stay upright. The high building set back behind a courtyard planted with tall fir trees is visible from a distance but the street entrance is small, an anonymous-looking wooden door in a blank wall.

The prosecutor's office is a powerful institution in Russia, combining oversight of policing, investigation and prosecution. According to its charter it has ultimate responsibility for 'bodies that conduct detective and search activity, inquiry and pre-trial investigation'; it oversees the 'interests of a citizen or of the State in court cases determined by law'; and it carries out 'prosecution in court on behalf of the State'. It thus partly performs the roles of both Scotland Yard and the British Crown Prosecution Service. This is where the Metropolitan Police's finest had come just weeks before, seeking the cooperation of Prosecutor General Yuri Chaika and looking for clues in the Litvinenko case. I was determined to follow their lead.

As in the Kremlin, my reception was warm and friendly. Two young detectives, Sasha and Kolya, took me through the usual security and a lengthy examination of my documents before walking me to the other side of the tree-lined courtyard and upstairs to a cosy, overheated second-floor office. The first surprise of the day was that the person who had been given the task of responding to my inquiries was not some grizzled old policeman but an attractive woman in her mid-thirties who introduced herself as Marina Gridneva, senior legal counsel and head of Yuri Chaika's information division. Before getting down to business she introduced another detective who would be sitting in on our conversation and together they produced a teapot and a large sponge cake topped with apricot jam. It was, explained Marina, home-made and she was sure I would like it. With a cup of a very unusual, aromatic tea, I ate two slices. The charm offensive seemed genuine and they laughed when I said journalists would certainly not get similar treatment from Scotland Yard.

But hospitality did not mean they were going to answer my questions. All my inquiries about the possibility of FSB involvement in Litvinenko's murder were met with a steely 'That is part of an ongoing investigation so we cannot comment.'

After twenty minutes we seemed to be getting nowhere. I decided to be a little provocative and quoted them Boris Berezovsky's assessment of the Russian prosecutor's office, *their* office, as 'an absolutely criminal, gangster organization that serves as an instrument of suppressing people and which has essentially the same mentality as Putin and the others sitting in the Kremlin'. But they were prepared for that approach too.

Without batting an eyelid, they replied calmly and evenly, 'There has been some speculation that we might swap Lugovoy and Kovtun for Berezovsky. Russian law prevents the extradition of Russian citizens to a foreign state. But on the other hand we continue to demand the extradition of Boris Berezovsky to allow him to stand trial here for crimes committed on the territory of the Russian Federation ... economic and other crimes, including actions aimed at the forceful seizure of power. Here are all the details of the charges we have brought against him. This is a full copy of the charge sheet and you are very welcome to take it with you.'

It was starting to look like I was in a chess game where my opponent knew all my moves in advance.

I persevered. 'What about the new laws of July 2006?' I asked, glad to be able to quote some legal stuff myself. 'I believe Federal Law N 153-F3 of 14 July 2006, passed by the Duma and supported by the Kremlin, allows the president to use the Russian secret services to eliminate "extremists" in Russia and on foreign territory, does it not?' I could see my words were having some effect, so I ploughed on: 'And what about Federal Law N 148-F3 of 27 July 2006, which specifically expands the definition of "extremism" to include anyone "libellously critical of the Russian authorities"? It looks like a pretty clear mandate to go out and kill people like Litvinenko, doesn't it?'

The two detectives asked for a moment to consult. They went to tap at the computer on the desk, and they phoned through to Sasha and Kolya to fetch them some documents. My recorder was running the whole time and the recording conveys an air of mild panic. Marina's voice is heard asking me to help myself to some more tea and cake while they sort things out. Then, after a lengthy pause, they are back with the explanation: yes, those laws were indeed adopted but they were not adopted with any evil intent. They were a response to the cowardly abduction and murder of five Russian diplomats in Iraq. President Putin had needed such legislation. Look, the next week he ordered the special forces to hunt down and destroy the killers of our diplomats.

It was an explanation of sorts. But what about the extension of the law to cover 'enemies of the state' and people who are 'libellously critical'? I quoted what Berezovsky had told me about the effect the new law had had on Sasha Litvinenko: 'After Putin signed the decree permitting the special services to kill, without judgement or consequence, so-called enemies of the regime abroad who in fact are simply political opponents, Sasha said to me that we were first on the list – him, Zakayev and me. The hit list didn't stop there, but we were the first.'

Marina Gridneva and her partner were reassuring: 'No, no. It was a law that was aimed at terrorists abroad. Litvinenko wasn't even an "enemy of the state", so it wasn't aimed at him at all.'

It seemed I was going to get nowhere. For forty minutes they had stonewalled me with a charming but immovable double act. So

I said, 'OK, thanks very much,' and they clearly thought the interview was over because they started smiling and suddenly became very expansive. Fortunately, my tape was still running to record what came next.

'Look, Martin, do you really think we'd bother assassinating a nobody like Litvinenko? Someone who left the country God knows how long ago? Who was no threat to us and didn't have any secrets to betray? . . . He just wasn't important enough. He didn't know any secrets that would be a reason for liquidating him . . . Do you think we would have mounted such a special operation to eliminate *him* . . . with polonium that costs the earth? That we would have spent so much money on *him*? My God, we could have used the money to increase pensions here at home. If we'd needed to eliminate Litvinenko, we would have done it ages ago.'

I thanked them and switched off the tape recorder. It was the closest I was going to get to an admission that such operations do after all take place. And if they take place, was it not possible that someone had his own reasons to conclude that Litvinenko actually was worth the price of a vial of polonium? Having spoken to the authorities, it was time to speak to the men at the coalface.

60

THE HARD MEN

I had talked to Andrei Lugovoy, through intermediaries, several times before I flew to Moscow. He and his assistants had been polite, helpful and informative. He had never seemed difficult, panicked or in any way threatening. In fact he had been more talkative and open to the media than one would expect from someone in his situation. I got the impression that Lugovoy was taking things calmly and felt himself in a strong position. We provisionally agreed we would meet when I came to Russia.

When I got there several conversations took place to confirm our arrangement, but there was, I felt, a certain cooling in the telephone discussions. I wondered if something had happened. Perhaps it was the announcement that Scotland Yard had sent a file on the Litvinenko case to the Crown Prosecution Service or perhaps it was something behind the scenes, but for the first time there was a certain reluctance to talk.

He was still insisting he was being interviewed by the British police as a witness rather than a suspect – 'There has been no change in my status, or at least there has been no official notification from the British side of any change' – but now he was much more cagey. He had, he said, been called to the Russian prosecutor's office 'seven or eight times since the British went away'. He 'wasn't ruling out' the possibility that he would travel to London if he was asked to do so, but he added,

I have engaged both Russian and British lawyers and I will take their advice on the matter. You know, there is such a thing in English justice as the right to a fair trial. And I would just like to know how we could get one in the atmosphere of psychosis we've seen in the British media, where they've portrayed us in such a way that ninety-nine out of a hundred British people are convinced we are guilty of this murder. So, to be honest, I really have to consider if it is worth going to meet people who from the very outset are so dead against us and so conditioned to make us the culprits in this affair.

It was, I thought, a reasonable observation.

Lugovoy said his former business partners in London had all suspended contact following the press reports about him, but he and Kovtun were continuing to get support and good wishes from ordinary Russians they met on the streets. 'They come and offer us a cognac or a vodka. They say, "Keep your spirits up, lads. We don't believe what they're saying about you, especially what they're all saying in the West." '

Lugovoy confirmed what Berezovsky had told me – that the two men had spoken on the phone on 6 February – but he would not comment on the contents of the conversation except to say that it was 'constructive'.

After days of phone calls, excuses and prevaricating, I got the distinct impression that Lugovoy had changed his mind about meeting me. I remembered the words Boris Berezovsky had said to me – 'I have the impression that he is not independent ... that there is someone standing behind of him that doesn't allow him to do this step' – and decided to confront him with my suspicions. I needed to discover if Andrei Lugovoy and Dmitry Kovtun, the men who were being so widely accused of putting the murder plot into practice, were independent figures or if they had ties and allegiances which determined how they acted. With unresolved questions over who had ordered the assassination and why, it was of vital importance to know if they were answerable to a specific group, whether inside the FSB or outside.

The decisive telephone conversation was fraught. From the outset Lugovoy seemed tense and quickly launched into a diatribe against the British press, saying they had convicted him without a trial. Then he turned his wrath against Scotland Yard, denying that a file had been sent to the Crown Prosecution Service and claiming that the British detectives would need to come back to Moscow again shortly. 'I'm tired of all this,' he said. 'I've got my life to think about. You know, they interrogated my wife for nine hours without a break. My wife! Nine hours!' He suggested he still could not give a definitive answer as to whether he would be able to meet me before I left Moscow. But it was my next question, asking if this was really a decision he could make for himself or if he was waiting for someone else to make it for him, that threw him into a towering rage.

'What are you saying? Are you asking if . . . ? Who decides? You what? Are you saying the FSB or something . . . ?' It seemed to be a sore point. Lugovoy was becoming increasingly indignant: 'You know what? That question you asked – Who makes the decision? – that's an outright provocation (*provokatsionny vopros*). You know what? I'm not going to have any meeting. I'm sorry; I'm busy.' And he hung up the phone.

61

POISON IN THE BLOOD

My conversations of the previous few days had elucidated some questions and left me puzzled on others. I had come to the conclusion that, despite all the accusations and beliefs of Boris Berezovsky and the exiled Russians, it was highly unlikely Vladimir Putin had ordered Litvinenko's murder, either directly or indirectly. There was no evidence, no precedent and no pragmatic reason for him to do so. I had spoken at length to men who are close to Putin, who spend many hours with him on a daily basis, and I felt their testimony on the subject was convincing. But, equally, I had been unable to rule out a freelance operation by the FSB or by a group connected with it. The reaction of the prosecutor's office suggested that no adequate measures had been taken to investigate possible FSB links to the Litvinenko affair, and that there may even have been a reluctance to probe too far in case embarrassing connections were discovered. My communications with Andrei Lugovoy had broken down over the vexed question of who, if anyone, he was answerable to, leaving me with the impression that he may not be an independent figure in this affair. But if Lugovoy and Kovtun really were connected with an organized group of conspirators, I was making slow progress in my efforts to discover who they might be. I had some leads I was working on, but so far with little result.

I decided to turn my attention to the poison that had made the Litvinenko case such a cause célèbre. Poison was much in my mind, and some chilling words Boris Berezovsky had spoken to me were constantly in my head: 'I can tell you, if Alexander had been killed by a gun or even by thallium, no one in this country would even remember his name now. The same in Russia. And it's the reality . . . only because he was murdered in a way that will not allow anyone to forget it, in a way that will not allow anyone to feel safe any more, *wherever they are . . .*'

I knew from talking to former KGB agents in London that somewhere in Moscow there was a clandestine secret service facility known as Laboratory Twelve or the *Kamera* (the Room), set up as long ago as 1921 specifically to develop traceless poisons which can be administered without their presence being evident in an autopsy. The location of the KGB poison factory is known to few people, but I was taken there by a former intelligence officer whose name I had been given by one of my contacts in London. The man instructed my driver to take a circuitous route through the Moscow backstreets and we eventually emerged into a nondescript street with lengthy low-rise stuccoed buildings on either side. None had nameplates but one had police guards at the gate, and this, said my new acquaintance, was Laboratory Twelve.

As we drove he told me he had worked briefly in the research department and assured me that its activities were still continuing, including research on radioactive poisons. He mentioned several instances of political poisonings that he assumed to be the work of the FSB, including Anna Politkovskaya, who was unsuccessfully poisoned before she was finally shot; the anti-Kremlin Ukrainian President Viktor Yushchenko attacked with dioxin; and the Duma member Yuri Shchekochikhin, who died from suspected radiation poisoning. But he wanted particularly to tell me about the case of Roman Tsepov, a former member of the security services who had acted as bodyguard to Anatoly Sobchak when he was mayor of St Petersburg, and even briefly to Vladimir Putin.

Tsepov had 'gone bad' and had links to crime groups. My contact said his death was the closest in its symptoms to that of Litvinenko himself and may link the FSB – or at least members of the FSB – with the London poisoning. Tsepov was forty-two when he died in September 2004. At first doctors thought he was suffering from food poisoning with violent vomiting and diarrhoea. When his symptoms intensified they had looked for evidence of toxic infection, but, just as in the Litvinenko case, none could be found. Tsepov's white blood cell count began to decline, his hair fell out and his immune system failed. The skin on his face, lips and tongue began to blister as if he was undergoing chemotherapy and his bone marrow was being destroyed. Just like Litvinenko, he died of cardiac arrest caused by massive toxic shock. Tsepov's post-mortem showed alpha radiation many times higher than a lethal dose.

My contact said the Tsepov case showed enough similarities with Litvinenko's to suggest that polonium had been used at least once before and that the confusing nature of its symptoms means it may have gone undetected in many other murders. I thought once more of Berezovsky's warning that few can feel safe when such methods are in play and I recalled the history of the Soviet and Russian security services from the Revolution onwards. After 1917 the Cheka – and later the OGPU and the NKVD – had terrorized Russians who fled abroad. The thousands of émigrés who settled in Paris in the 1920s lived in constant fear of murder or kidnapping by Red agents; propaganda from the Kremlin deliberately spread the message that no one was safe from its tentacles. Far from being ashamed at the activities of his thugs abroad, Stalin deliberately sought to foster the impression that the NKVD was all-knowing, all-seeing and inexorable in its pursuit of those who opposed him.

Just as in today's London, the émigrés of the 1920s had brought with them all the acrimony and hatred that had riven Russian society at home. Rival political groupings continued their feuds on the streets of Paris. Neighbours mistrusted neighbours, and after 1924 everyone feared the vengeance of Stalin. Few exiled Russians slept easy in their beds. Seemingly committed anti-Bolsheviks among the émigré community were blackmailed or bribed into switching sides and many became agents of the red terror. One of the most poignant cases concerned the husband of Marina Tsvetaeva, the great poet Anna Politkovskaya had studied in her youth. Sergei Efron had been a commander in the White Army, but homesickness led him to accept an offer of safe passage back to Russia on condition that he take part in an NKVD plot to murder a Bolshevik defector, the double agent Ignace Reiss. Sergei agreed and carried out his part in the plot, but when he and Tsvetaeva were taken back to Moscow, Stalin had their daughter arrested and tortured. She was forced to incriminate her parents; Sergei was arrested and shot, and Marina hanged herself in despair.

The night after I was taken to the poison laboratory, I went to the opera. It was a new production of Rimsky-Korsakov's *Bride for the Tsar* in the Tchaikovsky Hall with the tremendous Olga Borodina in the main role. It was only in the last act that I remembered the plot hung on the poisoning of a rival bride. The following evening I was at the Bolshoi's temporary home for their production of Shostakovich's *Lady Macbeth of the Mtsensk District*. I looked on with horrified fascination as the heroine murdered her father-in-law with rat poison and the dead man later rose from the grave to demand vengeance on his killer . . . There were strange happenings and ominous coincidences in the Moscow air. That night my sleep was disturbed by restless dreams of white powder and deadly, colourless liquids.

62
WEIGHING THE EVIDENCE

The more I probed, the more I was becoming convinced that Sasha Litvinenko had been poisoned by a group of people independent of the Kremlin but with close connections to the Russian security forces. The sophisticated planning behind the plot and the evidence of the poison factory strongly suggested the fingerprints of an FSB-style operation; the parallels with former crimes linked to the organization were too strong to be ignored. This did not necessarily mean the FSB had been acting in its own interests or on its own initiative; the security forces were so fragmented and out of control in the years following 1991 that individuals and groups within them were constantly taking on moonlighting jobs on behalf of paying customers. Today's security agencies are not homogeneous; they are composed of people with widely differing interests, and the unspoken truth is that neither the director of the FSB nor Vladimir Putin nor indeed any other Kremlin leader can be sure he controls them all (or even knows what they are getting up to).

I considered the possibility that a wealthy client or clients who had fallen out with Litvinenko over a commercial dispute might have hired FSB agents to carry out a hit for them. The idea was not impossible and if the murder had happened on Russian soil, I would certainly not have dismissed it. But the international aspect of the killing, specifically the fact that it was in a west European country, troubled me. Even the most reckless agent offered the highest fee would think very carefully before accepting it. The FSB may be home to some very ruthless people, but they are nonetheless professionals; they would know that the murder of a British citizen on British soil would inevitably stir up a hornets' nest of public interest and trigger an investigation by a police force which is not open to being threatened or bought off. For professionals with security service credentials murder in Russia was child's play; FSB-connected contract killings were rarely investigated and almost never solved. But accepting a commercial commission to kill abroad was an entirely different matter. The risk was just too great.

Amid the faded grandeur of my room at Moscow's once magnificent Hotel Budapest I sat and reviewed the evidence I had gathered. I listened to the recorded interviews and notes I had amassed, and I weighed the theories I had been offered by interested parties and impartial observers alike. I was coming to the end of a very long road, and my thoughts on the Litvinenko affair were slowly crystallizing into what I considered the only feasible explanation for the crime that had taken place 1,500 miles from here in the heart of London. By the end of the evening and with a bottle of Stolichnaya half empty, I knew I was looking for a group of killers with FSB connections. I knew it was a group with its own reasons to target Litvinenko, a group that could advance FSB interests to justify the murder, interests that would confer at least some immunity on it if the Kremlin were to become aware of what it had done.

I looked again at the Federal Laws of July 2006 and considered what my thoughts would have been if I were a former colleague of Sasha Litvinenko, if I had been biding my time waiting for the opportunity to avenge myself for the wrongs he had done to the service both before and after his defection to the West. It struck me forcefully that Litvinenko was right: the wording of the law – whatever the Duma's intentions in passing it – can be interpreted as justifying the assassination of Russia's enemies overseas. If I were one of the many FSB men who had suffered as a result of Litvinenko's actions, it would have looked like a golden opportunity to kill him with at least some pretence at legality. If I had to make a dispassionate assessment of all the possible consequences of such an act, as all security men are trained to do, I would say to myself that even in the worst case of being fingered for the murder I could argue that I acted in accordance with the law. My defence would be that Litvinenko was a traitor who had damaged the interests of the service and of the Russian state. Such a defence could not be advanced for a commercial assassination. It was a compelling consideration and it pointed me in a very specific direction.

63

MORE HARD MEN

There were a remarkably large number of people who matched the description I had come up with: current or former FSB men whose interests had been damaged by Litvinenko's actions and who bore a grudge against their author. It is likely that most of these potential suspects have remained anonymous and never spoken of their feelings about Litvinenko. That does not rule them out as suspects, but it does mean they are almost impossible to trace. Others, though, have been less anonymous. The FSB bosses such as Yevgeny Khokholkov, Alexander Kamishnikov and Nikolai Patrushev publicly accused of corruption by Litvinenko all have a strong motive to wish him ill. But those with the strongest motive, and who have made no secret of their feelings, appear to be those FSB men who sat before the cameras with Sasha at the infamous press conference of November 1998. All of them suffered as a result of their actions that day; all found their careers stymied; and most of them blamed Litvinenko for tricking them into taking part.

We have already noted that some if not all of these men accepted the FSB's offer to 'go back' and we must assume that the terms on which they were taken back included an obligation to inform on and work against the 'traitor' who had caused their problems. As we have seen, Mikhail Trepashkin says as much in his smuggled testimony and makes it clear that Viktor Shebalin, for one, continued to plot Sasha's downfall over the intervening years. The alleged 2002 plot against Litvinenko is a documented incident; there may be others.

It is an undeniable fact that URPO, the unit that they and Litvinenko worked for, was set up with the central purpose of 'neutralizing' inconvenient figures. And we have already discovered that the targets selected for neutralization were not confined to those designated by the political authorities running Russia – Litvinenko himself speaks of freelance executions ordered by individuals or groups within URPO and the FSB hierarchy. Motives included the commercial interests of security chiefs, criminal rivalries, revenge or simple payment. And although the name of URPO disappeared after 1998 there is no reason to believe that the concept of non-judicial execution was also abandoned. It seems more than likely that the FSB continued to maintain one or more similar units and that former members of URPO were assimilated into or attached to them. It could easily be the case that Sasha Litvinenko was assassinated by the same unit he used to work for.

Of the five officers who sat with Litvinenko on 17 November 1998 most are now uncontactable. Only the most senior of them, Colonel Alexander Gusak, has remained in the open. To test the theory I had built up of who might be behind the London poisoning I would need to seek him out. Remarkably, finding Gusak was not difficult. A full biography together with his home address appears on several Chechen separatist websites, with the unspoken suggestion that his crimes during the Chechen War may merit some retribution:

Alexander Ivanovich GUSAK, born October 19, 1957, in Donetsk, now Ukraine; ethnic Ukrainian; on FSB service from 1985 to 1998; married, two children; rewarded with two military orders and three medals. He is now vice-president of the Moscow building company Northern Building Group (Severnaya Stroitelnaya Gruppa) and the owner of a restaurant near the FSB Headquarters on Lubyanka Square in Moscow. His home address is ... He has close ties with a certain FSB officer, Malyshev, a friend and crony of Patrushev, the FSB Director General.

In fact the Chechens' information was a little out of date. I discovered that Alexander Gusak is now a lawyer, but his office is indeed on Lubyanka Square, diagonally opposite the towering mass of the FSB – formerly KGB – headquarters. Standing outside Gusak's office, I looked across to the empty patch of grass in the middle of the square. Until August 1991 an imposing statue of Feliks Dzerzhinsky, the founder of the Soviet security services, had stood here, but two days after the collapse of the August coup I had watched from this very spot as pro-democracy demonstrators attached a rope to its neck and dragged it to the ground with a crane. At the time we thought it symbolized the end of repression and murder by the security forces; now I was here to ask a former FSB man if those days really were a thing of the past.

When I had called to arrange the meeting Alexander Gusak had carefully taken note of all my personal details, including date and place of birth, former employers and time spent in Russia. He had said he was going to 'check me out', so I assumed he would know more about me than I would about him. I wondered if he still had access to the FSB's database in which I am sure I figure.

In person, Gusak is a lugubrious heavily muscled man with a deep voice and a clipped, military way of speaking, his short cropped hair and constant cigarette perhaps indicators of his former profession. He was pleasant and polite, but he clearly did not want to speak about the subjects I had come to broach with him. 'You know, if I start speaking about those things,' he said, 'they'll have to put me on trial for betraying military secrets.' It was a joke and he laughed – a short, nervous laugh – but he was not going to talk. Fortunately, my former BBC colleague Tim Whewell had better luck. In a rather tense exchange Tim asked him if he felt Litvinenko had deserved to die. After a long pause, Gusak replied,

> Betraying the motherland. Treason. For that – and I speak as a lawyer – what Litvinenko did comes under article 275 of the criminal code. And there are sanctions ... prescribed punishments. Up to twenty years in prison. But that's in accordance with the law. I was brought up on Soviet law. That provides for the death penalty for treason – article 64. I think if in Soviet times he

had come back to the USSR he would have been sentenced to death. I consider him a direct traitor. Because what he betrayed is the most sacred thing for any agent: his operational sources. His sources came to me and they complained that the British secret service officers had found them. And they asked me what to do. I'll tell you honestly: I didn't advise any of them to go and kill Litvinenko, though one of them did say, 'Listen – he's done you so much wrong – shall I bring you his head?' I don't want to say what I recommended those people to do. But I didn't tell them to go and kill him.

Gusak's denial of any role in the murder of Litvinenko must be taken at face value. He does, however, leave open the possibility that the other agents he mentions may not have been so restrained. And, speaking on another occasion, Gusak admitted he would personally have carried out a killing during his active FSB career, saying, 'If the director had given me the order, I would have carried it out – without written instructions.'

The evidence was mounting that some elements of the security forces were undoubtedly capable of assassinating a 'traitor' like Litvinenko and that they would not seek the sanction of the Kremlin to do so.

64

DIGNITY AND HONOUR

Sitting in the warmth of the new coffee house which stands in the front courtyard of the Moscow Conservatoire, I was reflecting on the contradictory nature of this weak, powerful, proud, humble, cultured, barbaric country that is Russia, a country that has produced the genius of Tolstoy, Dostoevsky, Chekhov, Tchaikovsky, Stravinsky, Shostakovich, Kandinsky, Chagall, Mendeleyev; and has thrown up the horrors of the Gulag, summary executions, the deportation of nations, mass repressions and deliberately engineered famines. The Russians themselves know about the schism; they feel themselves to be a nation torn between the softness of the west and the implacable cruelty of the east. In their moments of despair at the barbarism of which they are capable they ask, 'Are we Scythians?' *Skify li?* The values of life and power in Russia are different: the barbarity of one man's murder seems somehow diluted by the millions that have gone before. In this world taking a weapon and killing a man is much less likely to bring punishment and much more likely to bring a collective shrug of the shoulders. Society *accepts* what is done to the weak by the strong. It is the world in which Sasha Litvinenko's URPO meted out summary justice; it is the world that Vladimir Putin is trying to temper; but it is the world in which people like Alexander Gusak can calmly say they would carry out an unwritten order to kill.

Boris Berezovsky told me that he thinks Gusak is sick: 'He participated in very serious battles in Chechnya; he really killed people, you know how. Like many people who participate in these serious battles, he is psychologically sick. He was a killer in Chechnya; he got orders to kill people in Russia too. Did he deliver? I don't know. But I think he is a sick man.'

I am not so sure. Gusak was injured in Chechnya and has suffered reverses in his career but I do not think he is an anomaly. He keeps a portrait of Feliks Dzerzhinsky on his wall and he says he 'loves' the FSB director who was his commander in the 1990s. I also discovered by chance that Gusak has been a member of the Dignity and Honour organization, which groups former members of the security forces in a society devoted to upholding the ideals and principles that underpin the FSB and former KGB. And I remembered that Dignity and Honour is the KGB veterans' organization referred to in the papers Scaramella handed to Litvinenko at their meeting in the Itsu sushi bar on 1 November 2006. These documents, emails from the former agent Yevgeny Limarev, claim that Dignity and Honour was planning to kill Berezovsky, 'the number one enemy of Russia', and 'his companion in arms' Litvinenko.

> Names . . . are often mentioned in confidential talks of intelligence officers of Russia who work in SVR [the Foreign Intelligence Agency], Kremlin and SVR veterans' association Dignity and Honour headed by acting SVR Colonel Valentin Velichko. Abovementioned Russian intelligence officers speak more and more about necessity to use force against . . . Berezovsky and Litvinenko. An agent who works with Velichko's deputy has a local network of KGB agents at his disposal and prepares 'final act' (could be serious provocation or even assassination).

The email adds, 'Velichko's agents are presumed involved in the assassination of Anna Politkovskaya in October 2006, as well as in elaboration of other similar assassination plans, by order and on behalf of FSB/SVR.'

As we have seen Litvinenko did not take this threat seriously. Indeed, there is no proof that Dignity and Honour were behind the killings of Litvinenko and Politkovskaya and there are certainly other groups capable of planning such attacks. But Dignity and Honour, along with other similar KGB veterans' organizations, could easily fit the description of the fanatically loyal group of security service men which has been posited as the driving force behind his murder. Mikhail Trepashkin, among others, states that while the deed may have been done by people like Lugovoy and Kovtun, 'the initiative was coming from another group within the FSB ... The group includes *both active and former members* of the FSB.'

The Dignity and Honour foundation was set up in 2003 and its president, Valentin Velichko, is a former FSB colonel turned businessman. Born in 1949, he joined the KGB's foreign intelligence arm, now known as the SVR, and was posted to Amsterdam in 1984 under the cover of belonging to the Soviet trade mission. When his cover was blown in 1989 he was expelled and returned to Moscow. Dignity and Honour, which is believed to have over 3,000 members, has its own website, stating its key aims as 'helping veterans' and 'helping needy children'. Its ideals have a nationalist tone and include 'working for the spiritual revival of Russia'. A quote from Velichko appears on the website: 'We see our task as introducing law and order in the country with a view to establishing a dictatorship of law, where everyone is equal before the law. We are ballast. When the waters get choppy, we bring stability.' But he is quoted elsewhere as saying, 'We will punish those who rob Russia and the Russian people. There is a long list of so-called oligarchs, officials and politicians who used to make decisions in favour of certain clans.'

Velichko has denied that Dignity and Honour had anything to do with Litvinenko's death, saying Stalin-era assassinations of enemies had ceased. 'In those days there was a special department called V which handled the liquidation of political opponents.' But now, he says, there is no department for liquidations and there are no people in his organization wanting to settle scores with Litvinenko. He claims that Litvinenko was a traitor but was not killed by his agents: 'Who is Mr Litvinenko? A traitor. But I am against the elimination of traitors ... I have turned to religion ... Litvinenko, having betrayed Russia, was already punishing himself.'

Velichko's deputy, Viktor Afanasevich Dolya, indignantly rejects recurring suggestions that the organization has links to Lugovoy, Kovtun and Sokolenko: 'We have nothing to do with them. They have no relation to the foundation. If they do know something about our organization, it must be from the press or our leaflets. This link has been made with no grounds whatsoever. We know who made this link – Berezovsky.' And he is scathing about Litvinenko: 'Of course as a defector he damaged Russia's image. Everyone knows what he was doing – he was selling information for nice fees.' Dolya says he has no faith in Scotland Yard's investigation of the case: 'You have to understand this – the Brits are not looking for truth now. They are looking for a Russian trace. If they succeed in stitching the case up to Russia, the murder will be solved. If it turns out that the killers have nothing to do with Russia, we may never learn about the results. I think this could prove to be the case.'

65

A FINAL RECKONING

My unofficial driver, former *spetsnaz* commando and 'fellow Muscovite' was taking me to Sheremetevo Airport to catch the plane back to London. For all the days he had been driving me round the city to my public and clandestine meetings he had kept his opinions pretty much to himself. When I asked him about Litvinenko, he would pretend to spit and say, 'Akh, that's all politics.' But now I was leaving he leaned over and smiled his crooked grin. 'Did you solve it then?' he asked with a bit of a belly laugh.

Leningradsky Prospekt, the road to the airport, was clogged with crawling traffic; it looked like I was going to have time to give him the long version.

'I have a firm idea what happened,' I said, 'and a firm idea why it happened.'

'So was it the *spets-sluzhby* like I said?' I thought for a moment and then told him it wasn't the special forces in the way he meant it: it wasn't an official operation with all the paperwork signed and sealed by the Kremlin; Vladimir Putin had nothing directly to do with it. My driver grunted and nodded.

'It was a freelance operation by the FSB,' I said, 'or more exactly by members or former members of the FSB. It was an honour killing under the KGB code, a vengeance killing and a message . . .'

For the next hour I poured out my thoughts on the Litvinenko file and the conclusions I had come to. The traffic moved in fits and starts. The smell of diesel fumes permeated the cabin of the old Volga. My companion chain-smoked his way through a pack of *papirosy*.

★

It is the ceremonial character of Litvinenko's death that has stayed with me, the ritual nature of his dying. The use of a poison that destroys the human body from within, that takes days if not weeks to do so, that eats up the internal organs with no known antidote to its inexorable torture seemed to me to have something oriental about it, an air of exquisite eastern cruelty. It was without doubt the eastward-looking Scythian side of the Russian character at work. Sasha's was a deliberately inhuman death, and the killers knew it would be made horribly public.

But it was also an exemplary killing, exemplary in the sense that it sent a series of coded messages. The first was that traitors will not be allowed to live. The old KGB code of honour demanded that a serving agent coming across a traitor abroad kill him. Enforcement of the code lapsed under Yeltsin, but the law of July 2006 was a tacit indication that it should be revived. Oleg Kalugin, the KGB general I had known in Moscow in the 1990s before he defected to the US, says, 'Never forget, never forgive. They called [Litvinenko] a traitor . . . the one who will never be forgotten, will never be forgiven.'

The second message was more complex, and it took me a while to figure it out. At first I couldn't understand why Andrei Lugovoy had spent the evening before Litvinenko's assassination sitting over a bottle of wine with Boris Berezovsky. Lugovoy ostentatiously trailed polonium into his office – the evidence was left for all to see – and even Berezovsky seems at a loss as to why he was spared and Sasha was killed. The fact is that Berezovsky and Litvinenko were equally culpable for the 'betrayal and shame' of the November 1998 press conference, but only Litvinenko was punished.

Then I understood – the avengers were leaving a calling card. They were making a show of Berezovsky's vulnerability before sparing him and killing his lieutenant. It was a demonstration of power: the assassins were saying, 'We could have killed you, but we didn't; you were at our mercy and we spared you.' They had indeed been sent to kill 'Trotsky's dog', as Russian state television so sneeringly put it, but they were killing him at Trotsky's heel, and the intention was to splatter his master's shoes with blood.

The whole Litvinenko operation was built on intimidation, and it reeks of the testosterone-fuelled machismo I have observed so often in members or former members of the Russian special forces. Their existence revolves around absolute loyalty to the service. When an ex-KGB man says he 'loves' his former boss, it is not a figure of speech. But their attitude to those who fail the loyalty test is a crude, threatening, very Russian 'You fuck with us and we'll fuck with you.'

The Litvinenko murder and the swaggering foreplay with Bere-zovsky was explicitly designed to be disrespectful and insulting, to instil fear and paranoia. The perpetrators were saying, 'We know this is a Western country, but we have the power and you are not safe.' It is a way of thinking that is very Russian. I don't think we have it in the West any more. Mossad might, but even the pumped-up CIA prefers a modicum of discretion.

The third message was about the way the Russian security forces now view themselves, and this is more subtle. In December 1999, the day after he had hugged Boris Berezovsky and called him his brother, Vladimir Putin went to celebrate his election victory with his old comrades at the FSB. When the toasts came round and Putin proposed they should drink 'To Comrade Stalin' there was a shocked silence followed by a loud cheer. Putin opened his celebratory speech by jokingly telling his former colleagues, 'The agent group charged with taking the government under control has completed the first stage of its assignment.' After years of ostracism and plunging morale, the FSB took Putin's rise to power as a signal they were once again in the ascendant. Yeltsin had made sporadic attempts to curb the security forces, but there was never any equivalent of the 'de-Stasification' that took place in East Germany; the organization's structures had remained in place and now they were ready to reassert themselves. Under Putin the FSB has become more powerful and better funded, and, crucially, it has regained the confidence that it can act with independence if not impunity.

What about the law? Already in 1918 Lenin adopted a decree which allowed executions without judicial process. A document published by *Novaya Gazeta* five years ago purports to be a secret 1990s instruction to the FSB allowing non-judicial executions by units such as URPO. But the law of July 2006 is an open and official decree that very publicly gives the security forces the right to kill enemies of the state at home or abroad. For the disgruntled FSB men working on their plans for revenge against Litvinenko, it was a godsend.

One final development set the scene for the Litvinenko killing. Russia has an old tradition known as 'initiative from below'. It was stifled for part of the Soviet period under the deadening structures of 'democratic centralism' but has re-emerged in many areas of life under Putin. Once the president has set the tone, officials, bureaucrats and managers aim to please – they do what they think will earn them credit from the Kremlin. The Putin years have seen a new dialogue in which initiative is tacitly encouraged by coded signs of approval or simply the absence of reprimand.

The Kremlin officials I spoke to were honest enough to admit that Vladimir Putin was 'not fond' of Litvinenko, breaking with the official line that Sasha was of so little consequence the president never gave him a thought. We know Putin was not indifferent: Litvinenko had been important enough to gain direct access to him in 1998 with his allegations against the FSB, and Putin nursed a simmering resentment against him until his death. My Kremlin contacts responded to my questions and left me with the firm belief that Putin did not order the killing. But the very fact that the president was 'not fond' of a man set the scene for an initiative from below.

If Putin can be implicated in the Litvinenko affair, it is because he created the atmosphere and conditions in which the killing could take place, in which an enterprising group of current and former FSB men read the signals from the Kremlin and embarked on their own initiative. Putin did not make any secret of his contempt for Berezovsky and his coterie; Litvinenko left behind many bitter former colleagues who suffered as a result of his actions, and the combination of these two elements resulted in the operation that ended with polonium on the streets of London. Putin did not even need to say, 'Who will rid me of this troublesome priest?' His servants were ready and primed to 'do something nice for the boss'. Anna Politkovskaya was killed on the president's birthday; Litvinenko's death was perhaps intended as an early Christmas present.

Sasha's old comrade, Yuri Felshtinsky says Putin's reinvigoration of the security forces has fostered an air of lawlessness in which murder has become easy: 'The truth is that Putin has created a system where the FSB know very well that they do not need to ask permission to kill any more. And that is more dangerous than if they did need to ask Putin's permission to kill, because in that case you know at least that unless Putin gives permission to kill, then no one is going to kill. Those people who killed Politkovskaya and Litvinenko did not ask for permission, because they knew they do not need that permission; that no one is going to punish them for doing it. Now people on a relatively low level are making decisions about whether to kill or whether not to kill. I think this is the result of their understanding of Putin's desires.' As for Berezovsky, I have sat and talked to him for extended periods; I have observed his behaviour closely; I have looked him in the eye, and I have come away convinced that he is not guilty of killing Sasha Litvinenko. I find it inconceivable that someone with such a heinous crime on his conscience would be capable of maintaining the complete composure and assurance he displayed in our conversations, or the indignation he clearly felt over the death of his former protégé. He was exasperated by Sasha; he had had enough of the man's irresponsible tirades and had slashed his allowance as a sign of disapproval. He had fallen out with Litvinenko, but he did not murder him.

As for his close relationship with Andrei Lugovoy, I believe Berezovsky just made a mistake. He himself says he is not good at understanding people – 'I don't know who is traitor, who is good, who is bad' – and he didn't spot the potential double agent in his camp. Oleg Gordievsky told me, 'It's an old Russian tradition to invite old friends, but still keep your suspicions of them. Everyone told him to stay away from those people because they are provocateurs and Boris said, "Oh I know they are provocateurs, but I have a duty of gratitude to them because they protected me in my difficult times . . ." Lugovoy was certainly no friend of Boris Berezovsky; he was an enemy of mankind, a monster and a murderer.'

Yuri Felshtinsky concurs: 'On some level Berezovsky is very naive . . . There are too many people around him from all sorts of backgrounds, many from the special forces. Because Berezovsky was very close to power, one of the most powerful in Russia, he had to deal with all sorts of people; he couldn't choose for himself. There were good people around, bad people around . . . He didn't distinguish between good and bad, loyal and traitor.'

Berezovsky is not guilty of Litvinenko's murder, but he is guilty of manipulating his memory. At the end of our last meeting he said, 'I can tell you this is not the end of this story; it is not even the middle . . . In a week we will do something that will make sure people cannot ignore it.' A week later the newspapers duly wrote up the story of Berezovsky's 'challenge' to Lugovoy to face trial for Sasha's murder that he had told me about in our interview. Another story was drip-fed into the media the following week, this time that Boris Berezovsky had uncovered an alleged Kremlin plot against his own life. A series of new accusations was trotted out. Anyone paying attention could see there was some fairly cynical news management going on to keep the story constantly in the public eye. Berezovsky's PR professionals have turned Sasha Litvinenko's agonizing death into much more than a human tragedy – now it is a weapon, a piece of ammunition that can be exploited over and over again in the propaganda war against the Kremlin. Berezovsky is not squeamish about manipulating his dead friend's memory for his political ends, but I am convinced he did not kill him.

What can we say about Alexander Litvinenko himself? The grief of his father and second wife have been evident for all to see; one can only imagine the effect his death has had on his bereaved children. But Sasha Litvinenko knew the stakes he was playing for, he knew the ferocity of the war he was engaged in, and he did not recoil from it – quite the opposite in fact. His career was full of violence and his hands may not have been free of spilled blood, both in Chechnya and in Russia itself. The Berezovsky camp and its PR professionals have naturally sought to portray Litvinenko as a peaceful family man, an innocent bystander unjustly targeted by an inhuman Kremlin machine, but he was not. He was a player, a soldier, a fully cognizant participant in a war which has claimed casualties with numbing regularity. He knew what he was doing could expose him to mortal danger – and he continued to do it. The war for Russia's soul has been running since 2000 and will intensify in the run-up to the presidential elections in 2008. The commander of the army in power is Vladimir Putin and the commander trying to seize power is Boris Berezovsky. As in a real war, the commanders do not personally order the deaths of the foot soldiers; equally, a soldier with a rifle does not seek the personal authorization of his general before shooting an enemy. Alexander Litvinenko was not the first foot soldier to die in this struggle – many have gone before him. The way things are evolving, he will not be the last.

What can clearly be stated is that there was no shortage of motives for his killing. Alexander Litvinenko was a man who accumulated enemies with reckless abandon, who pitched himself against mighty figures and powerful interests, and whose obsessive, almost maniacal, character drove him to spurn offers of reconciliation and ratchet up the level of confrontation with his former colleagues and bosses.

Many FSB people hated him; many sought revenge for the 1998

press conference and his denunciation of his comrades. His former bosses resented his whistle-blowing about their alleged lucrative commercial activities. He reportedly betrayed covert agents in the UK and elsewhere who were rounded up and expelled. He transgressed against the honour of the service. He took with him 'a hundred kilos' of compromising documents about the FSB. Former colleagues of Litvinenko had grounds to fear he had access to damaging material regarding the 1999 apartment bombings, or the murder of Anna Politkovskaya. In the foreword to his book *The Criminal Gang from the Lubyanka* Litvinenko boasted of all the dirt he had on the corruption of his former comrades and seemed almost proud this would make him a potential target. He was not a spy and did not have state secrets that would betray the motherland, but he was an active FSB agent and did have secrets about the FSB and those in it. He betrayed his firm, not his country, and it was his firm that killed him for it.

The Litvinenko File is very much the story of a death foretold. As far back as 2000 his former FSB comrade Viktor Shebalin sent him a warning in the columns of the international press: 'Litvinenko, you had better come back and give yourself up. You have no other way out . . . Let me make it clear: we do not forgive traitors!'

Alexander Gusak, the man who had been Litvinenko's boss in the URPO execution unit, had denounced him for the ultimate crime of betraying fellow agents to the enemy, as well as revealing that current and retired FSB men were volunteering to murder him.

Mikhail Trepashkin exposed both the aborted 2002 attempt on Sasha's life and the formation in 2006 of a new hit squad to track him down, 'sanctioned at the very highest level [and] including both active and former members of the FSB'.

In the month of his death Litvinenko received from Mario Scaramella an emailed warning from Moscow that the Dignity and Honour organization of ex-FSB and KGB officers was planning to kill both him and Berezovsky.

The accumulated weight of evidence is overwhelming. Elements among Litvinenko's former colleagues in the FSB had not for a moment ceased to plot against him, and on 1 November 2006 they got him.

What can be said with equal certainty is that it was an operation long in the planning. Andrei Lugovoy first contacted Litvinenko at the end of 2005, setting up the business relationship that served as a reason for his and Kovtun's visits leading to the final encounter in the Pine Bar. According to Berezovsky, Litvinenko told him he had spotted the danger, but too late: 'He said clearly that there was no such thing as "formers" – meaning ex-employees of the KGB and the FSB. He believed that Lugovoy was simply fulfilling an order. The first stage was to get close to Sasha, to pique his interest with some information; the second stage was simply to fulfil the order – to kill him.'

If in fact Lugovoy really was a double agent, the planning for the operation had begun much earlier than 2005. Back in 2001 he had allegedly taken part in a botched operation to help Berezovsky's jailed business partner escape from Lefortovo Prison in Moscow. The prison authorities may have seemed suspiciously complicit in the escape, allowing the prisoner out of jail for a night at home, but then arresting both him and his 'rescuer' Andrei Lugovoy. Lugovoy was found guilty and sent to jail, but was quietly released very soon afterwards. According to Yuri Felshtinsky, it was a classic operation to create a cover story for Lugovoy 'proving' that he had fallen out with the FSB and demonstrating his loyalty to Berezovsky: 'I now doubt that Lugovoy really did spend time in prison. I think it was a put-up job. In theory he was sentenced to fifteen months for helping Berezovsky, but it seems to be a false story. It was to make Berezovsky feel Lugovoy was a victim who went to jail for him, so Lugovoy was made a friend of the family and all doors were open to him.' If the aim was to infiltrate him as a double agent into the Berezovsky camp, it means Lugovoy then spent five years or more as a 'sleeper', gaining the confidence of the enemy before finally carrying out his long-planned mission. It is fascinating stuff redolent of the old days of cold war espionage. Vladimir Bukovsky told me that such operations did not stop with the fall of Communism: 'That is the whole point of the Kremlin operations. They chose a guy who would have easy access to the Berezovsky circle. All the time Lugovoy was working for Berezovsky, he was remaining a loyal FSB man ... controlled by the FSB all the time.'

As well as being long planned, the Litvinenko operation looked to have had the backing of a powerful organization with access to such esoteric resources as polonium. And once again the evidence points to serving or former FSB officers. Lugovoy himself has no explanation for his and Kovtun's polonium contamination except to suggest it might have come from contact with Litvinenko. In an interview with the newspaper *Izvestiya* he claimed that polonium is often used by police and other agencies to tag counterfeit money and drugs that they want to track around the world, and suggested that Litvinenko could have been poisoned as a result of his own criminal activities. The *Izvestiya* interviewer jumps to the conclusion that Litvinenko was involved in drug smuggling: 'Maybe he was trying to assess the quality of some of his heroin en route from Afghanistan to the United States ... by taking a pinch and tasting it.' It is an ingenious explanation but unfortunately fails to account for the fact that Lugovoy and Kovtun were contaminated long before they met Litvinenko on 1 November, and long before he himself began to show any signs of polonium. The *Izvestiya* article suggests that the Russian state media is doing its best to defend two men who are regarded in London as suspects in a murder.

Lugovoy himself is an intriguing figure. He is independently wealthy with his own successful business and not in the first flush of youth, and yet he seems nonetheless to have been persuaded, or compelled, to take part in a tremendously difficult mission in a foreign country. A Russian businessman with a thriving wine and *kvas* factory to think about would never voluntarily have established links with a derided traitor and enemy of the state. Such a liaison would have put him in very bad odour with the Russian authorities and could have had extremely negative consequences for his commercial activities. Taking part in the Litvinenko operation clearly put Lugovoy's physical health at risk and his role left him very much exposed to the public eye. Just why he agreed to take part is open to speculation, but that he did seems to reflect the ability of the security services in Russia to command loyalty through idealism, encouragement or possibly coercion. The drawn-out nature of the operation hints at the complexity and persistence of the FSB's struggle against its enemies. It also raises questions of whether the Russian security services have now become a state within a state, and the extent to which they operate independently of the political authorities.

Groups such as Dignity and Honour are semi-official bodies but ultimately deniable if things go wrong. They have access to the FSB's resources and seem to enjoy the backing of its organization and networks. Scaramella's warning to Litvinenko on 1 November 2006 said, 'An agent who works with Valentin Velichko's deputy [head of Dignity and Honour] *has a local network of KGB agents at his disposal* and prepares "final act" (could be serious provocation or even assassination).'

As Velichko himself pointed out, there are organizations other than Dignity and Honour which enjoy the same semi-official relationship with the Kremlin and which group former and serving FSB agents. He claimed Department V, or Vympel, which used to carry out executions has been disbanded. It has not. As its other duties include protecting Russia's nuclear facilities against theft, Vympel members are trained in nuclear physics and they have access to polonium in the course of their duties. It is almost certain there will be no paper trail of orders and instructions leading back to the originators of the Litvinenko assassination. Such operations are carried out with deniable nods and winks, without formal recorded decisions. Litvinenko's widow Marina says the people who killed her husband almost certainly did so on their own 'initiative from below' and were motivated by a desire for personal vengeance: 'There will conclusion that the most likely suspects are to be found within the Russian security services, the FSB, GRU military intelligence, and the foreign intelligence agency, the SVR. I believe these men or groups of men were acting on their own initiative and for reasons internal to the security forces. They were not hired killers working for commercial or criminal interests but were acting to uphold the honour of the FSB and to extract revenge on a traitor to the service. It is not possible at the moment to name the individuals who ordered the assassination: many former agents, including the men who sat with Litvinenko at his 1998 press conference and the FSB bosses he named at it, had reason to hate him. And there are several organizations similar to Dignity and Honour which have the means and the motivation to participate in a complex operation on foreign territory. Because of Russia's extradition laws it is unlikely anyone will be brought to trial.

★

In the end the Moscow traffic cleared and I arrived at Sheremetevo Airport just in time to catch my flight to London. My driver, who had listened sagely to my explanations, gave me a Russian bear hug at the terminal door. I asked him what he thought. He stood for a moment, pretended to spit and said, 'Akh, for me it's all politics.'

In London's Highgate Cemetery fresh flowers continue to appear on the grave of Alexander Litvinenko. Mourners, admirers and casual sightseers frequently visit to keep his memory alive. Down a couple of tree-lined avenues, the brooding figure of Karl Marx looks on pensively in the London rain.

be no written order. They don't even need to say it outright. They just pass the word along the chain of command, "It would be a good idea to . . ." So it's not spelt out at all; it's just a conversation. I'm not talking about the man at the top. But maybe someone wanted to do something nice for the man at the top. Those people are maniacs. Normal people just can't find any logic in the way they behave. I think it is the system Sasha used to be part of. They don't act out of patriotism even though they boast that they do. They act from a terrible desire for revenge. In the system Sasha used to be part of they are all abnormal.'

Members of Dignity and Honour are sworn to uphold the KGB code and their rhetoric against traitors and robber oligarchs is at times less than restrained. Former KGB General Oleg Kalugin says the group is nostalgic for hard-line Soviet ways and is capable of carrying out assassinations: 'Absolutely; he [Litvinenko] was a traitor. So was I and a number of others. They have a list . . . Litvinenko? They would love to kill him.'

The fury of people like Alexander Gusak and Viktor Shebalin, the tacit encouragement of a state that has introduced laws allowing foreign assassinations and the new confidence of an FSB returning to its former glory have combined to set the stage for a very public demonstration of where the power lies in Russia today.

*

Some of the questions I posed at the outset of this book now have at least partial, if tentative, answers.

Who carried out the murder? Was it Andrei Lugovoy or Dmitry Kovtun? Were they part of a classic three-man troika? Was the third man Vyacheslav Sokolenko or an as yet unnamed and unknown *keelyer* who administered the actual poison? The conclusions of Scotland Yard will go some way to providing answers, although the apparent refusal of Russia to contemplate all extradition requests may prevent a juridical examination of guilt or innocence.

Who ordered the murder? My investigations have led me to the